YOU'RE BETTER THAN ME

YOU'RE BETTER THAN ME

A Memoir

Bonnie McFarlane

An Imprint of HarperCollins*Publishers*

HarperCollins books may be purchased for educational, business, or sales promotional use. For information please e-mail the Special Markets Department at SPsales@harpercollins.com.

FIRST EDITION

Designed by Shannon Nicole Plunkett

Library of Congress Cataloging-in-Publication Data has been applied for.

ISBN 978-0-06-231949-4

16 17 18 19 20   OV/RRD   10 9 8 7 6 5 4 3 2 1

CONTENTS

Foreword
by Anthony Bourdain

The tarmac at Heathrow was socked in with fog, my flight was canceled, and the Percodan hadn't yet started to kick in. I'd spent the night before (figuratively) jacking off advertisers and sponsors at a network dog and pony, and it'd taken an ill-advised number of negronis at the hotel bar to wash away the memory. It felt like I had a brain tumor.

Other than that, everything was fine.

Because there was a bright light in this otherwise dark, depressing picture: I finally had in my possession Bonnie McFarlane's manuscript. Things, I was able to remind myself, could be worse. I could be growing up on a farm in northern Canada, eating homemade ketchup and taking once-a-week baths in the same water as the rest of my family.

I could be a working comedian.

I didn't know who Bonnie McFarlane was when I first met her. She was introduced to me simply as "the writer" at a charity roast where I was to be skewered by a panel of friends, professional comics, and people who genuinely hated me. Bonnie had been hired to write jokes and insults for those few of the assembled who, though in possession of sufficient ill will, were incapable of articulating that loathing to comic effect.

She apologized in advance though she needn't have. Not to

me, at least. In agreeing to participate, the other chefs and television personalities on the dais that night had apparently forgotten that custom and tradition require everyone to share the pain of a roast. And on that night, no one got out alive. By the time dessert was served, there was blood and hair everywhere.

Mario Batali had to endure one fat joke after another after another. Rachael Ray, given one of the best lines of the night, had to tell a joke about giving Mario a blow job and him thoughtfully providing his own scrunchie to help keep the hair out of her face.

Guy Fieri ("what you get when Billy Idol fucks a panda") took it from all sides and limped out of the festivities leaking fluids from every orifice.

My friend Eric Ripert dutifully read Bonnie's lines to uproarious laughter, pausing intermittently to apologize to his targets.

The jokes were witheringly funny, merciless, inappropriate. Other comics—famous comics, funny comics—took their turns but I don't honestly remember them, because when Bonnie McFarlane stepped up to the microphone, she killed. She destroyed. She eradicated all memory of the rest.

I turned to my longtime agent, sitting next to me, and said, "Who IS this person, and how do we get her to write a book?"

Some people have a unique voice—a special way of looking at the world, seeing it, describing it. Others have a story. Very few people have both.

I had no idea when I first reached out to Bonnie that she had a story. Particularly *this* story. I just knew that she had a fantastic way of looking at the world, talking about it—and that I'd happily spend a few hundred pages hearing her talk about, well, anything.

I knew, too, that if I was put on Earth to publish anyone,

it was Bonnie McFarlane. Like so few people are able to do (only Richard Pryor comes to mind), she walks that tightrope between comedy and tragedy—brilliantly.

I am proud to bask in her reflected glory.

On that tarmac at Heathrow—and on the dais of that glorious roast—I was just grateful to be in the presence of a rejuvenating, excoriating genius.

YOU'RE **BETTER** THAN ME

Chapter 1

HOW I FAILED AT BEING A SERIAL KILLER, *or,* WHY I AM A COMEDIAN

Ask anyone, I'm weird. But not like weird, weird. It's harder to categorize than that. My weirdness is more unsettling because it can go under the radar for a long time before it snaps to the surface. You could be talking to me for an hour, maybe longer, and perhaps even enjoyably so, before the realization wafts up on you like a cool draft that suddenly becomes difficult to ignore: you're talking to a fucking lunatic.

I'm not sure how it happened. I can't for the life of me imagine why I turned out so odd. I mean, I'm Canadian. I come from a nice farming family. My parents are still married to each other. I saw them fight only once and they had the decency to go into the garage to hurl insults at each other so my sisters and I wouldn't be scarred for life. Eager for any kind of drama, I followed them out to witness the fireworks, which turned out to be a real disappointment. I only remember my father saying to my mother, "You're just like your sister!" My mother was crushed by the comment. "Take it back!" she whispered. These short outbursts were followed by long pauses where they stared at each other or their feet. I left during one of these endless lulls. Borrrring.

My mom didn't do drugs when she was pregnant. I grew up eating organic vegetables and I have three older sisters who turned out just fine. So why do I have six of the seven characteristics of being a serial killer and, worse, grow up to be a professional stand-up comedian?

Here are the seven signs of serial killers found on Wikipedia, the most factual Web site on the information superhighway. Can you guess which one I don't have?

- White Male
- Antisocial
- Abused: Mentally, Physically, or Sexually
- The MacDonald Triad: Fire Fascination, Bed-Wetting, Killing Animals
- Above Average Intelligence
- Violence
- Fetishism

1. WHITE MALE

It's true, I am white, but contrary to some of the rumors floating around, I am also a woman, born and bred. This is, apparently, the only part of the serial killer configuration that keeps me from wanting to see the life drain from the eyes of strangers. However, and I'm not sure this is relevant, when I was three or four years old, I started identifying as a boy and wouldn't wear a shirt around the house or during swim lessons. We swam in a huge body of water that bore the same name as the closest town, Cold Lake. The lake was not creatively named, by the way, and I suspect it might originally have been named Motherfucking Cold Lake. Still, we swam in it all the time and after the hypothermia set in, it was a pretty fun afternoon. The dude who gave me lessons was just a boy, maybe fifteen, and my topless heroin chic androgyny was not his cup of tea. He unloaded me as fast as he could, telling my parents I was a swimming prodigy of sorts, advanced for my age and could be moved into the older kids' group, where I very promptly nearly drowned.

But this near-death experience didn't stop the crossdressing. I wanted to be like my dad. I wanted the attention he got from my mom and my sisters and me. One of us would look out the window and see him walking toward the house from the barn after a long day of baling hay and milking cows. "Places! Places everyone!" We'd buzz around, getting coffee started and popping a few fresh rolls onto a chipped plate. He'd sit down at the kitchen table and they'd pull off his boots and I'd comb his hair. "Oh, Bonnie, you've got the touch," he'd say. He wanted me to be a hairdresser. Those were his big plans for me. I knew I could never do it because I have an intense aversion to small talk. Plus, I knew I could be anything I wanted to be in life if I were a man, so I refused to wear dresses, drank unsweetened iced tea out of a pickle jar, and answered the phone "Y'ello!" just like my dad. My parents didn't fret over my gender-bending and my mother even cut my hair short, but I think she did that so she had two fewer braids to tie every morning. In those days, you didn't spend a lot of time stressing about the weird stages your kids went through. I'm glad, because if I grew up in this decade, my parents would've changed my name to Benji and started saving for a sex change operation. Personally, I don't think women should get sex changes until all their good ladies' years are used up. As Chaz Bono taught us, you can go from being a fat old woman to a well-fed young man in the blink of an inverted vagina. Unfortunately, what Chaz Bono failed to realize was that getting an actual medical procedure is excessive. Many women have late-in-life sex changes using only the cruelty of time and their own natural hormonal shortages. One only needs to take a stroll through the Milwaukee airport to see how popular this method is.

I was a tomboy who had graduated to tom-man, though I never really had the party I thought I deserved for such a momentous occasion.

2. ANTISOCIAL

This one is true. I am antisocial. I realize, medically and psychologically, it might be more than just sitting by yourself at a party with a couple of celery sticks and a side of lumpy dip but I don't feel like researching the real meaning.

I think I actually have severe social anxiety. I don't take any drugs for it or have a therapist. No, I get through it the old-fashioned way, overcompensating by being horribly obnoxious. I don't know why it helps and I'm not even sure that it does, but that's how I self-medicate, by being an asshole. So fuck you.

I've heard about rape victims who, after their attack, pack on the pounds for protection so that no one will come near them again. Maybe this is why I act the way I do. I wear my assholeishness as a protective covering so that people steer clear and I can avoid small talk. It might sound insensitive, comparing my sweaty palms with rape victims' bodies, but perhaps it would help to keep in mind that at least I'm not out there killing innocent people.

People think it's odd to pick a profession where you have to stand up in front of strangers and try to make them laugh when social anxiety is one of your challenges, but that debilitating

4

feeling most people get when they have to do any kind of public speaking is something I'm used to. It's the same feeling I get if I have to order a pizza or poop in a public bathroom. No more, no less.

Since we've still got a few minutes left in this session, I'd like to take this time to say that I was not around many people other than my family very often. Sure, I'd go to school when forced, but weekends, holidays, and summers (if you can call them that in northern Canada) I spent talking to no one but my family and the animals on the farm. One of the animals, as I look back on it, was a pretty good friend.

The tradition in my house was to get a cow as a gift for our tenth birthdays. I don't know, perhaps it was an Ethiopian tradition passed down generation after generation. My sisters never even got off the couch to accept their cows. Never put down their *Little House on the Prairie* books to check out their bovine offering. "Dad, just give me the money," they would say. And he would "buy" the cow back from them and plop the sixty dollars into their bank accounts.

Now when my tenth birthday rolled around, I dog-eared that Laura Ingalls page, got my ass off the couch, and hit the fields to pick out my baby. My dad was a little surprised, but the truth was, they knew not to try to figure out what I was going to do. Do not try to second-guess Bonnie, y'all. I never met expectations. I always came in way under or way over. Or way to the side of things.

As I scanned the cows, lazily munching their cud, I was looking not for the prettiest one, or the one with the least amount of nose snot, or even the one with the best teats. No, I was looking for the fattest one. I was determined to get the most bang for my buck, and bingo! There she was, backlit in the morning sun. Her head turned, and she batted those big eyelashes at me and we made a connection. It was just like the meet-cute in a romantic comedy. She was for me, and I was for her. My angel, my soul mate, my—

"No," said my father, looking where my outstretched arm was pointing.

"Why?"

"Because you can't."

"You said I could pick any one I wanted, and I want that one."

"You don't want that one."

"I do."

My father kicked a lump of dirt with his steel-toed rubber boot and rolled a cigarette with one hand. He could do that. When I started smoking pot, I always thought about what an asset he would've been at parties.

"Please," I said in barely a whisper. I knew begging could send him over the edge. He didn't appreciate being manipulated, my father, and he was always on the lookout for it. Scanning the world for ways in which it was trying to use him was a passionate hobby of his. You had to be careful you weren't one of those ways. Maybe he didn't hear. Maybe I said it softly enough that he didn't perceive it as manipulation. Finally he said, "Okay. She's yours."

"I'll call her Bessie," I said, because that was the first name of my fourth-grade teacher and something about it made me laugh.

Bessie was young, but apparently this little whore cow liked to fuck. She was fat because she was knocked up, bitches. And before long, I had two cows. Doubled my investment like that (transvestite finger snap).

I also doubled my workload. After that calf was born—it was so cute for three days and then it started to look like a cow—I had to feed it and milk it, every morning and every night. And it also meant I had to figure out what to do with all that milk. She was producing about twelve gallons a day. I was drowning in it. My family didn't need it. They had their own milk from their own cows. I sold some of the milk and cream locally but it was still too much to unload. I made butter, I made yogurt, I made buttermilk, and then I came across an unusually good idea. I began making ice cream with a little electric ice-cream maker that my parents had packed away in the back of a cupboard. Cream and custard in the middle cup, ice and salt in the mote that went around it. I made a batch every night and then I sold it once a week at the farmers' market. To say my ice cream was a hit was like saying Bobby Orr was just a hockey player. When the market opened, customers ran like a herd of wild buffalo to my table and bought up all the product in a matter of minutes. I started with the basics—vanilla, chocolate, and strawberry— but as the weeks rolled on, I included raspberry swirl, rum and raisin, and Big Bubba's Brownie Bits Bonanza. I started getting orders for creamy pumpkin pie weeks in advance. People called my house asking for a special blend of fresh blueberry with tof- fee chunks. I filled every order, I answered every call. I saved every dollar. This ice-cream money would be my ticket out of here. It would fund my worldly travels. It would pay for my new life. And I needed a new life. Because let me tell you something, if you're a preteen and your best friend is a cow and you're sell- ing homemade ice cream at the farmers' market, you're in des- perate need of a new life.

But I had Bessie. And as I milked her every morning and every night, I talked and she listened. She was a great friend. I told her everything—my hopes, my dreams, my fears. The boys I liked, the girls I wanted to befriend, the stories I thought I might write, and the cities I might one day live in. Bessie became my closest confidante. She was my best ally. My dearest friend. And then a few years later, I ate her.

3. ABUSED: MENTALLY, PHYSICALLY, OR SEXUALLY

Here's something. I was never molested. That I can remember. But I'm not convinced it didn't happen. For one thing, I've seen a picture of myself and I was a great-looking kid. I mean, if you're into sloppy tomboys with home-cut hair and chapped lips (And really, who isn't? Am I right folks?), then I was hot stuff. Second, being that I'm a marginally to completely messed-up adult depending on what day of the month you catch me, I'd like to shift some of that blame on to something or someone else, which is why, whenever I'm at a family reunion, I whisper, "I forgive you," to all of my uncles and one of my aunts, just in case . . . In the hopes we can all move on, I'll forgive. But I'll never forget. Because, as I mentioned before, I don't actually remember.

But even if we're not counting these dubious abuses, there is enough mistreatment of me from my childhood that I do recall. I have suffered. Believe me, I have been through all kinds of horrors. For example, we did not have running water until I was six years old. We did not have a television until I was nearly ten. This is how I grew up. In the 1800s. But the worst of it was that I wasn't even aware I was being abused until I was much older.

If you're going to be poor and make all your kids sleep in the basement with mice and make them wear hand-me-downs and not have running water, can I suggest that you also keep them away from television? It's what my parents did for my sisters and me and we never knew what we were missing. Without commercials to let us know what toys we didn't have or what kind of clothes we should be wearing or what gadgets could make us really popular, we walked around in a state of ignorance without the foggiest idea that we were woefully living in the Dark Ages.

For example, after my family finally moved from a trailer

to the "shack," as my mother still unlovingly refers to it, we thought we were moving on up! My father traded some farm equipment for the old girl and had it pulled onto our property. It wasn't much bigger than the trailer but my father dug a basement for it, unfinished, of course, and full of mice. FULL OF MICE. And that's where my sisters and I all slept. FULL OF MICE, ladies and gentlemen. Full of mice! I'm not kidding. We would snuggle under the covers, quiet down for the night, let a few minutes pass and then one of us would sit up and go, "Boo." We'd hear all the mice scatter to the corners of the basement, squeeze into the holes and run through the walls. I don't know how many there were but it sounded like hundreds. Thousands. There were probably six.

There was one bunk bed and a double bed for all four kids and none of it was reserved. It was first-come, first-serve sleeping arrangements. We all wanted the top bunk because of the basement being FULL OF MICE. But one night my oldest sister told us something that we, the three younger sisters, barely literate and less wise, hadn't considered. "Mice," she said, "love heights. They crawl up the sides of the bunk bed to the tippy top and nibble on the nose of whoever is sleeping up there." We believed her of course. Who would lie about something so serious? And just like that, the top bunk lost all its desirability. My oldest sister reluctantly agreed to take it, so kind was she.

Without television, I didn't know how other families lived. Didn't realize, for example, that mice played a much smaller role in the bedtime rituals of most other children. I wasn't aware that not everyone else's entire family bathed in the same water once a week, water that began as snow and was melted in four enormous pots on the stove. I didn't realize that during the rest of the week, not everyone else took whore baths in the sink and relieved themselves in an outhouse. If it got too cold or too late to use the outdoor crapper, there was a pot in the corner of the bathroom that my father hauled outside and dumped somewhere every night. I don't know where he dumped it, and honestly, my curiosity was never piqued. "I must find out where my family shit pile is! I won't sleep until I know the truth!"

Even later, when we got running water, it was from a well. A well that could dry up and leave you without water for a lengthy amount of time. Look, I don't know the process it took to get that well primed and going again but you NEVER WANTED THE WELL TO GO DRY! God forbid! And so we were very careful to conserve water, and while we stopped all bathing in the same tubful, every bath was still a twofer. To this day I take the shortest showers on the planet and if I hear water running for too long, I get intense anxiety and need to cut myself until the feeling goes away.

Before we got running water, when I was still preschool age, I remember going to the house of a friend of my mother's in the middle of the afternoon on a Saturday for reasons I was not privy to. Perhaps they were comparing recipes or trading secrets on the best way to kill one's husband; I can't really be sure as I was too far out of earshot, sitting in the middle of a love seat in the living room with my winter jacket on, staring at a lamp with a base shaped like a pineapple, when a ten-year-old girl came walking down the stairs wearing sweats and a T-shirt, patting a towel on her dripping-wet hair. I was immediately confused. Why was she wet? Was it raining out? I looked outside, not a cloud in the sky.

"Why are you wet?" I asked. She raised an eyebrow and threw her towel into a corner. "I took a shower," she said, inflecting up on the last word like you do when you think you're talking to a crazy person.

"Where are you going?" I imagined it had to be a wedding

or a queen's coronation or maybe she was competing for Miss Cowbell, an annual competition at the local rodeo. But no, this was winter, that wasn't until spring.

"Nowhere." She was combing her hair with the fingers of one hand, flipping through a *Reader's Digest* Canadian edition magazinelet with the other.

"But you took a shower," I said as if she didn't know. A shower in the middle of the afternoon. On a weekend!

"Yeah . . ." The word was drawn out like I'm a crazy person again.

I couldn't process it. I asked her one last time where she was going. And then I asked her again. And again. And again. It didn't matter that she was giving me the same answer. I was like a CIA operative extracting sensitive information. I was this close to waterboarding her when she complained to her mom that I was "bugging the crap out of her" and my mother and I were politely ushered toward the door and I was driven to the hospital for a lobotomy. I still sometimes, to this very day, reflect on these events and think of her and wonder what the fuck she was doing taking a shower at three P.M. on a Saturday. I mean, c'mon! Even with running water, that's fucking bizarre behavior. But *I'm* the weirdo.

So, to recap, I grew up in a shack, in a frozen wasteland without television, without running water, and I slept in a basement FULL OF MICE. Still, if that's not enough to convince you that I was abused, I haven't even told you the cruelest part of my childhood yet, the most horrible thing I had to endure growing up, which is still difficult for me to talk about as it makes my stomach cramp just thinking about it: homemade ketchup.

Everything was homemade in our house. Now bear with me because this gets a little NPR.

Everything came from the farm. We ate meat raised just a

few feet from our bedroom windows. We slaughtered pigs and chickens, and the cows we shot in the head were hung in the garage until we butchered and wrapped them twenty-eight days later. Eggs were plucked from the chickens' nests every morning. In movies they always make getting the eggs from chickens look like a real walk in the park, accompanied by a lovely upbeat rhyming song, "I've got a hen for a friend! And she gives me eggs from her end!" but it's not like that at all. Chickens are disgustingly dirty creatures and when you walk into the pen, they flap around and the shit and germs dust up and coat the inside of your eyelids, your nose, and your mouth. And the eggs, everybody, come out of a chicken's ass. (Or a slot close to the chicken's ass—biology was never my strength.) So guess what? They're coated with chicken shit that somebody has to wash off! And by somebody, I mean the youngest person in the family. In my case, me. The whole process is so gross that if those little abortions weren't the best thing on the planet to eat, the most wonderful food ever, no one would ever put up with those fucker cluckers.

All our milk products were made to order. Raw milk isn't like the transparent, tasteless kind you pour out of a carton. It comes loaded with cream, and if you leave it for a while—just like the saying people have about talent—the cream rises to the top. Except in the case of fresh milk, it really is true. You skim the thick white cream off till you get to the blue-toned milk underneath, but no matter how many times you do this, you never get it all. Eventually you just stir it up and drink the equivalent of half-and-half. Butter had to be shaken in a jar with a spoon for hours with your left hand while you were reading or doing math homework or flicking boogers at your older sister with your right. My mother also made the best pickles. We'd pickle anything. Cucumbers, of course, but also onions and carrots and green beans and peppers and zucchini. And cabbage. My mother made sauerkraut in a big pot with a plate on top of the shredded cabbage and a rock on top of the plate. She kept the whole thing under her bed while it was fermenting. My parents' bedroom had the sharp smell of rotting cabbage that I'm sure any purveyor of fine candles would be excited to re-create under the German name, Sie Sind Sexy Sauerkraut.

My mother wasn't much of a cook but her baking won prizes at the annual fair. (This is the '80s. The 1980s. Why do you keep imagining women in bonnets and long dresses?) Wheat from our fields was ground into flour, which was then made into bread of all kinds. Delicious bread, of course, but it crumbled and made quite a mess at lunchtime. The other kids at school with their paperlike bread product that produced no crumbs at all looked at you like you were a dirty, filthy pig. Bathing just once a week in the same water as the rest of your family didn't really help that cause, either.

Vegetables, of course, were straight from the garden in the summer and in the winter fresh frozen. Jam, relish, tomato sauce, and yes, even ketchup was made from scratch. Now, it's interesting to point out that the tomato sauce and tomato paste were phenomenal. The freshest herbs and tomatoes cut from the vine just minutes before being blended into a smooth as silk tomatoey heaven couldn't have been kinder to the taste buds. But ketchup, made from nearly the same fresh ingredients, was a lumpy, sugary mess from hell. To me, homemade ketchup is the ipecac of condiments, vomit inducing. To this day I have an aversion to the stuff. Homemade ketchup is one of the worst things ever concocted and Heinz, in my opinion, is only slightly better.

But there, in the middle of a table full of food direct from the farm, was a bright spot, a sunny, backlit bit of gold. (Cue the Danny Elfman music.) Mustard! Because mustard couldn't be made, or at least we never tried. And it came in a bright yellow container with an actual label. From a store. I loved mustard. It was like a sign of something that was out there. That we weren't alone on this godforsaken planet.

Not to put too fine a point on it, but we were like miners buried alive. We were so starved for information from the outside world that when my older sister Audrey had a sleepover at her friend's house that included a TV dinner, she talked about it for years. Usually because we'd prompt her like a trio of Lennys from *Of Mice and Men*. "Tell us about the peas in the TV dinner again, sis!"

"Well," she'd begin as we gathered around her. "They were small, tiny actually, a greenish-gray and all exactly the same size . . ."

4. THE MACDONALD TRIAD: FIRE FASCINATION, BED-WETTING, AND KILLING ANIMALS

It's almost clichéd to point out that serial killers in their youth took joy in lighting fires and killing small animals. And I, though as of yet not a serial killer, also partook in these sordid activities, though joy didn't factor into it much. I lived on a farm, so yes, killing animals was something we did as a family. In fact, it was my job every spring to lop off the heads of the young hens. It was my job because my sisters were pussies and didn't seem to need my father's approval the way I did. "You sure can kill a bird like nobody's business, Bonnie." Melt.

If you want to kill a chicken (and you must want to because you keep asking me about it), here's how you do it. You start the same way as if you locked your keys in the car. Take a wire hanger and straighten it out. Turn the end back so you have a hook, but a narrow one. This is your chicken catcher. Take the chicken catcher into the chicken pen and start swinging. Eventually, you will catch one of those dirty birds by the leg. Carry it upside down, out of the pen. Throw it onto the chopping block as you pick up the ax with your other hand and swing down as hard as you can. Hopefully you'll slice it right across the neck, nice and clean. But not always. An inch to the left and you've cut into some of the precious chicken breast. An inch to the right and you've cut the head in half. It was precision work and I was always trying to get it just right, always working on the perfect execution. After being decapitated, the bird, or rather its body, will take off running like, well, like a chicken with its head cut off. Sometimes it ran like a dart in a straight line until it fell lifeless into the dirt. Without a head, it looked comically like those cartoons of ostriches with their heads buried in the sand. Sometimes the headless bird ran around in circles like a sadistic circus performer. Always good for a laugh. Very entertaining. The same thing will happen to a person, incidentally. A human head can remain conscious for up to sixty seconds. I don't know how scientists discovered this, but I imagine it went something like, "Marie, blink once if you can hear us." Seventeen headless bodies later and they had their results.

After the chicken's head was removed, my sisters and I picked up all the chickens, finding them like Easter eggs: "Here's one! Behind this bush." "There's one under the car!" We'd take them to my father, who was boiling water in a big vat over an open fire near the tree line. He'd dip the chicken into the water and tie it up by its ankles. The hot water would loosen the feathers and the hanging upside down would drain the blood from the bird. We'd rub our hands down the chickens' bodies to remove the feathers, leaving a bloody, feathered mess on the ground. Then we'd take the birds and put them in a large tub where they'd be taken into the house for my mother who would further clean them, cut them up, and freeze them for the winter.

During this entire process my sister Andrea would cry, but like the chickens she was crying about, she was not let off the hook. Sure we gave her concerned looks and occasionally patted her on the back, but she still had to scrape the feathers off the birds, letting her tears mingle with the blood and feathers beneath her feet.

Andrea didn't enjoy the killing, but she did enjoy the fire. So did I. We burned our garbage in two big oil cans out behind our house every second or third night. It was a fun thing to do. We'd throw in the trash and then light up an old cereal box and watch it catch on the grocery bag and then the sugar bag and the stick I was poking it with. Fire has such big ambitions. It wants to go everywhere. It doesn't think, oh, maybe that's not for me, let me just stay where I started.

So yes, I had a fascination with fire, but more than likely it was because of the absence of a television. If you take a look at the graph, once we got a television, our fire watching trended downward at a pretty sharp rate.

I did the majority of my television watching between the ages of ten and twelve because I spent a lot of time in the hospital with bladder problems, which brings us to the third element in the trifecta: bed-wetting.

When I was around six or seven years old, wetting the bed, my pants, and a snowsuit or two became something of a specialty of mine. This, it turned out, was just a starter kit to bigger problems, which involved the above mentioned inability to hold my urine as well as terrible kidney pains and life-threatening fevers. I was whisked around to countless doctors and specialists and had numerous tubes shoved up places I didn't know tubes could go. A common test, which I think they also use as a form of torture in Islamic countries, involved roughly shoving a tube up my pee hole and into my bladder to drain any pee that might be there. The tube was then used in reverse to fill my bladder with water containing a dye that could be photographed easily on an X-ray. They filled and filled and filled and if I started letting it out, reversing again the direction of the liquid flowing through the tube, they—the technicians—would get mad and say, "Come on, you can do more." It was extremely painful. Did I mention that? It hurt like hell. Then they'd remove the tube and ask me to hold in the pee while they x-rayed me this way and that way, and honestly, I felt like I could die from the pressure of having such a full bladder. I often wondered if my bladder could actually tear. It felt like it was tearing. "I think I'm tearing here!" But they assured me that my bladder was still fully intact. And then finally, they'd say pee, and I'd pee and they'd x-ray that and then they'd say, "Stop! Stop! Stop!" But you know how hard it is to stop midstream. It's hard. Then they'd say, "Finish up in the bathroom." And I would hobble to the nearest one, my gown wet with colored water and I'd pee until I could no longer pee. All this because I couldn't hold my pee.

The problems with all this ureter nonsense started in elementary school. I was fighting with a little girl on the playground before school and winning! After a brief wrestling session, the little girl tried to escape the situation with some dignity but I followed her around verbally abusing her. For one day of my life, I was not the bullied, but the bullier! And it felt great. That's the thing we often fail to pay attention to when we have the bullying discussion. How great it can feel for the bullier. When we focus on the victim all the time, we miss these feel-good stories. This was turning out to be one of the best mornings of my young life and I was feeling pretty proud of myself when we were handed a pamphlet with half a dozen pages and nearly forty questions and told we had thirty minutes to finish it. It was IQ test day. I wanted to excel if only to keep my ego feeling buoyed. I wanted to be a genius bully, not a stupid one. At about the eleven-minute mark I started feeling an intense sensation in my bladder region. A pressure, a tickling. I moved around uncomfortably in my seat and kept writing. My leg started to bounce. Then the other one. I squirmed. I exhaled loudly. But still, I kept circling. One page left. I could do this! I was capable of great things! Six more questions. A line began to form between my eyes that twenty-five years later, an unsolicited someone would suggest I correct with Botox. My head felt hot, my hands were sweaty, my panties were damp, damper, dampest. Five more questions. Four more questions. My inner thighs were wet. My bottom began to slip in the pool that was now on my seat. I stopped squirming. I felt relief. I heard the dripping of pee from the seat to the floor. I moved my feet out of the way and kept answering. Three more questions.

The kid who sat behind me tapped me on the shoulder. I turned with the wide-eyed universal look of bewilderment. What, young man, whatever could you want?

"Do you have to go to the bathroom?"

I shook my head no. And it was true. I was no longer sidetracked by that pesky feeling of needing to pee.

But now there was yelling. My teacher was standing in front of me, mouth agape, hands moving excitedly, but I tuned her out. I had a test to finish. Concentration, which no one thought was my strength, was now my greatest quality.

My teacher practically dragged me out the door, and I swear, that little girl, the one I'd bullied earlier in the day, what seemed like an eternity before, was looking at me with the smuggest look ever smacked off someone's face. But I didn't smack it off because I was being escorted by the neck of my shirt to the home economics class where I would be given a T-shirt and a pair of pants (with a hole in the crotch!) and my clothes would be washed and dried and folded by the sixth-grade class. "Okay, class," I imagined their teacher saying, "today we're going to learn how to clean the clothes of a six-year-old bully who wet herself while taking an IQ test. Okay, everyone, let's get those rubber gloves on. We've got work to do."

It was a tough day, The Day I Peed My Pants in School. The highs were high and the lows were wet. But then there was also the pity and the shame to deal with. The shame came not so much from peeing my pants, but from having to wear a pair of crotchless trousers for the rest of the day. I knew the kids were trying to be extra nice to me, they sensed the hell that I was personally going through, but for some reason it caused me to react unfavorably. As I was working on my letter *k*s after snack time, I realized my legs were not crossed in a ladylike position, the way one does when one is going commando in pants without a middle seam. I crossed my legs and looked up to see a little boy looking at me with a sad, pitying look. We made eye contact and he gave me a little smile, as if to say, "It'll get better." I gave him the finger.

5. ABOVE AVERAGE INTELLIGENCE

Yes, it turns out I scored above average on the IQ test and that was without even finishing the last two questions!

6. VIOLENCE

Our school still practiced corporal punishment. When kids did something wrong, like throw a snowball or roll their eyes, they got the strap. Several lashes on each hand. And then of course, when you got home, you got hit with the belt for getting the strap.

My mother taught at my school, but this did not save me from being hand-spanked on a fairly routine basis. In fact, after one incident where I skipped class to get French fries with my friends, I was the only one in the group to get the strap. And that's because when my mother told the school's disciplinarian to work me over, he obliged, though I can't be sure if he was giddy when he agreed. What I do know is he tenderly fingered a leather strip about the length and width of a ruler while he yammered on about responsibilities. I wasn't really listening. I was trying to pull a piece of hair out of my head. Rumor had it that if you laid a piece of hair on the palm of your hand before the strap made contact, the hair would dig into your skin and make it bleed, and if you bleed you can sue. And if you can sue, you can win. You can Sally Field this fucker. But I couldn't get a hair out of my head. I pulled and pulled but nothing. You can never get a strand when you need it. But kill somebody and they fall out of your head like you've just finished your first round of chemo.

The school's enforcer grabbed my right hand and instructed me to unfurl my fist. If I hadn't opened it, there would've been nothing he could do. Ah, if you could live life over again, I would've never opened my fist. I'd write a series of self-help books titled things like "The Art of the Closed Fist" and "An Open Hand Is a Smacked Hand." But I did open my fist. And it was smacked. Repeatedly.

I was sent back to the classroom with red-rimmed eyes, still sniffling, hands swelling like floatation devices being prepped for the beach. I couldn't even hold a pencil.

The boy who sat in front of me waited until the teacher was at the chalkboard and then he turned around and put a few slightly melted M&M's on my desk. I mouthed, "Fuck you." And then shoved them all in my mouth at once because it hurt too much to pick them up one by one with my throbbing, red fingers.

When I got home that night, I got my ass tanned by my

father. And that night I slept like a baby; I woke up every two hours and cried.

Still, being beaten by adults was somehow better than getting beaten up by your classmates. That was something people did in my school to pass the time. Guys, girls, it wasn't gender specific. And it always happened in the IGA grocery store parking lot.

There was a group of girls in my school who roamed the halls systematically choosing a new girl every couple of weeks to intimidate and abuse. I thought it was amusing until it was my turn. I knew I'd been chosen when they began making fun of my homemade, self-designed summer frock. I simply turned my stone-cold stare on them when they began mocking me. I didn't say a word. I just stared. I think it freaked them out. "What are you looking at?" they said, practically in unison. "Pig shit," I answered. And that seemed to make them angry. The blondest one drove her fist into a locker and they all walked away. My heart was pounding, but I felt I'd successfully avoided a painful interaction. Later that day, however, I was passed a handwritten note in typing class. It said: "Meet me tomorrow night in the IGA parking." Blondie didn't need to specify a time. Everyone congregated there the minute the grocery store closed at ten. I knew everyone had stopped typing to watch my reaction, so I read the note, swallowed hard, and then shrugged. "Yeah, why not." But really, why? I lay awake in bed that night going over my moves. But even if I connected, landed that one perfect punch, I knew it was going to hurt my fist. I was really, truly, overly concerned about hurting my hand. It's what I focused on. As I fell asleep that night, I decided that the best place to punch her, despite her rock hard abs, would be in her midsection.

For reasons I can't fathom now, I went to the IGA grocery store parking lot the next night after it closed. The girl gang was there waiting in a tight group, surrounded by kids who desperately sought their approval. Blondie, the ringleader, stepped out of the group when she saw me. I think I actually detected surprise on her face. The crowd gathered, and my adrenaline was pumping. She was talking shit and I just walked right up to her and punched her in the face. I don't know what happened to my midsection plan. She fell backward and I looked at my hand. It stung but not as badly as I had anticipated. Suddenly someone grabbed me and the next thing I knew, I was driving around in a Corvette with two semipopular guys. We were speeding through town without our seat belts on, yelling at people through open windows that I was a "killer."

"Can you slow down?" I saw no reason for more people to be killed.

"No way," the driver answered. "I have a need for speed." And he handed me a stack of speeding tickets. There were a lot.

The next day at school as I walked to my first class, people started chanting, "Rocky! Rocky! Rocky!" I can't say I didn't enjoy it, but it was short lived. I got another note. This one said to meet the ringleader during first break in the smoking area. Oh, man, this is it, I thought. This is where she gets even. I might've caught her off guard the night before, but now she was ready. I had two choices. I could kill myself in the bathroom or go to the smoking area and have her kill me. Either way, I was going to have to write a few good-bye/thank-you notes to the people who had been kind to me over the years.

But I finally had a reputation and it was one I felt was worth protecting. So on shaky legs I walked out to the smoking area. It was just her, without her entourage. She had a very large swollen nose and a black eye. I must've been staring.

"It's broken. But there's nothing they can do about it."

"I'm sorry."

"No worries. Don't worry about it." No big deal!? I broke your nose and blackened your eye! Don't worry about it? Okay. I won't.

"Listen," she said. "Do you think your mom could make me one of those dresses you were wearing the other day? It's super cute."

It would've been a nice gesture, an olive branch, a gift to say sorry I broke your nose! But no. Not me!

"I don't know. She's pretty busy. Summer is coming and all that. It's her busy season."

"Oh."

And that was that. We never really talked again. We'd smile sometimes in the hall, or I'd pass her the ball extra gently in gym class, but we never became friends.

My fighting career was over, too. No one ever asked me to meet them in the IGA parking lot after that. Thank God.

7. FETISHES

There was not a lot for teenagers to do in the town where I went to high school. There wasn't a movie theater, or a bowling alley. To pass the time we drank, we fought, and, of course, there was sex. Lots of it. You could see the effects walking through the halls of our high school in the form of pregnant girls lugging their book bags around. One girl a few lockers down from me had two babies at home and another one on the way, all before she was eighteen! I mean, clearly an overachiever.

Sex was something all the girls talked about. They talked about penis size, they talked about balls. (I didn't even know what balls were! I had no brothers; I was shocked to see them dangling there the first time.) They talked about blowing and sucking and how to lick the bedsheet to get the hairs off your tongue. And every few weeks one of the girls would say, "I think

I might be pregnant!" and the other girls would crowd around and pretend it was the best news they'd ever heard. "Ah, you're going to have the cutest baby!" "Danny is going to be so happy! He's going to marry you." Pause. "Oh, it might be Johnny's? Well, one of them is going to be so happy!" "We'll all babysit. I love babies!"

I realized how unbelievably, incredibly ridiculous this was. But I kept my mouth shut because I didn't want them to start chanting TIGHTY TIGHTY TIGHTY at me again.

So, you're thinking, sexual fetish, number five; I guess you didn't have that one. Well, I had the sexual fetish to NOT have sex, if that is in fact a fetish, and I think it is because I was particularly fixated on not doing it, which, among a lot of the girls in my school was very, very odd.

It wasn't that I was overly moral or waiting for Mr. Right or anything like that. I just thought, much like my hand in a fight, it would hurt. Every time I thought about it, I would cringe at the idea of the pain that it must cause.

Despite my reluctance, I lost my virginity at the ripe old age of seventeen. Alcohol was involved, of course. Had a snapshot been taken earlier in the evening, it would've shown me at a house party wearing mittens and holding a beer in each hand. Cops came, threats were made, and the least drunk among us jumped behind the wheel and sped off in search of a new location to finish whatever wine and vodka we'd manage to liberate from the previous party's home liquor cabinet. One of the friends I was with suggested we go to her house since her parents were out of town. At her dining room table, I guzzled wine straight from the bottle. I got the laughs I was looking for, but also double sight and slowed reaction time. Around the table were four or five girls and two young men who patiently sat through several hilarious stories my girlfriends and I told. Stories that took twice as long to tell as they should have because of all the "likes" that peppered our speech back then.

At some point, one of the guys took my hand and led me downstairs. As the room spun around me, he began kissing me and I eagerly kissed him back. He was older by five years or so, which at the time seemed impossibly aged and I'm sure that held some appeal for me. His breath was smoky, but I didn't mind though I was having trouble concentrating on kissing him and keeping his hands to areas of my body I felt were acceptable. As his hand made a mad dash under my shirt, I grabbed his wrist and held it. "Hey," I managed to say, my lips still making contact with his. He shook my hand off him and the next thing I knew I was on my back and he was on top of me. He was holding me down, tearing off my skirt, my tights, my panties—no one can say he didn't put in the extra effort necessary—and then we were having sex on the carpet by the coffee table. I wasn't quiet in my protests. I screamed, I cried, I yelled for help. Later, as I obsessively cleaned the red off the white carpet, my friend acknowledged that she'd heard it all. "It hurts for everybody," she said, without a twinge of guilt for not attempting to rescue me. Cries for help notwithstanding, she and the other girls had decided it was time for me to lose my virginity. I was so OLD, for God's sake. I was a dinosaur. I was nearly old enough to vote! And so my friends kindly looked the other way, charitably turned a deaf ear so that I wouldn't have to walk around with this horrible burden anymore. Thanks, guys! BFFs forever!

And for the record, I was right. It did fucking hurt.

My old ripened body took that sperm as fast as it could and bore a zygote like it might be my last chance to reproduce before I went through menopause. My body wasn't taking any chances. It was making a baby.

I didn't realize I was pregnant for months. I was gaining weight at a rapid pace despite only ever really eating pickles, but I never put two and two together. I never said to myself, "Hey there, little lady, ever since you had sexual intercourse, you haven't been getting your period, your breasts hurt, you're packing on the pounds, you've been throwing up almost every morning . . . think maybe you should pee on a stick, see what it says?" Nope.

It took a snide comment from my sister Audrey to bring it all into sharp focus. Audrey no longer lived at home. She had moved to Saskatchewan after high school to become a secretary but she'd show up every few months for a week or so to sleep and nap and eat cheese. One afternoon she woke up long enough to call me fat. "I'd think you were pregnant if you weren't such a virgin," she said before rolling over and going back to sleep.

But I wasn't a virgin. Somehow those words were the first seeds of the realization that I might actually be in a little bit of trouble. I made a doctor's appointment and a couple of nights after my exam, after bingeing on a jar of pickled beans, the phone rang. I answered it. It was the doctor. Or a nurse, I don't remember. Someone on the other end said the test results were positive. I thanked them politely and hung up. I sat on my bed and took a deep breath. I poked my head into the living room and asked Andrea to please come into my room. She did. I told her my situation. She cried. She cried harder than she did when she was butchering the chickens. I cried too but mostly so she would know that I knew I was a disappointment. Then we dried our eyes and went to the dinner table and ate dinner with the rest of the family.

"Where have all the bean pickles gone?" my mother asked. "I swear we made fourteen jars and there's only seven left."

The next day, I had a doctor's consultation with the

extremely religious Dr. Reilly (name changed, as if you care). I sat through a long lecture about sin and maturity and I think there was even something in there about kids eating too much sugar, but I wasn't fazed by any of it. I had made up my mind the night before, and knowing that I knew what I was going to do made me feel better. It made me feel safe. I was seventeen. I was poor. I would have enough challenges getting out of here.

"I want to end my pregnancy," I told him.

Dr. Reilly, of course, thought this was the worst idea he'd ever heard and he cleared his throat, gearing up, no doubt, for another long-winded lecture. But before he could launch into the perils of underage sex and red dye number 3 I cut him off.

"Can you do it?" His face turned white. It was against the law, he said, to get such things done in Canada. But even I knew there had to be work-arounds. "Call it something else," I said.

He shook his head dramatically. The only way I could get such a service done was if I had been raped. "Were you raped?" he asked.

"No," I answered. Rape happened in a dark alley or in a parking lot with a stranger. This was at my friend's house with a guy I'd known for at least six to seven hours. No. This was not rape.

And so, Dr. Reilly began a new speech. One in which I'd keep and raise the baby with the help of my family. He said there'd be resources I could use from the community. He said my friends would babysit. He was starting to sound an awful lot like a sixteen-year-old high school girl.

Dr. Reilly didn't believe in abetting young women seeking abortions and he didn't believe in patient-client privilege. He called my mom. I was in the waiting room staring at the wall when she walked in. Now my mother is a smart, educated woman, but I guess we are all prone to delusion. She asked me why I was there.

"Guess," I said, rolling my eyes.

"Tell me," she said.

"You know why," I said.

"I don't," she answered.

I looked at her carefully. She did have a deer-in-the-headlights expression on her face. Maybe she really didn't know. Maybe she thought I'd cut off a toe in home economics class or maybe she was hoping it was just herpes. Something I'd have to take care of for the rest of my life but not something she'd have to explain to her neighbors.

My mother kept secrets. I don't know what they were or why she had to keep them, but she didn't like anyone to know anything about her. She'd say, "I don't care what people think," but she did. She cared very deeply. Once she told me she didn't have a best friend. This was after watching the Bette Midler movie, *Beaches*. I felt sad for her, but before I could effectively translate those thoughts into an appropriate action, she shrugged and said, "I'm glad. I don't need anyone knowing all my secrets." What secrets, Mom!? That you dye your hair or have only seven pairs of panties? What?

On the way home from the doctor's that day, after she did learn why I was there, she finally turned to me and said, "What am I going to tell everyone?"

"Don't tell them anything," I said. "I'm not keeping it."

"Yes you are."

"No I'm not."

"Who have you told?"

"Just Andrea."

"You told Andrea?" My mother pushed her glasses up her nose. "Who else? What friends?"

"No one." It was true. I hadn't told anyone. Maybe I was more like my mother than I thought.

"We'll tell your father and that's it. Do you understand? Tell no one else. Not even Audrey."

I nodded. I suddenly felt very tired. I was struggling to keep my eyes open. To this day, great stress exhausts me. I was once watching a *Dateline* about a man whose wife was killed and he was brought in for questioning. He was a suspect. And while he was waiting to talk to the officers, he fell asleep. They noted that this was a sign of guilt, but I related. That's how I would react. (By the way, he did not do it. It was a scorned lover who killed his darling—albeit cheating—wife.)

"You're going to tell your father."

I forced my eyes open and looked at her. "Please, Mom," I begged. "You tell him."

She shook her head. "Oh, no. You got yourself into this mess."

She woke me up when she pulled the key out of the ignition. I walked slowly toward the house. My father was just sitting down for his afternoon coffee break.

I begged my mother one last time. "Please, Mom. Please."

"Nope," she said, staying put in the doorway. "Tell him."

"Tell me what?"

I told him, but he already knew. He could read the situation as soon he looked at his teenage daughter, eyes red from crying, and my mother, her thin lips pursed, disgust dripping from her elbows. There are only so many things "Tell him" could mean. My father stood up and gave me a hug. "You're not the first person it's ever happened to," he said, referring to my mother and himself.

I'll never forget him for that. It was an act of pure kindness that I so desperately needed then.

My father is a kind, generous man. A good husband, a devoted father. But he does have a quirk in his personality. My father has never said, "I love you," to me or to any of my sisters.

Never. Ever. And he has almost died three times. He has been lying on his deathbed but "I like you, a lot" is the closest he could ever come.

When I was four, my father had stomach and testicular cancer and, after a year of chemo, hospitalization, and having his internal organs removed, put in a bucket, cleaned in bleach, and put back into his gut, the doctors sent him home to die. There was nothing more they could do for him. And so, home to die he came. We all said our good-byes. Even me, young as I was; I didn't understand of course what was going on and I don't remember everything that was said but I do distinctly remember the three little words that were not said. My grandmother, my father's mother, drove from Saskatchewan to see him but good-bye was something she wouldn't say. She told him, as the story goes, that he had a responsibility to his family—to his wife, to children—and to his farm to get better and that is what he would do. No ifs, ands, or buts. My father's father died of a heart attack when my dad was only four and I suspect that my grandmother gave my father the speech that she had been working on, that had been festering for thirty-five years, one that she wished she could give to her own husband but could not.

My dad recovered but "I love you" never crossed his lips.

Not then and not the time he broke his back. And not the time his spleen ruptured, either. He is the last of a generation of tough-as-nails men who thinks it's faggy to show affection.

But he was kind in that moment. The fighting began later. We fought because I wouldn't tell them who the father was. And because I wouldn't stop saying, "I'm not having this baby!"

I did finally tell them what had happened. Teary eyed, I told them about the drinking and the sex, and I even told them about having to clean the carpet afterward. They said nothing.

Late one night, they came into my bedroom as I was about to fall asleep. In whispers, they told me the plan. My mother and I would drive to Oregon, to a clinic there. I'd have the procedure the following morning and drive home that night. I would get what I wanted. In return, I was never to tell anyone what happened.

I got up the next morning and walked into the bank. I removed all the money I had, all the money I made from my cow and my ice cream, so I could pay for the trip and the procedure. Turns out that money really was being used to get me out of this place.

One of the conditions of getting the procedure in Oregon was that I had to see a counselor the day before to make sure I was making the right decision. I went and explained flatly the events of the night and she told me that I was "raped." She used that word. Raped! She said, "Do you get that this isn't your fault?"

I didn't.

In fact, I chalked her up to a New Age-y liberal (a phrase my father liked to use) who didn't ever want to have to take responsibility for anything. I smiled and thanked her and the next day I got an abortion. An hour after that I drove the entire fourteen hours home because my mother just couldn't.

After about six hours of silence she said, "What are you doing?"

"I'm writing funny stories in my head."

My mother looked at me with repulsion. A look that said, "What the hell kind of monster have I raised?" and she leaned over and turned on the radio.

MY COPING MECHANISM HASN'T CHANGED much over the years. When a subject causes me inner turmoil, it fuels my creativity. I process the uncomfortable feelings by writing stories, telling offensive jokes, and making perverted macramé wall art. This probably makes me a weirdo, but not a serial killer, so hopefully you'll judge me on a curve. If you have the appropriate emotional response to things, congratulations, you're better than me.

Chapter 2

BEING BORN: I'LL NEVER DO THAT AGAIN

I was welcomed into the world the way anyone welcomes a mistake: with gnawing regret and the determination to make the best of it. My mother had her tubes tied shortly after I was born. She told me she had to beg the doctor to do it, since four girls born to a farm family served very little purpose and surely the McFarlanes wanted to try for at least a few boys. My mother, who was very young and very poor at the time, politely declined by screaming, "Make me barren or kill me now!"

Both my parents grew up on farms in Saskatchewan. They were bound to meet eventually, as the law of averages dictates that everyone in Saskatchewan eventually meets everyone else. Before Heather and Carle began their romantic-comedy movie montage, my father took a road trip west to the next province over, Alberta. He was visiting an old friend and I can't know for sure, but my guess is that he got blind drunk soon after he arrived because he spent nearly every penny to his name on three sections of unbroken farmland. Prior to the purchase he had nine thousand dollars burning a hole in his pocket for twenty years, an inheritance from his father who died when my father was just four years old. He asked little Carle to fetch him a glass of water but when my father returned with the H_2O, his dad was dead. He and his six older siblings managed the farm, all the boys dropping out of school after eighth grade to work the fields. Of course, this early commitment was rewarded, hence his portion, a whopping nine thousand dollars. And he put all of it toward that laughable piece of Northern Albertan farmland. Saskatchewan farmers looked down on Alberta farmers. Alberta was nice to look at it, but it was too hilly, too rocky, and too foresty for growing crops. The McFarlane clan was not impressed. It was a nutty thing to do. But back then, my father was good at making rash decisions. It wasn't until much later, with several near-death experiences under his belt, that he started to second-guess almost every single thing he ever did.

After that reckless bit of business, my father returned briefly to Saskatchewan and followed it up with three more devil-may-care moves. He met my mother at a dance, hit on her sister, struck out, and a few whirlwind weeks later knocked up my mom in the back of his sweet maroon 1959 Ford Meteor. The wedding was a few months after that, with just close family. In their wedding picture, my mother is wearing a navy suit with a knee-length skirt. If she was a wearing a little hat, she could've walked right onto Air Canada and gotten a job, "Coffee, tea, or me?"

Even at that young age, my mother was a pretty serious lady with thick glasses and a short sensible haircut, but I guess because she knew there wasn't going to be a honeymoon or even a party, she decided to get drunk at her wedding supper (wedding supper!). She even did the limbo despite the fact that she was three months pregnant. I've never seen my mother drunk, so it had to have been a pretty good supper.

Ten days later, the newlyweds struck out for their new home. In the flat land of the prairies, their families could watch them drive away for seven of the ten hours it would take them to reach their final destination.

It was a long, slow trip on bumpy dirt roads. They had a house trailer hooked up behind their half-ton pickup truck (which my father traded his beloved Ford Meteor for) and loaded it down with all of their belongings. It wasn't much. What they had in personal items would have fit in the overhead carry-on compartment if they were plane people. But despite my mother's choice of wedding outfits, they were not. When they got close to their plot of land, there was still a lot of snow, even though it was the end of April (Hello! Red flag, farming people!), and a huge hill, which nearly did them in. The truck-and-trailer combo was struggling to climb the nearly vertical Beaver River hill and it lurched and grunted and slowed to a hair-raising five miles an hour, even though the pedal was to the metal. My father told my mother to open her door and jump out if they started to go backward. Today we encourage pregnant women to stay away from soft cheeses and jumping out of moving vehicles, but in those days, they just didn't know better.

Luckily, my mother didn't have to test her jump-and-roll abilities and they made it to the top. I'm sure they were relieved, but the Beaver River hill was nothing, NOTHING, compared to the metaphoric hill they would have to climb nearly their entire lives.

Why did my parents choose to live in a place that routinely saw temperatures drop to forty below both Celsius and Fahrenheit? Why did they choose a place that was carpeted with rocks and trees but lacked people and roads? Why did they try to farm in such a cold climate with an exceedingly short growing season? My parents made this their home for the same reason anyone lives in a place that makes other people look around, turn up their noses, and say, "Why would anyone live here?"

They were poor.

When my mom stocked the kitchen for the first time, the groceries came to the astonishing sum of fourteen dollars and my parents knew they were going to have to tighten their belts. They were going to have to save for belts, then get belts, and then tighten them. They had a total of $1,400 to last until the next fall when they could start harvesting a crop.

First, though, they would have to clear the land and prepare the soil for the following spring. It was work fit for an Egyptian slave, and to think that one man chopped down all the trees by hand, pulled out all the roots, hauled away all the debris, and picked all the thousands of rocks off the property is as hard to fathom as the building of the pyramids. But it was done. And it was all done by my father. And maybe an alien or two.

My father, Carle, lost thirty pounds that summer. The hauling, chopping, pulling, and tossing of rock after rock, hour after hour and week after week was certainly part of it, but he also did Tony Horton's P90X Total Body Transformation. The more my father cleared the fields, the more it looked like he needed to do. So he'd work harder and longer and the harder and longer he worked, the less it appeared that he had done. Rocks started popping up from the center of the earth. Tree roots were growing without their trees. The earth was getting harder. The days were getting shorter. And his waist was getting thinner.

His bride was a terrible cook, which also helped with the weight loss. From the field, he would look over to the house and know that dinner was almost ready by the smoke signals coming through the open kitchen window. He ate the charred animal bits anyway. He ate the dry potatoes. He ate the bitter aspic.

He ate because he couldn't drink. Imbibing was a thing of the past. He was probably an alcoholic anyway, or at least well on his way to becoming one. He quit drinking by using not AA but another method that has worked for men throughout the ages: lack of funds.

Somehow they made it through that first winter and then the next and the next and they eventually got some pigs and milk cows. It was a lot of work for my father, milking twenty-six cows every day and trying to keep the milking equipment sanitary without any running water.

MY OLDEST SISTER'S BIRTHDAY IS early October. And my next two sisters were both born on March second, though they're not twins, they're exactly two years apart. I arrived the following year, three weeks late, at the end of March. My father's birthday is June first, and if you do the math, you can see that my mother and father had quite a lively sex life, doing it at least once every year on his birthday and conceiving a child 75 percent of the time.

When my mother got pregnant with her third baby, they decided the trailer was too cramped, so they started fixing up an old log house on the property. It was an enormous amount of work, but they made it livable. They dug a well. They got electricity. This year, the third year, the soil would be ripe and ready and the crops would be the biggest yet. They would finally be okay. They would finally be able to relax. All their hard work would finally pay off. Then, ten days after their third baby was born, the log house burned down. Standing next to the tree line, the spring colors just starting to emerge, the sun setting behind my mother, it probably made a beautiful picture, but out front, where she was facing, her whole world was going up in flames. So with three kids and two heavy hearts they all moved back into the trailer. Twelve months later, smiling through clenched teeth and stubbornly stuffing down their resentment, they welcomed me into the world.

I was born a relatively healthy seven-pound, two-ounce beautiful, yellow baby girl. I was yellow because I was born jaundiced, which means that there was excess bilirubin in my blood caused by an immature liver. It turns out that my immature liver was the ringleader that indoctrinated the rest of me, part by part, into a tragic life of scatological humor.

I was delivered into the world by Dr. Forest, a wild man with thick red hair. (I've changed his name in case you're trying to Google him.) In the northern Canadian Cold Lake Hospital, it was hard to get doctors and this one was probably hiding out from malpractice lawsuits, or maybe he just came for the all-you-can-eat Valium. It was entirely possible that he wasn't actually a doctor at all. He treated my dad's ringworm with diesel fuel from the heater in the office, and when my father had severe reactions to it, Dr. Forest laughed his maniacal laugh and said, "We cured the ringworm but almost killed the patient!"

My entire family was living in a one-bedroom, thirty-eight-foot house trailer in the middle of 480 acres of farmland with one inadequate road, no phone, and a lot of prairie bush. My mother was a substitute teacher in those days, but because they didn't have a telephone, the principal of the school would have to drive all the way out to their farm in the morning to see if she could come to work that day. I'm guessing she was last on his list of people to contact if they needed someone to fill in.

In the winter, the trailer would get so cold, Mom couldn't let her babies crawl around on the floor. Being poor sucks everywhere in the world, but it has its own special disadvantages in a brutally cold climate. It's one thing to have to go without, but if you're living off the land in a frozen tundra and you can't afford shoes for your kids, they can lose their fucking feet. And then you have to fill out forms to get a government-issued wheelchair and then you have to get a van . . . it's a slippery slope.

AS IF MY MOTHER DIDN'T have enough challenges, my parents' second child was born on a Wednesday. And Wednesday's child is full of woe. I never knew my sister was different until one day when we were cavorting at the beach and my sister Andrea, maybe six or seven, swatted my sister Lynn on the butt even though she was two years older! Andrea spanked Lynn. Lynn was older. This was a radical change in the hierarchy, in the power system. My little brain chugged and whirred trying to comprehend intellectually what I was now aware of emotionally. Lynn was younger than Andrea. Not in years, but in some other way. Andrea, though younger, felt she had authority over Lynn.

The thought rattled around in my brain for a while and I looked at Lynn through a different lens and started to notice things. She read the wrong words in books. My mother spoke to her in a slightly different cadence. My father always hugged her first when he came in from the barn. She pooped in the bathtub and wasn't beaten within an inch of her life. And I don't know about your family, but in our family, pooping in the bathtub was a major faux pas.

"What's wrong with Lynn?" I didn't know I was going to ask. I don't remember thinking, how should I frame this? It just popped out on a rare occasion when it was just my mom and me in the car.

"She's retarded, honey."

Oh.

And the car pulls into a parking space at the post office and out she goes to mail a letter.

I spent a few months making it my mission to "un-retard" her. (We eventually learned all the politically correct words to use, but in the beginning, "retard" was the correct word. But then people started using it to spice up their everyday language and new words were chosen and then people started using those words, and ever since we've just been trying to outrun the vernacular of the mean people.)

I was determined to crack the code of her brain and flip the switch that would allow her to think as easily as I could. I knew that if I just spent enough time with her, if we worked hard enough at it, she would learn to identify her letters as quickly as I could, count by twos, and learn all the colors of the rainbow. I tried to teach her her right from her left, "Your other left!" and catch a fly ball instead of running from it, "Don't be scared!" She'd stand there, eyes closed, letting the ball hit her in the head. To her credit, she never complained. She never whined that it was hard or begged to quit. She just jauntily went along with everything I tried to get her to do. And eventually she learned how to catch a ball and could tell her right from her left, but not because of me. She learned it at school like everybody else.

Our school system was not progressive for its time, so I have to assume there weren't enough funds for the special needs kids to have their own school and this is why they were integrated into our classes. My classes. I didn't have to look out for my sister Lynn. Didn't have to protect her from bullies. She was not bullied. She was not picked on. I can't speak for other schools, other towns, but it wasn't like how they depict it in the movies. In the movies they always make it seem like all the handicapped kids are getting rocks thrown at them all day every day. It wasn't like that for Lynn. In fact, she was very popular. Definitely more popular than I was. It wasn't just that they were nice to her. They liked her. She's funny. She's good with people. She's kind. She was able to banter in that small-talk kind of way that I was never able to do. She did not suffer from severe social anxiety.

In those days, Lynn had long, thick, pin-straight hair, parted in the middle; the popular girls would brush her hair at lunch and discuss which shampoo was the best and how if you stopped using your regular shampoo for a while and used another brand your hair would be super soft.

I, on the other hand, spent a lot of time by myself. Sometimes I went to the gym and spent the lunch hour perfecting my three-point swish even though I wasn't on the basketball team. Other times I went to the library and read. But mostly I spent the breaks washing the word "TIGHTY" off my locker. Yes, in my high school, having a small circumference in the vaginal area was an insult. I guess these fuck nuts wanted their lovers loose as a shower cap.

I'd walk by the guys sitting on the stairs and they'd all go, "Squeak, squeak, squeak." And my rejoinder would be along the lines of—and this is obviously a sign of the great comedian I would become—"Fuck off, asswipes."

I have always been trying to reinvent myself. Because when you're weird, you don't want to be weird. You want to be normal. But you can't be normal because normal is something you're either born with or you're not, like the "it" factor or a third nipple. So in your attempts to be normal, you make even weirder choices, like deciding you're going to jog the four miles to school instead of taking the bus (which I did because I wanted to use the shower at school!). You'd be better off just accepting your weirdness and making it your strength, but children lack that kind of perspective, especially when everyone in your family is constantly telling you how weird you are. And not in a cheerleading kind of way, either. I mean, I have an older sister who is mentally disabled, but I'm the least normal one. That's a pretty big accomplishment that I never got my trophy for.

Maybe I lacked proper socialization. In the summers, we

rarely saw our classmates. We were stuck out on the farm where our days were filled with feeding livestock, milking cows, pulling weeds, shucking peas, cutting grass, trimming hedges, picking raspberries, watering, digging, planting, stacking wood, hanging clothes on the line, fixing fences, and herding cattle. Then after breakfast we'd have more chores. Just last year I saw a special, with Diane Sawyer reporting, about the terrible conditions children of migrant farmworkers are forced to endure during the summer months. All the kids have to sleep in the same room. They have to get up at the crack of dawn and hit the fields, working through to dusk with just one lunch hour and two short breaks. I couldn't help thinking to myself, two breaks plus an hour off for lunch! These kids today . . . they are so coddled.

Sounds crazy, but as a kid I had a very strong aversion to this kind of rigorous lifestyle. People who are born into the farm life but don't enjoy laboring from sunup to sundown are diagnosed with a very serious illness: laziness. And like a tramp stamp, once you have the label, you can never bend down again without someone noticing: "Well, look who finally decided to do something." Once you are anointed as lazy, it is a lifelong label that no amount of success can ever undo: "Sure he's the star of the New York City Ballet, but he's such a sloth. Remember how long it took him to clean out the barn?"

To pass the time, I wrote books in my head. Later, after dinner or when I had a break, I would transcribe those thoughts to paper and hide them under my bed where the mice would nibble up the edges. Writing in your head while you're supposed to be pulling weeds is a good idea in theory. In reality, I pulled out all the baby radishes and left all the weeds.

After all the farm chores were done, after the supper dishes were cleared and cleaned and the clothes were taken off the line, we played games as a family. Board games, card games, occasionally charades. One of our favorite board games to play was called, and I'm not fucking kidding, FARM. We worked all day long hoeing and weeding and caring for livestock and then to relax, for pure enjoyment purposes, we played a game that simulated those exact same activities! It was so stupid and yet none of us seemed to notice the irony. One of us would flip a card, "Hey, I got a bumper crop! Right on." We worked hard and we played mildly.

One summer, as I picked and shucked, I wrote an entire book in my head called "Chicken Island." Hey, write what you know! I spent hours every night neatly writing it all down and drawing and coloring a few accompanying pictures. I fastened the whole thing together with brads. I made an actual book.

Quite proud of myself, I took it to school at the start of fourth grade and showed it to Allison, who shared a cubby next to mine.

"What is that?" she asked.

"I wrote a book!"

"Why?" She looked panicked. "For whose class? We had to do that?"

"No," I answered, slightly deflated. "I just did it. You know . . ."

Her eyes narrowed "You just wrote a book over the summer?" She looked like she had just eaten a diaper. I shoved the book back in my bag.

"No. Not really."

We never talked about it again. First rule of losers' club. Don't talk about stupid stuff you do in losers' club.

IN MANY WAYS, LYNN WAS my protector. She'd say to the other kids, "Be cool. This is my sister. Stand down, shorty." Or something like that.

After my other sisters moved out of the house, it was just Lynn and me still at home. We'd go to parties together. My mother always said I didn't have to take her with me, but I wanted to. I needed to. She would always say the right thing. "Great party. This dip is really yummy. Did your mom make this? I make a dip with mayonnaise. I love mayonnaise." And I would just stand there behind her smiling, thinking about what I would have said, like: "It's just going to get cigarette butts in it."

Lynn's blessing in many ways is that she looks mentally handicapped. She has the facial features of everyone with Down syndrome. The small wide-set eyes, the low flat nose that is too close to the mouth. And the oversize tongue that keeps her mouth open and lets it all hang out. It becomes a trick of habit to keep it closed, but she was able to do it, unlike my oldest sister Audrey, who was never very good at it.

Lynn's facial features send a universal message to anyone talking to her: keep your expectations low, this person might just be a drooling, blathering idiot. But of course, Lynn exceeds all expectations. When she speaks her eyes twinkle and they draw you in and make you feel relaxed. She can make you feel special. This is why people love Lynn. She makes people feel they are virtuous, charitable people. "Look at me! I'm being friends with someone who is not perfect! I am a good person!"

It's the people who don't look handicapped who have the real life of woe. How many times have you stood in the matrix, talking to someone who appears "normal" but you're unable to get through to them. And for a short time, before your brain is able to process that this person might be handicapped, your demeanor is like, "What the fuck is wrong with you? Were you homeschooled? Have you seen too many Tyler Perry movies?" And then suddenly, something clicks and you figure it out, but it's too late. Your true colors have already been exposed. And

this person, this handicapped person who doesn't look handicapped, deals with jerks like you on a daily basis. On an hourly
basis. Someone mean. Then nice. Or mean and then meaner
because they are mad that this person, this handicapped person who doesn't look handicapped, has exposed the asshole
they really are.

It was rare that my sister was teased at school, but at home
it was a different matter. At home, everyone got picked on by
everyone else. It wasn't exactly a free-for-all, but there was a certain gang mentality where, if someone started in on you, most
everyone else would likely pile on. I was told repeatedly that my
mother and father accidentally brought home the wrong baby
from the hospital! (Hilarious!) And not only was I the wrong
baby, but I was an aborigine baby (the horror!) and there was a
native family on the Cree Indian reservation wondering what to
make of their little white baby. (Little Running Nose!)

It was a never-ending jibe that I had to live with my entire
olive-skinned youth. I often shot back with gems like, "I guess
when you're head and shoulders more beautiful than everyone
else in your family, they start looking for answers." Now, people
always ask me how I got so good at doing roasts, and I think, "Jeez,
I've spent my whole life being roasted and planning revenge."

This hilarious zinger about my not being a product of my
parents once-a-year sexcapade was so persistent that I actually
believed it for a large part of my childhood. Then when I was
too old to believe it anymore, I just wished that it were true.
I wished that I had Cree Indian family who understood me
in a way this one didn't, and maybe even engaged in fewer
morning chores. I'd imagine walking up on the front step of
a cute house in a cute city like Moose Jaw or Red Deer and
my real mom would open the door and she would be beautiful, wearing a deerskin cape and knee-high moccasins, hair

braided with feathers coming down on either side of her high-cheekboned face, and just a little over a dozen years older than me. She'd look at me and know immediately who I was and hug me for six minutes straight without saying a word, just rocking me back and forth and letting the tears stream silently down her face. Then she'd take my cheeks in both her hands and look me right in the eyes and say, "Welcome home, sweetie. Welcome home." But let's be clear. That never happened. My family was actually my family.

I LEFT HOME IMMEDIATELY AFTER high school. I moved from town to town, city to city, searching for something but not knowing what. I went to college a little bit, I knocked around, I got fired a lot but I also got hired a lot. When I was living in Vancouver, I landed a job at a comedy club as a hostess. I was instantly addicted to live comedy. The first night, after the shows, which were the best shows I'd ever seen in my life, bar none, I sat in the greenroom with the comics drinking beer and shooting the shit. In this setting, for some reason, I felt the low level and not-so-low level of anxiety that I had hoisted around with me all my life ease and subside. I said unkind things, vulgar things, disrespectful things, and things that generally made people want to leap out of their chairs and strangle me, except these people (if you want to call them that) didn't contort their faces into angry scowls or demand I leave the area. These men and women laughed or shrugged or in a lot of cases said something even worse. In the context of the characters in the greenroom of that comedy club, I wasn't a wacky abnormality. In fact, in this setting, I felt downright regular.

No one put their hands on either side of my face and said, "Welcome home." But I knew I'd found my people. I'd made it home.

Chapter 3

THE COUNTLESS
STAGES OF DEATH

Let's back up for a minute. I sort of skipped over a lot of stuff at the end of that last chapter. I moved out of my childhood home and moved first to another small northern town called Lac La Biche. I worked as a waitress and an archeologist's assistant. It sounds interesting, but it mostly consisted of sleeping in a library. Then I moved to Victoria, British Columbia, where I worked as a hostess and a waitress at a cute tourist cafe. Then I moved to Edmonton, Alberta, where I went to the Northern Alberta Institute of Technology and took a course in Radio and Television Arts. At night, I worked as a waitress and also in a popcorn kiosk at the mall. Then I moved to Vancouver where I worked as a . . . you guessed it! A waitress. But also as a freelance writer! Ha, you didn't see that coming. During the day I was busy whipping up coupons, writing flyers about kayaking safety equipment and making menus that were funny yet informative. But that's not all. I was also working on a novel. And yet I was still having trouble paying the rent. What?! True story.

My boyfriend Justin (I've changed his name, incidentally, though he did look like a Justin) was between bartending jobs. Justin was (and maybe still is) an extremely handsome, down-on-his-luck guy who kept getting fired for stuff that was not his fault. On more than one occasion the unlucky bastard was unfairly fired from his place of employment despite the fact that he was an honest, hardworking, level-headed young man who never showed up late.

Anyway, because of my unrealized talents and his bad fortune, we both struggled to find an affordable place to live. We ended up sharing a micro studio apartment. I can't remember the name of the building, but for our purposes we'll refer to it as Papillion Towers. Justin was a whopping six four, so I tended to hover in any space he wasn't using. When he was in the bathroom, I would do high kicks and stretch until he came out.

Justin had thick, dark hair and blue-green eyes. It's only looking back that I realize how truly good looking he was and how rare it would be for me to be intimate with anyone again who so closely resembled an actual man. I'm not the type to sit around bragging about old boyfriends, but Justin really was a fascinating fellow. He could eat atomic-level hot wings without tearing up. He was fond of every alcoholic beverage ever invented. Louisiana hot wing vodka would've had a very good customer in him. And he excelled at crossword puzzles, something I was never able to master. The way I do crossword puzzles is really more of an exercise in Googling.

Unfortunately, he had a real passion for drinking just past his limit and would sometimes pass out in weird places, like the refrigerator* and my cute neighbor's apartment. Sometimes he lost his keys, and once he got detained trying to break into his own home. He probably wouldn't have gotten stopped but he argued with the cop because he didn't realize it was a cop. Yes, the cop was wearing a cop uniform but a cop should also imme-

---

*On a scale of one to ten that this really happened, I give it a five.

diately show his cop badge. That's my opinion and I feel pretty strongly about it, if only to avoid issues like this one.

But with Justin unable to secure employment without a good reference and my novel only three pages done, or on a more positive note, 324 pages from completion, we were broke and the rent was calling our name. Or more accurately, our landlord was.

One afternoon after my daytime waitressing shift had ended and I had spent most of my tips on tequila shots, I licked the salt from my upper lip and went into the bathroom to steal a couple of rolls of toilet paper. I was eager to get home, use a little of the contraband, and take a nap before tackling the night, but as I passed through the kitchen, I overheard a cook tell a prettier waitress about a comedy club downtown, the Punchline, that was looking for a hostess. He had me at hostess.

I went straight to Gastown, a hipster part of Vancouver's downtown, and got the job. I was really good in the interview as I recall because I was quite drunk and therefore sociable, charming, and witty despite the lime stains on the front of my blouse. I was ecstatic because in my inebriated state, I thought that I could write jokes and sell them to comedians! I even had a few good ideas about the neighborhood we were in, Gastown! I mean, are you kidding me? My professional writing career was about to go epic.

My actual job as a hostess was just to sit people close to the stage on a first-come, first-served basis. Sometimes people would tip me like it was a Las Vegas revue, but as I snatched the bills from their outstretched paws, I always felt guilty. They were already getting the best seat I could give them based on how quickly they'd parked the car.

Once the show was going, it was easy. I just stood at the back and watched the comedians while stealthily sipping some kind of lethal alcoholic concoction the bartender whipped up for me in a coffee mug. Occasionally, I was required to approach a table and warn them with a whisper and a friendly smile that if they continued to talk, I'd have no choice but to have the bouncer escort them out. Interestingly, it's exactly what I still do between sets.

It was a learning experience watching the comedians do show after show, tackling pretty much the same material with varying results. At first, like everyone else, I was shocked to learn the comedians were too lazy to write an entirely new act every night and instead had the audacity to trot out jokes that they had performed just twenty-four hours earlier. Of course, I wasn't aware at the time that writing jokes that actually work is as difficult as two full-grown adults having satisfying sex in a bathtub. As Mitch Hedberg famously said, "Beware of the comedian who leaves the room for twenty minutes and comes back with twenty new minutes of material."

The club was an inspiring environment and I dedicated myself to writing a few jokes every night after I got home. Of course, I didn't neglect my girlfriend duties. I still fought with Justin and occasionally whipped him up a burger before he zonked out. I didn't tell anyone I was writing the jokes. I thought I'd wait until I amassed a pretty good load, maybe a hundred or so, and just really blow them away with the sheer volume of my funniness.

After a few months, I decided to take what I'd written to the club and show the comics what I had: seventeen quality jokes, many of them scatological puns on the word "Gastown." Did I have any takers? Between bouts of genuine laughter, the comedians, who did not read the jokes or seem to have any interest in my writing whatsoever, told me, "Dumb idea. We write our own jokes. Even if we didn't, we don't have any money to buy jokes!" Wait! These guys were the cream of Canadian showbiz and they didn't have any money? Where were our priorities as a society? Was this the kind of world I wanted to be living in?

The fact was, writing jokes wasn't going to pay the rent and doing them onstage myself would still keep me in the red, so I figured I might as well try. Logically, it didn't make any sense, but neither do reverse mortgages and people do that all the time. I was going to go for it.

THE PUNCHLINE, THOUGH BLISSFULLY UNAWARE of things like drinking and drugging during a shift, had two hard-and-fast rules for the support staff: no fucking comedians and absolutely, positively no being a comedian. I had a boyfriend, so I was pretty good about the first rule. But the second one was starting to feel like a fence that was keeping me from greener grasses. (I know. I'm still doing farm metaphors.)

I waited a year before I finally had the nerve to jump that fence. I had amassed a lot of jokes and I realized if I ever wanted them to see the light of day, I would have to perform them myself. I organized and memorized to the point that the words meant nothing to me anymore. They became a collection of mere grunts and pauses. On a few occasions, I recited the grunts and pauses for my friends, most of whom begged me not to go through with it.

I didn't think I was doing something so outrageously out of character. I was already immersed in showbiz. I was a published pamphlet writer who had also written two diner menus. Hundreds of eyes read my words every month! And yet, so many of the comments I got were along the lines of:

"I don't think of you as a funny person, so it'll be interesting to see what happens."

My best friend told me, "Don't do it. Don't do it. Don't do it." It was like I was telling her I was going to walk drunk and naked into a frat party in the middle of a three-day weekend. But I would never do that again.

I think when you tell people you want to be a comedian, their comments reflect their own fears and insecurities. My sister Andrea worried that everyone would hate me, but she won't leave the house without full hair and makeup and a winning smile, even if she's going to get her hair and makeup done. When my sister Audrey found out that I was planning to try my hand at stand-up, she told me, "Well, we'll see if you actually go through with it. It's one thing to say, it's another thing to do." Then she added, without irony, because let's be honest, the most annoying people in the world don't get irony, "I know I'd be great as a comedian but I just don't have time to do it." Only my sweet sister Lynn gave me both encouragement and constructive advice: "Good for you! Don't fall off the stage!"

My parents refused to talk about it at all. That's how my parents disagree with me. Deafening silence. As a punishment, it's a tricky thing to master, but they're pretty adept at it. However, I offer this tidbit as a cautionary tale. I once gave my husband the silent treatment for an entire week, at the end of which he declared, "Hey, we've been getting along pretty great lately!"

My parents are still reluctant to discuss my stand-up career. Instead I regale them with funny stories about my "pet-grooming" business. They are particularly fond of my dramas with Poopsie, the poodle who likes to heckle me while I'm in the middle of a joke. I wonder if they think, "Boy, she sure tells a lot of jokes at her pet-grooming business."

My boyfriend, Justin, was kinder about my ambitions than I expected. I was worried that he'd be horrified that his girlfriend wanted to stand in front of strangers for laughs. But when I told him, he only said, "You know who would be good as a comedian? John! You should get him to go with you. He's hysterical." The comedians were more encouraging. "You're weird," they told me. "That'll make it easier." At last I'd finally be able to put that character trait to use.

But I was my own worst critic. I berated myself mercilessly. "You don't sound like a comedian. You don't look like a comedian. Comedians don't eat pickle-and-mustard sandwiches for breakfast." My inner critic also has a German accent, which somehow makes it worse.

WITH MY PARALYZING SOCIAL ANXIETY, I could hardly order pizza without being completely drunk. How would I ever be able to go onstage? Completely drunk, as it turns out.

I decided to do stand-up for the first time in secret at the competing comedy club. I was hoping if it went badly, no one would find out and I'd still have a job to go to Thursday through Saturday nights. And if it went well, then I'd quit my weekend job and become famous within the week. I chugged my two free beers and several ones I'd paid for and waited backstage for someone to call my name.

While some comics shadowbox to rid their tensions before a show, my fight was strictly with my sphincter. I really wanted to turn back and run out the exit, but I was unable to move. It felt like someone had switched my Doc Martens with cement shoes and then waited to see if I would notice. I did. But I didn't do anything about it. My nerves were so taut I could hardly breathe, let alone move. And then, just when I thought I couldn't take it anymore, that I was going to pass out, all of the fear drained from my body like the air going out of a pool toy. It was like I had used up all the adrenaline and the anxiousness and nervousness but still had some awkwardness in the old reserve. I could breathe and I could move, but not in a natural way. The emcee called my name and I moved to the mic with the grace of a toddler who was just learning to walk. It was much brighter onstage than I had imagined. I couldn't see the audience. I couldn't see anything. I put a hand up to my eyes to shield the light from my delicate retinas and forced a smile. They laughed. I hadn't even said anything and they laughed! They liked me. I began my series of grunts and pauses and they laughed again. And then they laughed again. By the end I felt confident enough to take the mic out of the stand but then I realized I was out of jokes so I tried to fit it back in the curved slot and it refused to go. I kept trying even while the emcee stood next to me and watched. I eked out a few more giggles with that unintentional bit of physical comedy and then handed the mic to the emcee and scurried off the stage. I could hear them applauding for me as I dipped behind the black curtain. I stood there for a moment taking it in. It felt amazing. It felt better than anything I had ever felt in my whole life and I had ridden a cow wearing a cape before. I felt renewed. I felt charged. I felt like taking a tequila shot.

As I tipped back shot after shot, little did I know that I was celebrating my first hit of crack, and there would be no turning back. I couldn't wait to do stand-up again. The next seven days were agonizingly long but eventually, as almost always happens, Tuesday rolled around again and with it came another open mic and another chance to experience the magic I had felt the week earlier. This time, I brought my boyfriend and a couple of his friends. I was ready to show off.

I felt the same nervousness I had the first time and the same sensation that I should've worn an adult diaper, but this time, the feeling didn't subside. I was forced to go onstage carrying the weight of all my anxieties on my shoulders and cement shoes on my feet. I got to the mic. I forced myself to smile using a sense-memory technique. My lips curled up at the edges, but this time the audience didn't laugh. I made it through my first joke. They didn't laugh. Halfway into my second joke a guy yelled out, "Next!" I laughed at that, so it's not like I didn't get any laughs during the set. Then I proceeded with my grunts and pauses.

A mere few seconds later, the same guy who so cleverly yelled out "Next!" bellowed, "Show us your tits!" The audience broke up like they'd never before heard such wit. And it was during this deluge of mocking laughter that I had a moment of clarity. I realized that the people down there in the audience, the people judging me, were idiots. They were letting me know I was lame by drunkenly one-upping me with a tired old cliché. Unfortunately, the teachable moment passed before I could school them, and then someone, a shadow of a person, of the same height and build as my boyfriend, stood up. The lights were burning holes in my irises, and even though I squinted, I couldn't quite see what was happening, but I could feel the energy in the room changing. That standing shadowy figure yelled, "Fuck you, asshole!" It should be noted that the shadow, of the same height and build as my boyfriend Justin, also sounded a lot like my boyfriend Justin. I'm not saying it was my boyfriend Justin. I'm just saying there were some striking similarities.

The laws of cause and effect and alcohol being what they are, the heckler yelled back something along the lines of, "This has nothing to do with you, fuck face." This begat a series of back-and-forth insults that I can't remember exactly but I'll bet my Nano included some of the less endearing expletives from the English language. I stared out into the murky darkness, watching shadows move clumsily around the tables, listening to the action like it was a radio play, but I never stopped grunting and pausing exactly as I had planned. The ship was sinking but I, like the band on the *Titanic,* was passively going down with it. It never even occurred to me that it might be reasonable to leave the stage, to excuse myself from the distasteful situation.

And then someone threw a beer bottle that hit the heckler directly in the back of the head. If my boyfriend Justin threw it, and I'm not saying Justin did throw it, but if he did, I'm going to go ahead and guess that the bottle was empty. Justin was not one to waste good alcohol. And I'm going to further assume that an empty bottle to the back of the head doesn't hurt as much as a full one, and perhaps the heckler, who was crying and screaming at the top of his lungs, was overreacting just a smidge.

The bouncers (who had been playing Parcheesi in the alley until now?) suddenly swooped in, grabbed the shadow that may or may not have been my boyfriend Justin, and dragged him out of the show room, followed by about sixteen people shouting and pushing one another.

I don't know if anyone was still watching the stage, but I was still up there, professional as a nurse at a nudist colony, finishing up my last joke, grunt, grunt, pause. And then finally I was done. "Thank you! That was a lot of fun! I'm Bonnie McFarlane. Good night." I easily rested the mic into the stand, overcoming at least one of my previous challenges. I waited for a moment to soak up my well-deserved applause, but if there was anyone clapping for me, I couldn't hear it over the discord that was still emanating from the back of the room. I was disappointed, to say the least.

I shuffled offstage and walked past the frazzled assistant manager who was standing behind the black curtain, his eyes wide. He was breathing from his open mouth. "What the fuck?" he said, as I groped around in the dark waiting for my pupils to dial down, hoping the lights hadn't rendered them useless forever.

"What?"

"If there's a barroom brawl going on, you get off the stage."

"Oh."

"You didn't see the red light? You didn't see me waving you off?"

"There was a lot going on. It was hard enough just to concentrate on the jokes."

"Was that your boyfriend who threw the beer bottle?"

"I don't think so. Justin would never do that."

Eventually, my eyesight came back and I made my way to the lobby, but I was unable to locate my boyfriend or any of his friends. The heckler was still on the premises. He was yelling at the manager, surrounded by his friends who were trying to calm him down. Also in the mix were some girls who love drama, several cops, and a couple of paramedics who were bandaging up the heckler's bloody head. Staff members zipped around frantically, audience members were trying to get their money back, cops were taking statements, and it was all intermittently colored red and blue from the lights of the cop car parked on the sidewalk out front.

As I stood in the midst of all this action, not one person said "Good show!" or asked me for my autograph. Such was the life of a performer, I thought, as I left without so much as a tip of the hat and began the three-kilometer walk home. Two blocks into the walk, one of my boyfriend's friends stepped out of an alleyway and told me Justin wanted me to meet him at a nearby bar.

"Why did he leave?" I asked. His friend looked at me like I was the dumbest person on Earth and then explained what he couldn't believe I didn't already know. Justin had thrown the bottle. The heckler did want to press charges.

So he did throw the bottle!

But it wasn't his fault! He was sticking up for me!

Poor Justin.

I elbowed my way through the Tuesday-night crowd at our meet-up location and found Justin at the pool table furiously knocking balls into the pockets. I reached up and rubbed my hand through his short dark hair and told him, "It's not your fault."

"I know it's not," he said angrily. "It's your fault."

Justin was never charged with assault.

JUSTIN AND I HAD A rocky relationship before that open mic. We fought about a lot of things, but my stand-up quickly made its way to the front of the line. He didn't like anything about my new career. He didn't like listening to my jokes. He didn't like that I was hanging out with so many dudes all the time. He didn't like that my priorities were shifting away from him. He didn't like hearing, "Is this funny?" fifty times a day.

I didn't like fighting with him either, but I just couldn't stop doing stand-up. I couldn't stop talking about it. I couldn't stop obsessing about it. I went to bed thinking about jokes. I woke up trying to write jokes. Needless to say, in those early days of stand-up, I had a lot of jokes about going to bed and getting up.

I wrote jokes while we were fucking, I thought about jokes while we were eating, drinking, dancing. Once we were watching a very emotional *Dateline* special about a guy who spent twelve years in prison for a crime he didn't commit. "Oh my God," I said, brushing away a tear, "there's a joke in there somewhere." Justin jumped up off the couch and grabbed his jacket. "You're fucking crazy," he said, and left the apartment.

I unfolded my legs and thought about it. Maybe I was sick. I kept hoping that the next joke I would write would be the breakthrough joke that would open the floodgates to writing all kinds of amazing jokes and I would start killing. Because, as crazed as I was about stand-up, I was not doing well. I bombed.

I bombed. And I bombed. And I fucking bombed some more. It was horrible, scary, pathetic, and thrilling. I was powerless to stop. I was addicted. And like any dependency, this one would take me down as quickly and as swiftly as any meth habit. But even if I managed to keep my teeth, I'd lose my job, my house, my relationship, and did I mention my job?

Word of my second-ever time onstage made it to the back offices of the Punchline Comedy Club, where I imagine the manager checked the rules, noted that I had broken the second one, and immediately fired me.

But it turned out fine. Less than six months after my first open mic, I started going on the road. At the time, I felt things were not progressing nearly fast enough, but now as I look back, I wonder what I could possibly have been doing onstage for up to half an hour each night. I do recall pretending to be a hypnotist once, as a kind of "bad hypnosis character," but instead of comedically failing to hypnotize the people who came up onstage, most of them really did what I asked them to do. I think we can assume that most people who go onstage to be "hypnotized" are probably just hams who enjoy the attention without having to be responsible for their behavior.

Of course, most of the time, I just did straight-up comedy. At least, I thought so. As a way to calm my nerves before shows, I would tell myself that they, the audience, didn't know I wasn't really a real comedian. In fact, if I could muster up enough confidence, fraudulent as it might be, it was possible that they'd not only believe I was a comedian, but a good one. Looking back, I have to assume I wasn't fooling anyone but myself. Still, I got a lot of work opening for C-list comics in D-list rooms. I mean, I was young, marginally attractive, and had no nose hairs. What middle-aged comic wouldn't want to take me on the road and teach me everything he knew? I went on the road with an insult comic. I learned the art of insult comedy. I went on the road with a juggler. I learned how to juggle. I went on the road with a guy who did dick jokes and I touched his dick.

In Canada, working comedians did an enormous number of one-nighters. There were only eight or nine actual comedy clubs in the whole country, so the rest of the gigs were in bars scattered around the more urban areas of the rural north. Towns that had names like Moose Jaw, Saskatchewan; Kelowna, British Columbia; and Medicine Hat, Alberta. We'd get to a town, do a show in a bar, and the next morning drive six hours to another town, do another show in a bar, and so on and so on for two or three weeks at a time. We did it without podcasts. Without cell phones. Without GPS. While the touring comedians in America were all doing similar jokes about airline food and the cramped seats in coach, Canadian comics all had a bit about folding a road map. We were always on the move. We performed for a deserted mining town, a little fishing village, a farming community. It's a different kind of entertainment business when the booker has to check the *Farmers' Almanac* before agreeing to a show three months out.

Somewhere along the British Columbia coast, in the town we were to play that night, we drove down Main Street at rush hour. There was just one guy on a bicycle rolling through the stop sign. If a tumbleweed had blown across the street and gunfight music started up, it wouldn't have surprised me. This was a ghost town. When we checked into the motel, I got my key, which was an actual key. This should've been a red flag, but I ignored it and went to my room. I swung open the door and was mildly impressed by how big the room seemed. But as I lifted my bag I realized there wasn't anything to put it on. Something was missing. I couldn't put my finger on it at first but in time it came to me. There was no bed. I walked back down to the front desk. "Sorry about that," the fat guy said, "we haven't had anybody stay here in a few years."

Hotels with beds were not necessarily a step up. One hotel room I stayed in had a thin mattress that was perched atop a couple of slabs of wood. "My bed is really hard," I complained to the front-desk clerk. "That's your opinion, eh?" He looked up from his comic book, we stared at each other for a long time, and then I went back to my room and laid down on my bed until my shoulder blades started to bleed.

Despite the subpar accommodations, I slept a lot. I also pretended to sleep a lot because the amount of information I was being given by the headlining comedians I was traveling with was exhausting. They all loved "teaching" me everything they knew. "Always smile." "Start with your best joke." "End with your strongest bit." "Never do more than three tags." "The truth is always funny." "Take the mic out of the stand." "Time plus tragedy equals comedy." "Pace back and forth." "Never laugh at your own jokes." "Two lines of setup are all you should ever need." "Talk about yourself." "Talk about the world." "Talk about your family." "Never swear." "Talk like you talk." "Ironic observations never get a laugh." "Do callbacks but never on a Sunday." "Leave the mic in the stand if it's a long, half-filled room and the average age is under forty-five." I would close my eyes, pretending to sleep, but all the while I'd write novels, screenplays, and jokes in my head. The tricks from the farm were still helping me along.

BEFORE SHOWS, I WAS ALWAYS sick to my stomach. After shows, I was exhausted from the nerves. Onstage, I was almost always heckled. These rural Canadian towns had some tough customers who were as desperate to get a little attention as they were to get some teeth. I don't think they were trying to be terribly mean, but they were testing me. I was young, female, and as I mentioned before, had no nose hairs. I was a real rarity for these cold-weather locals.

The men might've heckled, but the women would sometimes get downright physical. And not in a stripper, slap-you-with-their-boobs kind of a way. Sometimes I'd look at the audience before I hit the stage and think, There's not one person in here who hasn't wrestled with a grizzly bear and won. Once a woman jumped onstage and punched me in the arm. I hit her with the mic, but it was exactly like hitting a tree stump. Maybe not exactly like hitting a tree stump. When you hit a tree stump, you don't generally make it more upset. At one point, she had me in a headlock until someone—I couldn't tell you if it was a bouncer, her boyfriend, or a Sasquatch—dragged her offstage. I was a little dizzy. By all accounts, she had won the fight, but I steadied myself and said, "I should've known by all your facial hair you had a lot of testosterone." Applause break.

Another time, a woman heckled and I retorted. She kept going and I realized right away that I was much better at this than she was. She must have realized it too, since she threw her beer bottle at me in frustration. Luckily, she missed by several millimeters, and it shattered on the wall behind me. I was shocked but I immediately said, "You can't play on my soft-ball team." The audience shrieked and applauded as she was escorted out of the club by the management. What I lacked in wit, I made up for in speed. I learned when something happens, you comment on it as fast as possible. I could've said, "Your mom," and it would've gotten the same laugh.

One particularly harrowing night, I was relentlessly heckled by someone at the back of the room. I couldn't figure out who it was, and so I could never really best them. It's an unsettling feeling not being able to see your attacker. I started to feel like the victim in a 1940s horror movie: "Who's there?" "Who are you?" "Please, I want to live." When I finally finished the show, I went to the back bar, ordered a beer, and asked the bartender if he knew who had done that. "It was me," he said with a little laugh. "Thought I'd help the show." Needless to say, I did not tip him the full 8 percent I was accustomed to tipping back then.

The shows were always something of a crapshoot. I never knew how it was going to go, and I felt I had little to no control over that. Sure, I was getting better at dealing with hecklers and there were lots of instances where I was able to ad-lib a funny exchange with a drunken audience member, but improvising and getting big laughs during these situations sometimes made the rest of my act even harder to do. It was difficult to follow these combustible moments with actual jokes. I was almost always disappointed after my sets, regardless of how they went. I usually had a drink or two while watching the headliner, thinking that it must be wonderfully comforting to know that you're going to do well, to be sure of yourself, to know you can take this audience and make them laugh and giggle where you want them to.

WHEN THE SHOWS WERE OVER, I went back to my room to write and watch TV. Most of the guy comics I worked with back then stayed at the bar and partied with the locals until the wee hours of the morning. They welcomed the opportunity to be surrounded by adoring fans. And by adoring fans, I mean sluts. Being on the road and picking up dudes is not nearly as fun for a girl comic. First of all, great catches aren't really hitting up the funny ladies, and second, I didn't want to die.

Sometimes after a show, a waiter or local chamber of commerce member would offer to smoke me out and I'd go outside to the parking lot and take a few puffs off a joint before heading to my room. One night, I was doing just that with the bar's manager and one of his friends, whose appearance was a mystery to me, as he stood in the shadows. I could see only his fingers as he handed the joint to me after sucking in a few hits for himself. After a few rounds of this, I put the joint to my lips only to realize it had gone out. The mysterious friend finally stepped out of the shadows with his lighter, flame flickering between us. The glow of the light glinted off his cold sore like a coal miner's hat on a diamond. I realized just then that I'd had enough, I was good. I was more discerning after that, screening the dots and scabs on people's faces before smoking up with them.

We, the comedians, smoked and drank all the time. It was like an ongoing episode of *Mad Men,* only inside a rental car with the windows rolled up. I don't know why we haven't all died of cancer. It wasn't easy to be hale and hearty while drinking and smoking pot every night. I tried to fit in a prison workout of sit-ups and push-ups whenever I could, and I was a "just about" vegetarian. I couldn't have cut out meat completely in the northern wilds or I would've starved to death.

On one of our many sojourns for food along the unpaved road of Canadian showbiz, we stopped at a little diner in Slave Lake, Alberta, where I ordered the vegetable soup. Within the first two spoonfuls I chewed on something that could only be described as meat. I flagged down the waitress. "I ordered the vegetable soup," I said with a passive-aggressive shrug that said, You really fucked up but I'm going to be nice about it.

"Yeah. That's it," the waitress said.

"But there's meat in it."

"So? There's vegetables, too."

Somehow, this didn't feel like I thought showbiz would feel.

Chapter 4

ALL THIS VENEREAL DISEASE AND NO ONE TO SHARE IT WITH

Not long after I started doing stand-up, at just barely twenty-three, I was talking to an established comedian who was shocked to find out I was dating a regular Joe who was not in the biz. "It won't last," she told me. "Your boyfriend is comedy now." If this was true, I was certainly spending a lot of time with my new beau, Comedy, on the road, in dark bars, trying to get strangers to like me. When I was home, I would detox by sleeping and napping, which I then punctuated with short bursts of binge eating. Then, when I had my energy back, my real boyfriend Justin and I would fight. We'd fuck. We'd fight some more.

Justin and I felt our relationship would flourish if only we had a few more feet of space, so we signed the lease on a new, bigger, more expensive apartment. I was working pretty frequently as an opening act and he had picked up a few shifts bartending at nights. Together, we'd be able to cover the costs. We were to move in three weeks later.

A few days after we signed the lease, a well-respected Vancouver comedian (he'd been on local television, for God's sake!) asked me to open for him on a two-week tour of British Columbia. First, however, I was required to pass inspection from his wife during a dinner at their apartment. Justin refused to escort me on the grounds that it sounded boring. I was inclined to agree but I wanted the work. I stood in their doorway brushed and flossed and in my best men's button-down as the buxom blonde gave me the once-over. I had nothing to fear. She was warm and funny and we got along great although the dinner was more wine than food and there was only pot for dessert.

Still recovering some seventy-two hours later, the local comedy star and I were over four hundred miles away performing the first night of our tour. I did okay every show and he murdered every night. I'd leave the bar after his show and go to my room, while he, the comedy star, remained, surrounded by admirers both male and female, pounding back slippery nipples along with some other shooters with blatantly sexual names.

I, on the other hand, partook of more domesticated activities, like washing my panties in the sink and using the highly promoted "color" television. I also spent many a night pining over my boyfriend who never answered the phone. Once, I sat listening to the busy signal for hours until I finally got the operator to cut in on the call. I told her that I was trying to get in touch with him because his wife had just had a baby. She came back saying the phone was apparently left off the hook. No one was there. This went on for two weeks. Mr. Married closing the bar and me moping around my hotel room, manually changing the channel on the TV and calling my boyfriend and letting it ring seventy-six times in a row.

Finally, two long weeks later, I arrived home. I was excited to see Justin, but the minute I walked in, I knew he wasn't there. If he was asleep anywhere in the apartment, I would've seen his feet as soon as I opened the door. I eventually tracked him down after making a series of landline phone calls. Back then, when you wanted to find your boyfriend, you had to have the tenacity of a New York City detective or a debt collector. I eventually found the little rascal at his friend's house where, according to my sources, a huge blowout party was taking place. I knew where it was so I wiped a wet cloth over my stinky pits, greased down my cowlick, and hopped on a bus. The bash was indeed a blowout and, after weaving through what seemed like thousands of twenty-somethings, I still hadn't reunited with Justin. No one seemed to know where he had gone. A woman he worked with approached me and told me he had gone to get more beer. Sounded plausible. Then she got me a beer from a tub of about 750 beers on ice.

As I cracked open the Bud, we had a conversation that went something like this:

"So, you just got home from vacation?"

"No, I'm a comedian. I was on tour. Two weeks."

"Oh, wow. That's interesting. You ever cheat on Justin? You can tell me, I won't tell."

"No. Never." And it was true. I never had.

"You think he would ever cheat on you?"

"No."

"You sure?" What the fuck was this chick's problem?

"He would never cheat on me. He's very loyal." This was Justin's best quality. I know this because he told me so.

"Guys are assholes."

"Maybe he's back with the beer." I stood up but she took my hand.

"My boyfriend cheated on me. I didn't think he ever would but he did. Just be aware of the things that are going on." I was starting to make sense of her babbling. Her boyfriend cheated on her so she was projecting her problems on to me and my perfect relationship. Ugh. Girls. Drama, am I right?

And then, thank God, I was saved from this nut job. Justin entered the room. I jumped up and ran over to him, but he seemed less happy to see me. His arm was draped around a girl I had never seen before. Out of respect for me, he dropped his arm and put some space between them. I was already going in for a hug and was unable to stop myself. As he patted me on the back like we were bros, all the pieces of the puzzle came together and made a very clear picture for me. You didn't have to be a rocket scientist. It was obvious Justin had a sister he'd never told me about.

Later that night, in our apartment, he finally took me by the shoulders and shook me. "I've been cheating on you!" he yelled. This came as a complete shock. He did not have a sister. Justin left me curled up on the bed as the sun was coming up, and just as I'd started another round of snot-generating sobs, the phone rang. I immediately choked back the tears and answered with a cheery, "Hello!"

It was Mrs. Married, the wife of the comedian I had just been on tour with.

"Hi, Bonnie, just wanted to warn you that one of the hotels you stayed at last weekend has crabs."

"Crabs?"

"Yes."

"Ohh-kay."

"Did you get crabs?"

"Are you talking about the food or the bugs?"

"The bugs. My husband got crabs from the hotel bed and I just thought I should contact you to let you know. Did you contract crabs?"

"No." But I didn't sleep with any skanks, I thought to myself.

"Can you check?" What the fuck? I think I'd know if I had crabs. I couldn't tell if she really thought she was doing me a favor by telling me the hotel had crabs or if she was trying to find out if I gave it to her husband. What could I do? I played along.

"Yeah, I guess my room was clean. I got lucky."

"Just check."

"What do you mean?"

"Comb your pubic hair and look."

I gave it some time, holding the phone away from my head and then I lied, "Yup, just checked. Nothing. Sorry about your husband."

"Just thought I'd let you know."

"Awesome. Super appreciate it. Thanks."

After I hung up, I parted my hair down there in the middle and then went back to sobbing and blowing my nose with a sock. Five days later I moved by myself into the bigger, better, more expensive apartment I was supposed to share with Justin. Here I was living the crab-free dream but I didn't have anyone to celebrate it with. And just three short months later, I got evicted.

Chapter 5

NAME YOUR OWN CHAPTER

I had a lawn sale that netted me almost forty dollars and I gave away everything else I owned, including my bed. You can't sofa-surf hauling around a California king. It didn't take long before I was running out of friends. Asking to sleep on someone's couch rates right up there with, "Can you pick me up from the airport?" and "Will you carry my baby to term?" Also, I wasn't the neatest person in the world, but what really got on people's nerves was my endless asking, "Does this seem funny to you?"

One night, at a party, I took a break from cornering people in the living room and the kitchen to talk about how shitty my life had become and descended into the basement to do it. It was there that I ended up smoking a joint with three guys I knew from somewhere. They were friends of someone I knew from somewhere else and they all lived together in a house nearby. After hearing about my bouts of homelessness, they decided, right then and there, while I was waiting for them to stop bogarting the joint, that I could stay in their garage until I got back on my feet. Not an apartment above a garage like the one Fonzi lived in, you understand. A garage garage. With a car and a motorcycle and grease spots and the kind of exhaust fumes that kill people when they want them to. And occasionally, even when they don't. They didn't have to ask me twice.

I needed a few things. High on the promise of a roof over my head and, of course, cannabis, I exited the basement carrying a mattress. That's right. A mattress. As luck would have it, there were several piled up against the back wall, and without thinking about it too much, I grabbed the least bed-buggy-looking one and walked right out the door with it, thanks to my Irish-bred back and shoulders that I had inherited from my thatch-carrying ancestors. Several blocks later, I was at my new garage. I dumped the four-inch-thick twin bed in a corner on the oil-stained cement and crashed out. Home: only slightly less comfortable than living in a cave.

When it rained, which was only nine solid months of the year in Vancouver, the garage would flood, but it never reached my mattress for some reason. I had, either out of sheer luck or by God's grace, picked the high ground for my sleeping space. Since I was an educated white girl who knew the local language and was currently living in a garage, I think it was the former. I kept a pair of rubber boots next to my stolen mattress that I would pull on when I woke up, and I splashed over to the industrial sink where I would, yeah, sometimes I would. If it was late at night or too early in the morning to use the bathroom upstairs, I would. I'm not proud of it. But I did. But only number one. Never number two. I wasn't a monster.

As sad as I was about Justin, I tried to get out there and date as much as possible. Hey, a girl's gotta eat! But then the guy would drop me off after dinner and I'd wave and coyly say, "Thanks, I had a great time." Then I'd reach up and pull the garage door closed, real cool like. Most of the time it was just easier and warmer if I stayed the night at a dude's house. Also, as a nice parting gift, I would wear one of his T-shirts home and expand my wardrobe. I stole all the shampoos and soaps from the hotels I stayed at on the road. I shoved crackers and packets of ketchup into my backpack. I only drank when I worked because then I get could get them for free or at least for half price. I learned that if you "partied" onstage, people in the audience would buy you drinks, so I did that. I remember a few days on the road where I puked the entire way to the next gig. But I got my money's worth of drinks! Way to beat the system.

When I wasn't on the road or doing stand-up or on a date with someone I barely liked, I sat on the edge of my mattress with my notebook on my lap, keeping my feet out of the water, and thought, Okay, what can I write a joke about? What's funny in my life? What's different and interesting? And then I'd think, Why, there's nothing interesting about me. Nothing at all! And I'd toss my notebook next to my pillow, lie back, stare at the ceiling, and think about all the ways I could win Justin back.

Looking back, I was actually, really, seriously depressed. Living in a flooded garage probably didn't help. Justin was my first real love, my first real heartbreak, and the first guy I ever peed on. I was in bad shape. I cried all the time. Before my shows, after my shows, sometimes, not often, during my shows. I called my mom.

"This pet-grooming business is harder than I thought it would be," I said.

"You've always been good with animals. You'll be fine. I'm making you a quilt with poodles on it."

One night, after a marginally good show at the weekly Yuk Yuk's open mic—and by marginally good, I mean no one called 911—the club manager told me about a contest they were having. It was Yuk Yuk's Search for Canada's Funniest New Comic. I signed up because, quite frankly, I had nothing better to do and I needed something to take my mind off Justin. That, and one of the prizes was a new twenty-six-inch television and Justin really liked televisions. I also figured being in the contest would get me a few more minutes of stage time, which I realized I really needed if I was ever going to crack this nut. My performances onstage were hardly met with enthusiasm. I was the kind of comic other comics would tell that they liked my jokes, but the audience would throw things at me.

The night of the first leg of the contest was important and I knew I really needed to do well, but I couldn't get my head in the game. Turns out, not being able to concentrate was, for me, the key to succeeding. I won. The next week, I won again. And somehow, on a wing and a prayer, I won the whole west coast leg of the competition. No one was more shocked than I. Don't get me wrong. I wanted to win. I hoped I would win, but I didn't think it would actually happen. If there was one thing my upbringing hammered home, it was never to expect to have fate on your side. I was so stunned that I could hardly muster up any enthusiasm for the win. But as I walked onstage to accept my "prize," I realized I should do something to show that I was grateful. I put my hand in the air and jumped up and down twice. This embarrassing clip is what they showed on the local news channel. I watched it on my new twenty-six-inch-screen television set, which I kept at a friend's house. I couldn't keep it at my place. Where was I going to put it? Next to the motorcycle?

Winning also meant going to Toronto to compete for the main title, Yuk Yuk's Funniest New Comic in Canada. This meant I had two round-trip tickets for me and a guest. Justin wasn't going anywhere without his new girlfriend, so I was stuck with an extra ticket. My problems were solved when a waitress from the Punchline asked if she could buy it from me. She was from Toronto and was itching to go back. I was thrilled to have someone to go with me.

The waitress, Lynn Shawcroft, was a little crazy back then. On the way to the airport, she stole a baguette from a restaurant and we ate it all the way to the terminal in the back of the cab. This was back when stealing was still considered a crime and people thought carbs were a good way to start the day. Lynn turned out to be a wickedly smart and funny companion and we hit it off immediately. She had me laughing from takeoff to touchdown and it wasn't long before Justin and my garage woes were off my list of things to think about. She remains my best friend to this very day.

TORONTO FELT LIKE AN ENORMOUS city, and it was, in fact, big by Canadian standards. The population hovered somewhere in the neighborhood of two and a half million people. As Lynn and I walked down a couple of its older, crowded streets, I couldn't help but think, Wow, everyone is a cunt. Later, when I was more worldly and better traveled, I realized what I experienced was only cunt lite. New York and Paris were the cuntiest cities in the world, far cuntier than Toronto. In fact, in a global ranking of the cuntiest cities, Toronto was way down near the bottom of the list, coming in at a lowly number forty-three. Even Copenhagen beat them by a pretty decent margin. But I was still a simple farm girl who expected children to shake your hand when introduced and gentlemen to tip their hats when they passed you in the street.

Despite being out of my element, I again won the night and was crowned Yuk Yuk's Funniest New Comic in Canada. When I went onstage to accept my award, I had only one thought in my head bouncing around like a tennis ball caught in a cylinder: don't jump. So I said a polite thank-you into the mic and headed off. Mark Breslin, the owner of the Yuk Yuk's chain, made me come back onstage to say something else. I say "made me," but he was little more than five feet tall and I had fought a couple of girls in high school, so I take that back. He didn't make me, I returned of my own free will.

"What do you think?" he asked. "You won."

"It's good," I answered, leaning toward the mic. "It's better than losing."

I sensed the audience and the judges were disappointed. They wanted me to say something amusing and charming but I was only good at being funny in those days if I was being subjected to the worst situations, like waterboarding or getting my eyebrows waxed. When good things were happening, I felt totally powerless. I had nothing to overcome. I couldn't get my adrenaline to pump if it wasn't an actual life-or-death situation. Instead I smiled with my tongue in my teeth and baby-waved with both hands until I was booed off the stage.

Lynn and I were having a grand old time in Toronto. We were the belles of that male-dominated comedy-world ball in the way that only two young girls who can drink grown men under the table can be. I was still riding high from my win and the clubs were giving me spots and so we decided to cash in our return trips and stay. Moving across the country took only one phone call back home. "Hey, guys," I said to my housemates. "Go ahead and throw out that mattress. I'm not coming back."

Lynn and I moved in with her friend who lived in a really spectacular apartment owned by her father who, just weeks prior to our moving in, had passed away. His bereft daughter, Lynn's friend, was always cleaning out his closets and giving us socks and belts and cologne, all of which I eagerly accepted. I was only sorry my feet were too wide for his fancy wingtip shoes.

I had made it out of my farm life and managed to survive not getting hit by a bus in the big city. I had accomplished the Canadian Dream, which consists of knowing the name, birth date, and goal stats of every hockey player in the world, and making a quilt from scratch. But I wasn't done. I knew if I wanted to be an international sensation of stage and screen, I'd have to pop across the border to the good old US of A and take a whack at the aspiration no other country could boast: the American Dream.

Chapter 6

IT'S NOT ME, IT'S U.S.A.

My goal, at this point, was a lofty one. It was to meet and become besties with comedian Janeane Garofalo. I started formulating the plan one night while I was alone in my hotel room after an uneventful show in Mississauga, Ontario. I was snipping away at my toenails with Dennis Miller's late-night talk show droning on the TV in the background. I was mostly ignoring it, unwilling to haul my bag-of-bones self across the room to change the channel manually, and even less willing to use the remote that I was sure had been in at least one orifice of a prior guest. Instead, I actively tried not to listen. The banal banter of famous people on talk shows fills me with a kind of white-hot indifference. I can't imagine who is interested in these canned conversations and yet, someone is, because there are 407,000 of them on television at any given time. It's the number one job for white men after dressing up like Santa Claus.

That night, Dennis introduced, "My friend Garofalo!" It was the first time I'd seen her. I put down my toenail clipper and watched her from start to finish without so much as blinking. I didn't want to miss any of it. She was magical. Cool, effortless, funny, weird. She was the first female comedian I had seen who I didn't just enjoy, but who I also wanted to *be*. I even did her act several hundred times alone in my room to the mirror and maybe once onstage at an open mic. I loved how the jokes sounded coming out of my mouth. I thought the way she swaggered around the stage and didn't hide her disdain for the audience was so cool. I had other female comedy idols, too. There was Gilda Radner, Jane Curtin, Joan Rivers, Carol Leifer, and lots of others, but they didn't speak to me the way Janeane did. She was new school. She was young and spoke the way my friends and I did. Justin was out. I had someone new to obsess about.

A few nights later at a friend's house, I saw a show called *Caroline's Comedy Hour*. It taped in New York City. My plan started to take shape. I decided I would get on that show. I'd still be a long way from Hollywood, but at least I'd be in the States. I'd figure out how to get across the country after that. Project stalking Janeane had begun. Now it sounds creepy, but back then it was also kind of creepy. However, unlike these lazy cyber stalkers of today, back in my day, you had to get up off your ass to achieve your perverted desires.

I was going to America.

First stop, America's number-one comedy show, *Caroline's Comedy Hour,* which filmed on location at Caroline's, on Broadway, New York's premiere comedy club. I called information and asked them for the number of Caroline's Comedy Club in NYC. They gave it to me. I hung up and immediately dialed again. Someone answered, "Caroline's Comedy Club." I asked for the television show. They didn't know what I was talking about. I said, "Who decides on the comics?" They put me through to someone else. The person answered the phone with a thick New York accent. "Joe."

I launched with, "I'm the funniest new comic from Canada. Do you choose the comics for the show?" He said, "Yeah." I said,

"Well, I want to be on the show." He kind of laughed, and I imagined him leaning back in his chair thinking, This girl has pluck! But instead he said, "You think you can just call up and be on the show? How long have you been doing comedy?"

"A year."

"Are you funny?"

"You can't tell? I thought that was your job."

He laughed at that. "Okay. Are you cute? It's a visual medium."

"I don't know. I don't have a full-length mirror." That was true. I got him to laugh again.

"This is so weird," he said, "but here's what I'm going to do. I have some workmen in my office fixing my ceiling. I'll put you on speaker and if you can make them laugh, I'll put you on the show."

I had my notebook out in front of me, ready to go, because I thought this might happen. I actually thought this was how you got on TV, you call up and tell them some of your jokes and they let you know right then and there. So without thinking it was strange at all, I did some of my jokes for the booker of *Caroline's Comedy Hour* and the workmen in his office. I could hear them starting to laugh. I milked it. I did crowd work over the phone, in another country, to workmen I couldn't see. All those hard nights, with the bright lights in my eyes and hecklers who were hiding in plain sight as bartenders and middle-aged women with calf tattoos, was finally paying off. I was killing. Well, I don't know if I was killing, but I was certainly making an impression. And when I had gone through every joke in my book, Joe took me off speaker and said, "Damn it. I am giving you the show!" I wasn't that surprised. I still kind of thought, Well, this is how it's done.

"Do you have a manager?" he asked.

I didn't. I didn't even know what a manager did. The first time I even heard the term "manager" in relationship to comedy was a month earlier when I got a letter, sent to the local club in Toronto, Yuk Yuk's. The letter writer said he was a comedy manager and had seen my picture in a local magazine when he was at the Montreal comedy festival that summer. The article was about Canadian comics, and in a sidebar, they had a picture of me and a blurb that I had won the third annual Funniest Comic in Canada contest. I was not aware of the magazine, the Montreal festival, or that the contest was only in its third year. I also didn't know comedy managers existed until that letter. Overwhelmed by the information, I did what any up-and-coming comedian would do: I didn't respond. I shoved it in a desk drawer and didn't think of it again until right that second.

"A manager?" I somehow conjured up the name. "Yes, I do." And I told Joe his name.

"Oh, I know him. I'll set it up." Wow. Showbiz was welcoming me with open arms. And people said getting on television was hard.

I hung up with Joe, dug around for the letter, and finally found it next to a picture of Janeane. I dialed long distance again. I thought about reversing the charges but hell, I was going to be rich soon. I'd figure out a way to pay for these two international charges later.

"Hey, Jeff?"

"Yes."

"It's Bonnie McFarlane. I just got a spot on *Caroline's Comedy Hour* and I told them you were my manager."

"Because I am!" he said and laughed. And then he told me what a manager did. It made no sense then and it makes no sense now. But somehow these magical elves have cast a spell on comedians that leads them to believe they are a necessary part of the process. I will always appreciate what Jeff did do for me, though: he hooked me up with an immigration lawyer who set me up with the proper paperwork to get into the country so I'd legally be able to work there. Then he booked me at the hotel Chez Jeff. "Don't worry," he said, "I have a fiancée." And I accepted the fact that a woman loved him as a pretty good indicator that this man was probably not going to kill me, even though the arrest of the Canadian serial killer team Paul Bernardo and his wife, Karla, was still fresh in the air. But come on, it's hard enough finding someone who shares your passion for Sudoku, let alone another person who is down with killing innocent women. Not everyone was going to get as lucky as Paul and Karla. I bought my bus ticket and found a seat for the ten-hour trip. Not too close to the front, not next to the bathroom, and popped a CD into my Walkman.

Forty minutes later, we were at the American border where we all got off the bus in single file and one by one were vetted by a border-patrol guard. There were only about three things a Canadian could do to get denied entry into America in the days before terrorists used it as a revolving door for high-risk jihadists. You couldn't have fruit, have visited a farm in the past thirty days, or have purchased only a one-way ticket into the country. I had purchased only a one-way ticket into the country.

I explained that there was no financial incentive to purchase a return for the same day and that I fully intended to return to my homeland, a land I loved more than anything. But this border guy wasn't so sure. He didn't want to encourage homelessness, he told me.

"I know," I said, "I used to live in a garage but now I have a home. A real home. A guy died and so my friend and I moved in."

The border agent flipped through my notebooks and his face crinkled up in an expression of pure bewilderment. "They're jokes," I told him, but that didn't seem to clear up any confusion. "Well, a lot of them are not really funny, yet," I explained. "A lot of them are just premises that I'm working out." A lot of them kind of look like the ramblings of someone off their meds, I realized. I had to convince this guy to let me in.

"I have an immigration lawyer and the paperwork for a visa waiting for me."

"I have a TV SHOW!"

"I'm going to meet my best friend Janeane Garofalo!"

My pleas couldn't penetrate the heartless border agent and he directed me to the waiting area for the next bus back to Toronto. Entry denied.

The entire forty minutes home, I bounced around in my seat, crying and feeling sorry for myself. What was the point in trying? Nothing ever worked out. My ship was coming in and I was on a bus back to Toronto. But the next morning I awoke with new resolve. If at first you don't succeed, buy a plane ticket. A round-trip plane ticket. I had to clean out my bank account and use all the pennies at the bottom of my sock drawer, but I managed to scrape up enough to cover the amount and have forty dollars left over for spending money. At the airport, immigration detained me again. I must have fit some profile because for years crossing the border, I would get stopped, searched, and harassed. Nowadays of course, they focus primarily on terrorists and frisking the elderly, but back then, keeping disenfranchised youths from entering America seemed to be the exclusive objective.

On this particular trip, it took me four hours to convince the border police to let me in. I pulled out all the stops: the baby voice, crocodile tears, and a few empty threats. Finally, they stamped my paperwork and allowed me entry into the U.S. of A., probably because they were impressed with my character work and knew I'd make a fine addition to an improvisational comedy troupe.

I just made it onto the last plane of the day headed for Newark, New Jersey. That night I had an industry showcase that my (hopefully) not homicidal manager had set up, and then I would tape my set on *Caroline's Comedy Hour* the next night. I wasn't sure what "industry" was, so I wasn't terribly nervous about the actual showcase, but I was worried about getting there on time. Back then only people who worked at NASA had cell phones and I knew it might be tricky to try to meet up with someone you'd never met before in a city you didn't know toting a suitcase that didn't have wheels. Yes, the rolling suitcase had been invented; I just didn't have one. Because I was broke. That was another thing that worried me. I had no credit card, nothing in my bank account, and only forty dollars Canadian to my name. That was about $1.20 in American funds. If I didn't hook up with Jeff, I'd likely end up being exactly what those border guards were trying to seal America against: impoverished Canadian whores.

It wasn't a particularly long flight, but it was long enough for me to spill an entire Coke down the front of my shirt. That's right, I'd convinced the flight attendant to give me the entire can of Coke instead of the two ounces with an ice cube and I spilled it. Sorry.

After I arrived, I dragged my suitcase off the baggage carousel, hauled it to the bathroom, removed a wrinkled shirt, and changed into it. Then I lugged that suitcase through the airport, wishing I had packed my things in a wheelbarrow. Eventually, I made it to the cabstand. Many cabs and several humiliating attempts later I was finally able to convince a driver to take me to New York for the two Canadian twenties I was waving in his face. I was on my way to New York City!

I **SHOWED UP AT THE** World Famous Comic Strip Comedy Club where the industry showcase was in full swing. I knew my manager was Jewish, but the place, quite frankly, looked like the after party for *Fiddler on the Roof.* I didn't know where to start. Thankfully, my manager found me. My plaid wood-chopping flannel jacket, along with my inability to curb my "Sorrys," were straight out of his Dummy's Guide to Spotting a Canadian. We shook hands and he introduced me to his absolutely drop-dead gorgeous fiancée who towered over him. They reminded me of Boris and Natasha, and in my books, anyone who looks like a cartoon character has to be okay.

About a minute later, I was going onstage for my first-ever stateside set. I don't recall how it went, honestly. I was in a bit of a fog and my left arm felt like it was dangling from my shoulder, lengthened from the drag of my non-rolling bag, as my knuckles scraped the stage. I waved good night with my short arm, relieved that the whole ordeal was over.

When I got offstage, I did what all Canadians would do in that situation: I sought out a cold Australian beer. I drank down half the Foster's in one beautiful, refreshing gulp. Then my manager, doing what managers do best, introduced me to another manager. This one was the manager of the club. His name was Lucian.

"You're an interesting performer," Lucian said. "You walk a fine line between irony and satire." I had no idea what he was talking about. To me, the best compliment has always been and will always be, "You're funny." So I just nodded and smiled and pretended to understand.

"Shall we go into my office and talk about it some more?"

Normally, I would never turn down the opportunity to talk about me or things I'm involved in, but it had been an exceptionally long day. I was almost done with my beer and I really wanted another fourteen.

"I'm just kind of burned out. Thanks anyway."

He looked slightly taken aback, shocked by the rejection. But he seemed like the kind of man who kept his emotions close to the vest and he recovered pretty instantaneously. I was glad. I had more important things to talk about than my comedic tone. "Do comedians get free beers?" I asked. "And if so, how many?"

Many weeks later, a few comedians in the greenroom of another comedy club were sharing stories about their "Lucian talks." Turns out every comedian who auditioned at the club was subjected to a discussion with Lucian about their performance. At times he could be very harsh. "Shave your mustache, you look like a pervert." "We've got enough white guys, thanks anyway." "Your accent turns people off." After the critique, he would either say you were passed at the club or you weren't. For me at least, turning down the invitation for the critique worked out in my favor. I started getting on the lineup after that about twice a week, and sometimes I even got spots on the weekends. It was a pretty good haul for a new comic, but I was not grateful in the least. I lacked what most young people lack in situations like this: perspective. I had no idea that there were other people, people just as talented or even more talented than I was, struggling to get any spots at all.

That's how it was for me at the beginning. Call a club, ask for a spot on a TV show, get it. Tell a club booker you don't feel like talking to him and get spots immediately. Bomb and bomb and bomb and then win the Funniest New Comic in Canada contest. But not all my naiveté worked out so well.

In Canada, you don't greet people by kissing them on

the cheek. You stick your tongue in the person's eye and say, "Damn, girl." At least that's what my gym teacher used to do. But in America, I was introduced to the kiss on the cheek and it made me feel like we were rehearsing for *Masterpiece Theatre.* I didn't like it. So when a tall, intimidating talent manager met me for the first time and leaned in for a kiss, I decided to put a stop to it. "Hey, I'm not comfortable with kissing strangers," I told him with a twinkle in my eye. "Let's hold hands for a bit and see how it goes." He was clearly offended by my boorishness and has NEVER let me forget it. I didn't help matters much a few years later when he and his wife asked me to come for dinner and I said (as a joke!), "I couldn't think of anything worse!" It might've been a funnier joke if I had followed it up with, "I'm kidding, I'm kidding, I'd love to come. What can I bring?" But I really didn't feel like going, so I said, "I'm kidding, I'm kidding, but really I've got something I'm pretty sure I have to do."

But my biggest blunder, my most pedestrian mistake, came the night after the showcase. I woke up early, the way one does when one wakes up on a stranger's couch in a foreign country, happy to have woken up at all, and immediately felt an uncontrollable nervousness. It was the day of my big television taping. I was going to be on American Television. It was not even eight A.M. and I didn't have to be there until four. What was I going to do all day to keep my nerves in check? I started snooping, and after looking through every cupboard in my new manager and his fiancée's brownstone, I realized that they had everything I needed to make cinnamon buns. I got busy baking right away.

Who gets up and makes cinnamon buns in a stranger's house? Someone who is aware of her baking talents! If my manager had been using his head, he would have positioned me right then and there as the next *funny* Martha Stewart who isn't so great with flowers or crafts but who is equally as good at insider trading.

Baking cinnamon buns in this guy's house wasn't weird to me because I baked all the time. When I was growing up, I baked. When I had an apartment in Vancouver, I baked. Obviously, the seven months I spent living in a garage limited my confections output, but in my friend's friend's dead dad's apartment in Toronto, I baked. Baking relaxed me. So, there, my first day in a New York City Upper West Side brownstone, I mixed, I rolled, I baked. All day. When it was finally time to go, I had about six dozen rolls packed up and ready to take to the taping. I was sure there would be a lot of guys throwing around cables and apple boxes and cameramen swinging around those massive contraptions, all of whom would likely welcome a fresh, warm cinnamon bun. And it might even be a good way to meet some new folks, eh?

I walked in, nerves sleeping comfortably after overdosing on carbs, and put the rolls on a table. With the wave of a hand, like a queen to her subjects, I crowed, "Come and get it." People stopped what they were doing and looked over, unsure if I was someone they should invest another second looking at. I could see my manager was having second thoughts. He was doing that thing you do when you're with a crazy person. You start laughing too loudly and giving a few "fun" reasons for why the person they are with is crazy: "She's Canadian!" "She's from a farm." "She thought this would be funny." No, I didn't. I didn't think it would be funny. Who thinks slaving over a hot stove all day is funny?

The smell brought a few people over to see what I had brought. As I arranged them on the plate, I could hear them grumbling.

"What are these?"

"Are these cinnamon buns?"

"Where's the white icing?"

"How come there's no icing?"

I don't make them with icing. They don't need icing. They are perfectly delicious without icing.

"I never had a cinnamon bun without icing."

"Are you Americans fucking for real? I mean, come on! These are homemade! These are not factory produced at some fucking mall outlet!" I rolled up my sleeve. "See this burn mark? This is from making these fucking rolls for you people!"

Let's just say very few people ate the cinnamon buns. They were probably nervous because of the big show. Hey, you don't want to eat my cinnamon buns, fine. I don't care. Don't eat them. I'm not going to force you to eat my buns. Assholes.

My manager escorted me backstage to where I would be getting my makeup done. Despite the disappointment with the cinnamon buns, I managed to remain bright and lively. "This is my first time getting my makeup professionally done!" I confessed excitedly. And then I never stopped chatting. I don't know if it was sugar overload or nerves, but I was being very charming. I'm sure they loved my nonstop stories about the farm. "I had a cow! And made ice cream!"

Joe, the voice that had booked me on the show, entered the room. He introduced himself. I smiled as brightly as I could.

"Oh, hello," I said. "We finally meet in person!"

"You are cute," he said, and I think he sounded relieved.

"It's all because of these two hotshots," I said, pointing my thumb toward the women in charge of my head's appearance. I was being incredibly delightful.

"Are you nervous?" he asked.

"Not yet," I said, "but I'm sure I will be."

"You'll be great," he said.

"Have a cinnamon bun!" I called out after him. "Home-made. No annoying icing."

"Oh, I like the icing best," said the makeup girl.

"Me, too," said the hair girl.

What did they know?

As I was walking from the hair and makeup chair to the bathroom, I saw the audience come in and my captivating smile faded. There were black people! Right up front! And other skin tones I didn't recognize. And girls who looked like they'd been run over by a bus only moments earlier, carrying shopping bags that had seen better weeks. These didn't look like happy-go-lucky Canadians or even the rough-and-tumble small-town Northerners I had experienced. These people didn't look like they would waste time beating you senseless if you didn't make them laugh. These people looked like they would kill you if you didn't make them laugh. My stomach started churning. My mouth wouldn't fully open. Not only had I lost my ability to natter on nonstop, I had lost my ability to make saliva and, in turn, talk. But there was nothing I could do to remedy the situation except get on the toilet and try to push all the anxiety out through my asshole. I was in there for a while. An assistant producer knocked on the bathroom door. "You're on next. You okay?"

I was not okay. But it was a rhetorical question. There was no turning back. I heard my name and I walked onstage as if in a dream, and not the good kind, either. The kind where your legs don't work and you aren't wearing any pants and there are people who look like they might kill you.

I said the words to my jokes, but without my sparkling personality, they just didn't make sense. I chalked it up to another bomb, but this time it was caught on celluloid for posterity. I headed offstage and back into the bathroom. And I cried. I cried and I cried. And I cried. Finally there was another knock on the door. "We need you for one last shot," said the PA.

I took a deep breath and exited the bathroom. I must have looked like shit because the PA literally gasped.

"One second," she said. She came back with the makeup lady.

"Oh my God," said the makeup girl. She began wiping and reapplying like she was taught by Mr. Miyagi from *The Karate Kid*. Wipe off, wipe on.

I had to go back onstage. They needed one final shot that would be used at the beginning of the show. As the voice-over introduced who would be on the big program that night, the comedians would smile, wave, give a thumbs-up, or in my case, fight the urge to crumple to the floor in the fetal position. If I had been auditioning for the part of an American hostage forced by a terrorist group to make a video saying I was being treated well by my captors, I would have easily gotten that part. But this wasn't an audition for a heroic character in a docudrama. This was a comedy show. I remember the cameraman getting frustrated. He kept saying we just need a few more seconds of a full smile. Let's try again. Just keep the smile . . . You can do this . . . let's try again . . .

After what felt like hours of Sudanese torture, I was released. I changed into my street clothes and made my way back into the show room. The audience was gone. The grips were ripping up the cables. The club was resetting for business as usual.

My manager was doing a little spin control with Caroline's owner, aptly named Caroline, and the booker, Joe. But there was no way to spin it. I had blown it.

I decided that no matter what, I would never let my nerves get the best of me again. I was not going to let opportunities slip away because of nervousness. How lame. And as I made that decision, I looked up and I saw Janeane Garofalo. JANEANE

GAROFALO! My best friend. My American Dream! Not in Los Angeles, California, but right here in New York City!

I watched Janeane as she walked in slow motion toward the stage. I don't know if she was walking like that on purpose or if, in retrospect, I remember it like that for cinematic purposes. I guess it's also possible she was just a slow walker. Anyway, she made her way to the lap of a cute guy who was sitting on a chair on the stage, just hanging out there, comfortable as could be. I think he might have been a writer on the show but probably wasn't because, as I said, he was cute. Janeane, now perched on his lap, said something and he started to laugh. Then he said something and she was laughing. They were being really funny with each other, though I couldn't hear what they were saying.

I just stood at the back of the room while grips worked around me packing up cables, watching Janeane and the cute maybe-writer flirt and laugh.

Then an ugly guy approached me.

"Hi. I'm a writer on the show."

"I'm sure you are."

"Yeah. I felt bad for you."

"I'm fine."

"I heard you were crying pretty hard."

"It wasn't that hard. It was a lot, but lightly, over a long period of time. There was no snot or anything."

"Anything I can do to make you feel better?"

"No thanks."

"Really?"

"Really."

"Anyone you want to meet or anything?"

I finally turned and looked at him. That's when I realized he was not just a writer on the show but a messenger from God.

"Yes," I said, "I want to meet Janeane Garofalo."

"Really? I thought you'd want to meet the host or Caroline but okay."

The writer led the way and I followed him up to the stage. "Hey, Janeane," he called out to her. She was still on the cute guy's lap. She didn't look up. "Hey, Janeane!" he called out five more times. She finally looked over.

"This is Bonnie. She was on the show tonight." Janeane looked at me, not in a welcoming way, but also not in a dismissive way. She just looked at me. This was my chance. I'd tell her how great I thought she was, how I'd come to New York first and then was going to go to L.A. just to meet her and, "Wow, what a world, here we are!" I'd be charismatic and smile and we'd go for a beer and be friends. Instead I just stood there and said nothing because of nervousness! I didn't even offer her a cinnamon bun.

"Okay," she said, slightly annoyed, and then went back to laughing with her cute friend.

The ugly guy and I walked away. Then Jeff, my manager, came and escorted me out. "They'll still air it, I think," he said as we climbed the thousand or so stairs out of the club. "They can fix some of it in post." As we waited for a cab, he turned to me. "Don't worry, you'll do more television. You'll be fine."

I was fine. I did do more television. I did actually speak to Janeane on several occasions, but we never became the best of friends the way I had hoped.

No, for me, finding friends was a little like that old saying about shooting fish in a barrel. First the fish really have to want to be shot.

Chapter 7

LITTLE AIRLINE
BOTTLES IN
THE BIG APPLE

I officially moved to New York City (or more to the point, officially didn't move back to Canada). I know. This kind of move was becoming something of a habit. But the border guards would be happy to know that my manager wanted me there legally and so he hooked me up with a lawyer who scored me a working visa. Then he snagged me an apartment in Harlem. Fresh from Canada, I moved into a large one-bedroom apartment at 125th and Broadway. I didn't realize this was an interesting choice of locale for a white girl until I started telling other white people I lived at 125th and Broadway. They would hug me and say, "I'll try to make it to your funeral but I can't promise anything because I'm super busy right now with all my irons in the fire but if I can, I'll try. Nice knowing you!"

It sounds racist now but back then people said, "irons in the fire" all the time. Also, this is pregentrification but post Cotton Club. I should mention that my neighbors were all very nice, I had no problems with anyone, except for the one guy, and there's always the one guy who ruins it for everyone else, who failed to hold the door open for me one day, and normally I wouldn't make a big deal about it, but it was raining out! Still, I try not to judge the entire community by that one selfish individual.

While the common consensus seemed to be that I was going to die living in Harlem, I was not afraid at all. I mean, I was afraid of talking to people on the subway and answering the phone if I wasn't expecting a call, but certainly not afraid of dying in my neighborhood. However, full disclosure and all that, I should point out that people who lived in Harlem did sometimes die. It's possible someone is doing it right now. The person who lived in the apartment before me had, in fact, succumbed to the long sleep, but not because of an untreated knife wound in the gut the way my mother predicted I would probably go. She died of old age.

The apartment belonged to my manager's fiancée's grandmother. Our luck crisscrossed—hers bad, mine good—and just days after I arrived in New York, I moved in while the family attended her funeral. They allowed me to live there for a measly $500 a month while they tried to sell the space.

My Harlem pad had all the furniture and amenities I could ask for. In fact, there was still food in the fridge until I ate it and her clothes were all still hanging neatly in the closet until I wore them and then left them in a pile in the corner. I also, and this I'm less proud of, drank all the little airline bottles of alcohol that she had painstakingly collected over the years. Lemon gin, so yum, am I right?

It's true that this was the second time in ten months that I had moved into the fully furnished apartment of a dead person but, despite how that might come across in a *Law and Order* episode, I was not a dangerous predator. I was more of a hermit crab. In the months after moving in, I spent most of my time moping around the apartment, wearing a dead woman's nightgown while drinking lemon gin with expired cranberry juice and watching television.

I was hopelessly homesick.

Americans tend to think of Canada as just another state, like a big Maine or a small Colorado, but with less electricity. I remember Sarah Silverman asking a group of us once, "Do you ever wish you could just up and move to another country?"

I perked up. "I did!" I said.

She looked at me like I was lying. "You did? Where?"

"I moved here from Canada."

"Oh," she said, narrowing her eyes as though I'd slipped through an antiquated loophole. "No, like a real other country."

Believe it or not, Canada is a real other country, folks. It really is. It IS!

I'm sure you already know some of the differences between the countries, like Canada has socialized health care and we don't border Mexico. But there are also differences you might not be aware of, like the fact that we use the metric system for measuring everything, not just our drugs. Also we tend to jingle when we walk because our money consists mostly of coins, and we speak at a lower volume in restaurants.

And then there's this thing about race that we treat differently. In Canada, race isn't something we concentrated on. Sure, there are black people, but out of respect, you pretend they are white and one never mentions it. I spent a lot of time describing people in Canada like, "The guy with the curly hair and brown eyes? He loves chicken wings. You know the guy I'm talking about? He loves hip-hop and carries a basketball. He's never met his dad. You know, he grew up on the south side. His name is, like, Jamal or Micah? You know who I'm talking about? He always dates blondes who could stand to lose a few?" But we'd never say "the black guy" because we didn't want to seem racist.

New York was different. Comics onstage would look into the audience and say to someone, "What are you?" What are you! In Canada you could know someone from the cradle to the grave and you'd never ask, "What are you?" Sure, you'd speculate with friends, but no one would ever ask someone to their face. The boldness of it made me cringe. But the audience member would appear unfazed by such a query and would shout it out, loud and proud, "Half Irish, half Rican!" The audience member never realized that this was a not-so-clever way for the comedian to set up the phrase, "So you'd drink the alcohol that was meant to clean your stab wounds!" I was even more amazed that many comics didn't need to ask the audience member what a woman's background was. They simply determined her nationality from her skin tone and the diameter of her hoop earrings.

I was afraid that I would never be able to memorize enough stereotypes to excel in this environment. Not while I had a six-pack of brewskies and a hockey game to finish. Luckily, race jokes weren't actually a requirement. New York was experiencing a serious comedy renaissance and the only thing I truly needed in order to be a part of it was an original comedic voice. It was the late nineties and there were amazing comedians everywhere, and all of them were as different and unique as snowflakes or parole letters. Louis C.K., Sarah Silverman, Todd Barry, Marc Maron, Jim Gaffigan, Greg Giraldo, and of course the two Daves were king. Chappelle and Attell. The first time I saw Chappelle he blew me away with his white-guy voice. "I think I'll wear my cardigan tonight. Feels a little cool." The audience would roar because it felt fresh and funny. I'd never heard anyone make fun of the way a white guy talked before. Why, it was absolutely revolutionary, darling.

The next night Dave Chappelle stopped me as I was heading into the comedy cellar. "You a comic?" he asked. "Yes." I was so excited that he recognized that in me. I obviously had a comedic air wafting up off my droopy shoulders and likely it smelled like peppermint schnapps. I still had a half-full airline bottle in my pocket. I looked deep into his bloodshot eyes and realized he wanted to ask me something. Perhaps to write with him? Maybe open for him? The possibilities were endless, even though I really can't think of more than just those two right now.

"Can you go in and find out what time my set is?" Okay, that was slightly deflating but I returned shortly with an answer.

"Eleven fifteen."

"Cool." I didn't talk to him again until late August 2004.

And then there was Dave Attell. It was an understatement to say he was respected. He was the New York comedy scene's prized possession. He was talking about his balls and killing hookers and the first time I saw him, it made me realize I would never be the world's greatest living joke writer. He already existed. I knew I wouldn't be the best comedy performer in the world. I might've been Canada's funniest new comic, but in New York, my compliments were more along the lines of, "Well, you're really speaking English up there."

I showcased for a lot of agents and casting directors but generally did not make much of an impression. My manager really wanted me to get a spot at the Montreal comedy festival, but I bombed through that audition, too. I didn't go on the road that often and whenever I did, my social anxiety came flooding back because I'd have to talk to people who were not comedians. My coping mechanisms were one of two extremes. I either went out of my way to keep quiet and took to wearing an "I Hate Cats" button, which certainly discouraged all the chatty Cathys who wanted to gab on a train. Or I overcompensated by sharing too much, asking too many questions, or reading aloud from my journals until I was removed from the quiet car.

Once I went to Princeton to open for a comic at Catch a Rising Star. I took the train into central New Jersey and as I checked into the hotel, I found myself using coping mechanism number two, the Overshare. I began talking to the front-desk clerk in a very loud voice about my life. "I'm a comic," I announced. "I'm at Rising Star! Here all week!"

"Great."

"This is my first time in New Jersey, so this is really exciting. I've been to New Brunswick but the one in Canada. Not the one in New Jersey. I'm Canadian. Grew up on a farm. I've milked a cow."

"You're in 405. By the elevator."

I got fired after the first show and had to check out the following morning. As luck would have it, I got the same desk clerk. "I thought you were here all week?"

"My grandmother died."

She shook her head sadly and said sorry, but I think she knew I was lying.

I WAS STARTING TO THINK that perhaps my forte was not public speaking. Perhaps my talents were not meant to be enjoyed on a stage under a spotlight. Perhaps my talents would be better served silently, as a writer. When one door closes, another door opens—usually a refrigerator. And between PB and J sandwiches, I managed to throw together a few packets of writing samples. I was determined to get myself a staff writing job on one of the late-night shows.

I am still waiting to hear back from every show I submitted to.

I complained to my manager.

"Who cares?" he said.

"I want to be a writer."

"You're not a writer," he said, "you're a performer. You're

going to act." And he gave me the name of an acting teacher. Luckily, there was another comedian in the class I could talk to, Jim Gaffigan. He was literally the funniest person I'd ever met, so I told my manager he should manage him. My manager said, "He's not a performer. He's a writer." My manager was clearly a guy who knew what he was doing.

Jim and I started hanging out. He was friends with Greg Giraldo, so Giraldo got me as part of the Gaffigan deal, like it or not. We'd all hook up after shows and toss back a few Red Stripes. Greg was married at the time, so he would usually check out around midnight. Jim was a pack a day smoker and a hard drinker, but he was also disciplined, so he usually went home shortly after Giraldo left. I, on the other hand, never got in a cab to go uptown to Harlem until someone took a cigarette out of my mouth and informed me that I had lit the wrong end.

I was drinking a lot because I couldn't seem to get into the groove of New York's comedy scene. It's definitely the hardest place in the world to do stand-up, which is why some of the greatest comedians in the world are born out of this scene. You have to get good, fast, or get out.

I was terrified of working weekend spots. The clubs were packed tight with bridge and tunnel folks from Long Island or New Jersey who had worked hard all week and wanted to see a show and get drunk, not necessarily in that order. As a comedian, if you showed weakness, they'd descend on you with a mob mentality usually reserved for rioting and looting after a Stanley Cup loss.

One Friday night, I was booked to perform at a small club called the Boston Comedy Club, despite the fact that it was located in New York's West Village. I stood in the back of the room and tried to manage my nerves. The place was hot because so many bodies had jammed into the narrow windowless club.

The air was thick with the smell of B.O. and cheap draft beer. Todd Barry was onstage. He was doing well. I was heartened by this. He was able to engage the audience despite the fact that they were raucous and he was low energy. But he offered me a false sense of security, and even that was short lived.

After Todd, Judy Gold took the stage and destroyed. And when I say destroyed, I mean take no prisoners, behead everyone in the audience, laughing-till-you-puke destroyed. I had never in my life seen a woman command a stage like that. It was incredible, but it also made all the liquids from my mouth dry up and the palms of my hands drip with moisture. I wasn't sure I'd be able to hold the mic, let alone talk into it.

As each act went up, the crowd got more and more manic. By the time the comedy duo Red Johnny and the Round Guy took the stage, the crowd was completely frenzied. They were HIGH ENERGY!!!! They had MUSIC!!!! They had a LIGHT SHOW!!!! The audience was SCREAMING with delight. And I was up next. I would've walked out of the club if I thought my legs would be able to carry me that distance, but I only made it as far as the emcee. He was a young guy who looked much older than he actually was. I said to him, "Can you do some time between them and me? I'm going to die up there." He put a fatherly arm around my shoulders. "No problem," he assured me. "Whatever you need." I exhaled a little. Maybe I had a chance.

Red Johnny and the Round Guy stepped off the riser and the emcee stepped on. The audience was applauding. They were whooping. Even white people were standing in front of their chairs doing a little chicken dance. They were acting like they'd just seen the best thing they'd ever see in their whole lives. The emcee leaned into the mic. "Red Johnny and the Round Guy!" The audience gave it up AGAIN!

My knees were knocking together, which I hoped might help

me with my timing. Then, as promised, the emcee began a joke, to put a little distance between the greatest act they'd ever seen and me, the most nervous act they'd ever see. "I was in the gym the other day," the emcee began. "And I was in the changing room . . ." Someone in the audience cut him off by yelling, "FAG!" and without missing a beat, the emcee said, "Our next act comes to us from Canada. Please welcome Bonnie McFarlane."

They started booing me before I even made it to the stage. They might've been booing my ungainly gate, the fact that I was from Canada, or because I was a girl. I don't know. I didn't have time to process any of that. I just took the mic and started my act the way I always started. "Good to be here. You look like a nice audience. And by nice, I mean unattractive." More booing. Loads of booing.

People have always said I have a lot of stage presence, that I have confidence when I'm up there. I don't know what I'm projecting, but inside, I'm nothing. I'm horrified. I'm terrified. I'm a bag of drowning kittens. But somehow, some way, I just kept talking. I shrugged off their hatred. I smirked at their loathing. My face said I'm high-fiving myself. Then I got off, head held high, and mumbled a couple of "Whatevs" as I walked outside. I made it around the corner of the club before I started sobbing uncontrollably, wondering to myself why I still hadn't invested in a tube of waterproof mascara.

"Allergies," I said to some staring tourists.

Then a guy I'd never met before approached.

"You a comic?" he asked. I guess I had that comedic stench wafting up off my shoulders again.

I nodded.

"Me, too," he said. "Where are you from?"

"Canada."

"Never been. Look, this is a tough city. I know. I'm not from here, either. And it takes a while to get your New York legs. It takes a while to figure this place out. Trust me, I know."

I started to feel better. I took a deep breath. "Where are you from?"

"Jersey," he answered without a hint of insincerity. I looked up and to my left. Like, right there? I don't know. Who am I to judge? Maybe the guy did go through a lot. He did have to pay a toll and stuff.

A WEEK LATER I WAS back on a bus headed to Canada.

Despite appearances and the fact that I was carrying a pair of shoes in a plastic bag, I wasn't giving up. I was repaying a visit to my homeland to tape a comedy special for Canadian television and would be returning to New York just two days later. The proof, of course, was my round-trip ticket, which I had already purchased, and the dead woman's shirt I was wearing that I had vowed to return.

I was handpicked to perform on the special by the series producer, Joe Bodolai, who I'd met in Toronto after winning the crown of Funniest New Comic in Canada. He was a very kind man who would champion me for many years. He was the real deal: a former writer for *SNL*, American expat, and the original creator of *Wayne's World*. I was extremely grateful for the gig, even though I was convinced I would disappoint him and he'd regret giving me a shot.

The day of the taping, I spent the entire afternoon in the hotel gift shop, shopping for just the right outfit for my Canadian television debut. I wanted to pick something fabulous because, being that it was a Canadian TV special, I knew at least seventeen people would see it. I settled on an orange T-shirt that was one or two sizes too small. It was so tight that you could see the indentation the straps on my sports bra made into my back fat, so I made the ingenious decision to not wear a bra at all. Before you condemn me as a harlot hell-bent on getting male attention, keep in mind that I was still pretty unclear of my gender at this point, although I was almost sure I should've been getting my period by now. I had never walked more than three steps in a pair of high-heeled shoes and my outfits consisted mostly of men's button-downs and gentleman jeans because I liked that extra room in my crotch.

When, during the sound check, I casually asked if anyone could tell I wasn't wearing a bra, I literally thought the two hundred grips and gaffers who magically appeared before me eager to help by staring at my chest were just being kind. They were so adamant that the shirt looked good, I wore that shirt on two more television appearances through the years. So ubiquitous was that shirt during my televised stand-up career that the animators for the *Dr. Katz* show drew it on me for that appearance.

The special went well. I would have to say my Canadian television debut was 9.5 out of 10 compared with my American television debut, which was anal rape. After the show I was feeling fantastic. I was giddy with possibility. Perhaps stand-up was something I could actually be good at! I wished I could do another show to keep chasing that dragon. It's best that I didn't, though, because, like crack, the next hit is never as fun. It's a cycle of diminishing returns.

After the show, I connected with my old pal Lynn, who was still living in Toronto and who was now also doing stand-up. She had a way of being incredibly supportive while also subtly letting you know you got lucky with the audience. She was a great friend to go out with because we both liked to drink the same amount. Is there anything worse than partying with a friend who after only half a dozen drinks wants to go home and curl up with a good book?

That night Lynn and I met up with several other comedians. As I was among friends, I regaled them with stories not of the farm, but of my American exploits. I told the story of bombing on American television and made them laugh at my failures in the New York clubs. As I looked around, I felt a warmth creep up on me. I said "a-boot" without backlash. I threw out a couple of "eh's" at the end of my questions without worrying about creating a negative stereotype. I sang a few of bars of "Oh, Canada" and then mumbled the rest. Lynn and I walked back to my hotel, ordered room service, and crashed. It was truly one of the best nights of my life, except for the hour of stomach cramps I got after bingeing on pizza and pasta at one A.M.

The next morning, I had a pretty consistent throbbing in my temples, which was made worse by the ringing of the hotel phone.

"Hello?"

It was Joe Bodolai, the series producer, calling to tell me how proud he was of me for doing such a great special and not drinking too much before the show. I was proud of myself too, because it's always a tough thing to control for any performer with access to unlimited amounts of Kokanee beer in the greenroom. When he told me to have a good trip back, I realized I really didn't want to return to New York. I blurted out everything. I told him how I couldn't make friends. I was failing at stand-up. I auditioned for the Montreal comedy festival and didn't get it. I had only two airline bottles of lemon gin left. And then he said this: "I believe in you. I believe in your talent." It's weird what keeps you going. Joe Bodolai's belief in me was something I held on to. I needed it. When you have so many reasons to quit, it's nice to sometimes have someone convince you not to.

We'll stay in touch, he said. And we did for many, many years.

I hugged Lynn at the bus station and she gave me some things to make my trip more palatable. Her strict instructions were to drink the entire bottle of water and take half the Xanax she provided. I drank half the water and took the whole Xanax and was back at the New York Port Authority in no time, where they poured me off the bus.

Chapter 8

FRIENDSHIT

Once you go black, you never go back. And I'm talking about humor, folks. I've been with plenty of black guys and gone back to white guys, FYI. I assume we're all on the same page in categorizing Jews as white?

Here's the thing: Comics can be very dark. We often joke about things that are troubling and humorless to regular people. We're like ER nurses who use gallows humor to cope after a long, hard shift that includes terrible images of headshot wounds, missing appendages, and cafeteria food. Except we do it without the annoying inconvenience of trying to save lives. This is why I prefer the company of other comedians. You don't have to defend your attempts at humor and no one ever asks what school you went to.

I hate going to parties where there aren't any other comics. Both times I've been invited to a comic-less party, I've instantly felt completely out of place. First, there's the problem with saying you're a comedian. It never goes well. There are too many dumb questions you're expected to answer, and a lot of it involves explaining why you aren't on *Saturday Night Live*. So I usually lie about that. I just lie and lie and lie. And while lying about your profession, your income, and the amount of scientific studies you've had published is an enjoyable way to pass the time, occasionally you run across someone who actually knows you're completely full of shit and then you have to lure them into a spare bedroom and stab them to death with your pocket knife before they have a chance to tell anyone.

Second, people who do not spend the majority of their time in bars talking about Spanx and pony porn to drunk people still have an instinct for being socially appropriate. That can be annoying because every time you're even a little bit offensive, they tend to point it out, either with a gasp or actual pointing. I loathe the idea of having to curb my unseemliness around regular people so much that my family physician is a part-time comedian, known at night as Dr. Comedy; my tax guy does a little stand-up on the side; and yes, I bought life insurance from a man who opens for me sometimes on the road. He's terrible at crowd work though, because he always ends up asking the audience about their medical history. It was this pathological desire to be with other socially immature individuals that compelled me to seek out comedians as my first order of business anywhere I went.

Making comedy friends in New York was challenging. For a long time, the closest I came to having a group of comic friends was hanging out in the kids' department of the Salvation Army with all the broken toys. One of my first attempts at striking up a comic friendship was with Sarah Silverman. I saw her for the first time, midset, at Stand Up NY. It was love at first sight. She was fabulous. She even got a heckler and handily bested him. "You look like Rocky," she told him, "from the movie *Mask*." She was young, pretty, boyish, poised, commanding. We'd be perfect together. I immediately imagined us huddled over coffees in the late afternoon trading punch lines, discussing the genius of Bette Midler and *SCTV*. I'd share my secret theory on how you could tell the size of a comic's junk by how far he holds the microphone from his dick. If he doesn't even take it out of the stand, forget about it.

After her set, while she was retrieving her backpack from a bar stool, I told Sarah how funny I thought she was and waited for her to be dazzled by her comedy doppelganger. (That'd be me.) She couldn't have been less interested, which goes to show how popular she must have been already. Back then, if people told me I was funny, I would've followed them around for two weeks brushing their hair and doing their laundry.

Another female comic—I'll withhold her name because the story is unflattering and since she is now quite famous, I may need her to write a blurb for the jacket cover of this book. She was almost famous even then, and she immediately took me under her wing and listened intently as I talked about the difficulties I faced in translating my Canadian material for an American audience. "What do you open with?" she asked. I told her. "It's funny," she said and shrugged. "I don't know why it's not working for you." Then she went onstage and did my joke verbatim. For the record, it killed. I, on the other hand, stammered through a new, untested opening joke that did less well by quite a large margin.

I wanted to make friends with girl comics, but there were a lot fewer women working the clubs in those days. Why, with all the cursing and drinking and aggressive behavior, it just wasn't a suitable environment for a young lady. As a comedian, you don't even get that many chances to work with other women. Having two female comedians on a three-person show is rare. Generally speaking, club owners feel that zero women comedians on any given night is about a perfect number, although they will occasionally fill one of the slots with a comedienne every few years, just in case Gloria Steinem shows up to protest. That way, they can pull out the promotional flyer to show her proof of having booked a woman at least once since they opened in '82.

On the other end of the spectrum, club owners like to do an all-lady show once yearly to get all the women comics in and out in a single weekend, which also cuts down on the number of times they have to clean the ladies' room. They like to promote these shows as though they are promoting a night of family friendly prostitution. They give the shows names like Ladies of the Night, Hot Babes of Comedy, and Anal Whores. If there are two women on a show, often they are given a single spot to share. Co-headliners, co-middles, a female comedy emcee team. And there were those conjoined twins who stated in their rider that they had to have separate dressing rooms. That was fine; it was the fact that they requested their own mics that eventually stalled their careers.

The comedy climate being what it was, I, for one, was quite surprised when I showed up at a club on Long Island not long after I had moved to New York to see another woman on the bill. We weren't even sharing the middle spot. She was the emcee and I was the opening act. This was tantamount to Comedy Heresy, but no one really seemed to care or say anything about it. The headliner, obviously, was a man. He had called me the night before and offered me a ride to the club. He told me to meet him in the alley where he kept his car. This is probably one of the reasons there aren't more women in comedy, if you think about it. Meeting guys you've never met in dark alleys for rides to places called Chuckles probably stokes some pretty intense fight-or-flight responses in women who are wired normally.

Not me! The minute I saw a shifty-looking white guy in a wrinkled suit sitting in his car reading the entertainment section of the paper, I jumped right in. And sadly, as a result, I was forced, against my will (as the word "forced" implies), to listen to a full blow-by-blow account of how he and his writing partner were nominated for an Emmy for writing an episode of a popular sitcom. The experience was infinitely worse than being raped and left for dead in a Dumpster, if you ask me.

I don't want to spend too much time on this, but I think it's an important teaching moment. Let me make it clear that Mr. Headliner was recounting how he was nominated for an Emmy, not how he won an Emmy. I think if you win an Emmy, you can talk about it a little bit, but even by male egotists' standards it's kind of a blowhard thing to do. But if you're only nominated, I'm sorry, modern manners dictate that you wait until the conversation turns to "Has anyone here ever been nominated for an Emmy for writing an episode of a popular sitcom?" Then, by all means, you should sheepishly jump in and reluctantly explain how you lost the award. While he yammered on, I feigned the old, "I'm beat," and pretended to sleep.

Once we made it to Chuckles, things started looking up. For one thing, they had fried pickles, which I liked to eat with blue cheese dressing. Two, as I mentioned before, there was another female on the bill, and she was fabulous. I hadn't yet met her, but judging from her eight-by-ten promo picture that was stuck in the window, I was fully convinced she was cool as they come. In her picture, she wasn't giving a thumbs-up or opening her mouth to a fantastical degree the way Jenny McCarthy does in EVERY photo. I think some girls think this is the universal sign for "I'm funny! And I take it all without gagging!" Of course, if you can take it all without gagging, you really don't need to be funny, and I should also point out that in my experience, some guys like gagging, but I digress.

This funny woman kept her face in a natural, not-trying-too-hard, straight-to-camera pose. In more recent years, she has gone on to do some pretty amazing things, like creating at least one of your favorite TV shows and defending your lady parts as an avid and vocal feminist. I didn't know then, of course, that she would become the sage political commentator and writer she is now, but I did have big plans for the two of us. At this point, I'm pretty sure you know what I was going for. Coffees, huddling, joking, writing . . . it was the same imagery I'd had with Garofalo, and then after that, Silverman. I had one fantasy that I was recycling, superimposing the head of my new friend interest onto the old one. I was a fantasy hack.

I accosted my soon-to-be new best friend immediately and tried to bond with her. She was playing it cool. She'd been doing this longer than I had and possessed a combination of hostility and indifference that probably kept less desperate folks at arm's length. I, however, had not traveled all the way from Canada to let a little cold shoulder derail my dreams of having a best comedy pal. I always found her lurking in the hallway, the alley, the bathroom, the bar three doors down. "Hey, you!" I'd shout once I'd zeroed in on her location, and her shoulders would sag as I enthusiastically approached. Somehow, by the end of the weekend, I had convinced her to give me her digits, but I waited a full twelve hours before dialing them so I wouldn't look pathetic. I reached her bright and early Sunday afternoon.

"Hey, it's Bonnie."

"Oh. Hi."

"Listen, I love your clothes and I think you said you got them from a secondhand store and I was thinking we could go and hang out and maybe hit up a few."

"I'm busy."

"Maybe tomorrow?"

No answer.

"Wednesday?"

"Look," she said, expelling a heavy sigh, a sigh that says, "Why won't you get this?"

"I don't want to be mean," she began, easing me into the second half of the statement that was sure to be mean. "But I already have enough friends."

I don't like to think the problem I was experiencing with getting new friends was entirely because of my "European-style" hygiene. I believe this is a problem single adult women without kids face all over the world. How do you make friends once you've outgrown the "Wanna play?" phase of life? Moms, of course, have the parents of their kid's friends to hang out with, whether they like it or not. But if you're not going to a big office every day or joining a coupon-cutting class, it's slim pickings. You can't exactly ask a woman on the subway for her phone number because you notice she's reading a Woody Allen book that you yourself have memorized from cover to cover.

I sometimes went to a screenplay-writing group at a Barnes & Noble. We were asked to write our names and addresses on a sheet of paper that was passed around the room. When I got the sheet, I noticed the woman who handed me the clipboard, the last one to write out her name and address, lived just one block from my house. Excitedly, I wrote out my address and then showed her the sheet, pointing out the one-block difference. Without saying a word, she stood up and found a chair on the opposite side of the room. That didn't feel good.

Strange women who try to befriend other strange women are considered, by and large, to be strange. And so, I met a lot more men.

Chapter 9

SCREWING UP, DOWN, AND ALL OVER TOWN

Meeting men can be difficult for a young woman. Trying to discern their intentions often takes a bit of detective work that almost always ends with a hand job. I am still trying to figure out what young Marc Maron wanted with me.

I met Marc at the Comic Strip. His first order of business was to let me know that he was currently employed by Comedy Central and that he knew how to use a teleprompter.

"If you need anyone to show you how to use a teleprompter, I can show you," he said.

I didn't know what a teleprompter was, but I didn't want to look foolish, so I rolled my eyes and lazily intoned, "Everyone knows how to use a teleprompter."

"Not true!" he countered. "You've got to read at the right speed. You've got to know when to breathe."

"I read at a good speed," I said. "I breathe without even thinking about it. It's like second nature to me."

Mark moved closer. He got more aggressive. "It's an important skill to learn if you want to work in this business!"

His dedication to the subject freaked me out and I tried to

steer clear of him. But every time I was within earshot of him (and I'm only exaggerating slightly for effect), I could hear him talking about the importance of the teleprompter and how it was not the easiest thing in the world to learn.

One day I was hanging out at my manager's office (which shows you just how few friends I had, as no self-respecting comedian would hang out with his or her representation) listening to him roll calls while I tried to unknot the laces in my boots when Maron called.

"Oh, Marc Maron," Jeff said, raising an eyebrow in my direction. "What can I do for you?"

I made wild motions for my manager to not let on I was there. My phone phobia dictates that sometimes I need time to prepare. Jeff put Marc on speakerphone without giving me away.

"I need Bonnie's number," Marc said, getting straight to the point.

"Oh, what's it regarding?"

"I just have to ask her something."

"What?"

"Really? I have to tell you what I want to ask her? What is she, the queen of England?"

"No. She's Canadian. She's new here. She's a little naive—"

I cocked my head and scowled. I was not naive! How dare he! Although this speakerphone thing was pretty cool.

"Before I give out her phone number," Jeff was saying, "I want to make sure people have good intentions."

"I'm going to marry her."

"Really?"

"No." Marc was getting very aggravated. "Just give me her phone number. I want to teach her how to use a teleprompter."

The teleprompter again! I was starting to think that maybe he really did want to teach me how to use it. Or maybe he was somehow getting a kickback for each comedian he got hooked on it. Maybe there were two competing units and once you learned the one, you couldn't possibly use the other. Like Mac and Windows. Or maybe "teleprompter" was code in some circles for blow job or 69. Maybe I was naive because I only knew the code for anal sex, which is when someone picks their nose with their thumb.

One thing was for certain: at some point I was going to make it my mission in life to find out exactly what a teleprompter was. Jeff took down Marc's number and said I'd call him but I never did. Once I realized that a teleprompter was just the thing people read their lines from while on television, I was almost positive I could master it on my own.

Another time a comedian who is now possibly the most famous comedian in the world, but who was just another dude comic back then, asked me straight out if I wanted to go out with him. When I declined, he said, "Don't you know who I am?" Of course I didn't. I had just moved from Canada. I didn't know anyone or even the fact that comedians could be "someone." In Canada, comedians weren't even billed by their names. Just generic "Comedy Tonight!" He must've noted my confusion because he added, "People think I'm like . . . you know . . . people that matter think I'm . . ." He didn't want to say it because he knew that finishing that sentence would make him sound like an asshole, but I figured he either meant "very talented" or "hung like a soup can." He did hold his microphone about halfway down his body. Either way, I wasn't interested. One, I have a tiny vagina. And two, I wanted a friend, not a relationship. Of course, I don't think he really wanted a relationship, either.

Comedian-turned-*Wipeout* sports announcer John Henson once invited me out for breakfast. I went because I had never been on a breakfast date before. I mean, I'd gone out to eat after drunkenly fucking someone, but never showered and gotten dressed at my own home alone and then met someone at ten A.M. for steak and eggs. Also, he ordered oatmeal! In my experience, when you go out for breakfast, you order eggs. And toast. And home fries. But in Rome, do as the Romans. I ordered oatmeal, although I believe I called it porridge, as we did in Canada. John and the waiter laughed and laughed. "With a side of gruel," I added, hoping to make it seem like I was kidding. But they couldn't hear me over their laughing fit, which had infected the other customers. A few cooks even came out of the back to see what was going on.

After the oatmeal, we went to his apartment, which was located about five steps from the doors of the diner. He lived on the top floor of a quaint, three-hundred-story walk-up. Now I understood the oatmeal. A ham-and-cheese omelet and climbing those eight thousand stairs would've resulted in cardiac arrest. Finally, with the help of two local Sherpas, we made it to the building's summit and his apartment. After catching my breath and possibly hepatitis from lying on the landing between floors 104 and 105, John asked me if I wanted to smoke a little pot. Before noon? Are you kidding me? Yes.

He passed me a bong. "You ever see one of these before?"

I had no idea what it was, but with my extreme intelligence, I assumed I could fake my way through it. "'Course," I said as I turned it over to look at the bottom, the way every bong aficionado does. Bong water flew everywhere. Well, I say everywhere, but really it was limited mostly to my shirt and pants. John laughed for a very long time and I fully expected the waiter to poke his head in and say, "She do or say something dumb again? What'd I miss?" John curbed his mocking laughter long enough to show me how to use the contraption, which really wasn't that complicated and from what I'd been told, much less intricate than learning to navigate the teleprompter.

I'd gotten high before of course, but a bong high at 11:35 A.M. was a kind of high that went over and above what I was looking for. I was spending critical seconds analyzing which way I should move my head, when it was actually my hand that I needed to move to scratch my nose. Natural movement seemed to be a thing of the past. Then, just when I was formulating how John would have to become my nurse, bathing me, wiping me, and, ironically, spooning porridge into my perpetually half-open mouth, he stood up and announced he was going to back to bed. He went into his room and closed the door.

I sat there for an excruciatingly long ninety seconds and then, after trying to exit through the broom closet and the bathroom, I found the door leading to the million-stair march. I walked down, down, down until I got the bends. With my ears bleeding and my clothes still soaked in bong water, I hit the streets of New York ready to take on the world, if I could just figure out which way was north. Why was it that you could never find a Sherpa guide when you really needed one?

I DID DEVELOP CRUSHES ON comedians I thought were talented. I usually let nature take its course, and before anything happened, which is to say that I'd see them sloppily hitting on a skank or do a hack joke and I'd lose interest. But there was one comedian I couldn't get out of my mind. I wanted him inside me but not necessarily in a sexual way. I wanted his comedy in me. He exhibited little to no interest in me and so I was put in the uncomfortable position of having to be the pursuer. Hard as it might be to believe, I was terrible at being the hunter. With men, that is. With deer and fowl, I'm actually pretty good. With men, I have an interesting sexual pathology where I need to be the one pursued in order to get turned on. Most of my sexual interludes sound something like this. "No. No. No. No. No. No. No. No. Please, I don't want to. No. No. No. No. I shouldn't be doing this. Why am I doing this? No. No. No. I shouldn't be doing this. I can't stop doing this, even though I should stop. I should really stop. Yes. I should stop. Yes, yes, yes. Oh, God, yes, yes, yes! Don't stop. Don't stop. Don't—oh, you're done? I shouldn't have done that. That was really not something I should've done. I've got to go. Tomorrow? Same time, same place?"

Even after I got the comedian to notice me, it was hard to get him to stick around with all the no's. He'd go to kiss me, I'd back away, no, no. No. And he'd go, okay, and then he'd leave. I mean, what the fuck? (Feminists, don't write me letters. I understand I'm fucked up.) My attraction to the short, pudgy fellow grew stronger every time I said I could care less about him, and I eventually decided once and for all that I was going to bed him. After a set where I did marginally well, I had enough confidence to track him down. I went to a bar where he was known to go. He wasn't there. I went to another. After I frequented seventeen bars where he liked to hang out, I gave up. Halfway through my second beer, I remembered another bar he went to sometimes, right next to the first one I'd checked out. I walked the sixteen blocks back to the bar, wiped the sweat from my brow, and entered looking like a Muppet who'd fallen into a puddle.

There he was, sitting with a bunch of people who were not comedians and so I pretended they weren't there.

"Hey," I said as I squeezed in next to him. "What are you doing here?"

"The girl raised by wolverines," he quipped about my appearance and I took that as a flirtatious invitation to stay.

Most of the people he was with were doing coke in the bathroom. I did a line too, to be polite, but coke is not my drug. I just never liked it. It never gave me the euphoria that people claimed to get after doing it. The first time I did it, I was bored at a party and then I was just bored longer and faster. But that line did give me the extra push I needed to continue into the night. After all, I did walk approximately the same route of the New York City Marathon trying to track him down. I was on a mission to close the deal with us once and for all.

The party moved from the bar to the object of my affection's apartment. Of course, I'd been outside his building many times, but never inside. This was a big step. Unfortunately, I was there with seven other people who were unable to pick up on social clues about overstaying their welcome. There was also one girl there who had flawless skin and bright white teeth and who kept looking at my "date" like he was the most important dude she'd ever met. I gently shoved her out of his eye line several times, but she'd just apologize politely and move back into his view. Well, honey, you can laugh as loud as you want at his jokes because I am going to win this little contest. Let the waiting games begin!

My man's apartment was exactly as I imagined it. Tiny, cramped, messy, VHS tapes against the wall, a few notebooks on the coffee table, hundreds of half-smoked cigarettes in the ashtray. He only smoked his cigarettes halfway because he had read that the last half is where all the cancer is. Isn't that adorable? Not only was he funny and quirky, he was also health conscious. That's where we'll write, I thought, looking at the coffee table. Then I looked over at his bedroom. That's where we'll do everything else. The TV was in there and, judging by the takeout bags, that's also where he ate.

My daydreams were interrupted by the nightmare of people

on coke, talking and snorting. This party was never ending, like a Sandra Bullock movie. Surely they'd run out of coke at some point! I mean, coke doesn't grow on trees! Or does it? I'm not really sure what a coca plant looks like. It could be treelike. I'm just not sure. Although, I'll bet if you asked this group, they'd all start talking at once, excited to tell you the answer.

I hoped my soon-to-be lover appreciated what I was going through for him. I didn't particularly enjoy talking to non-comics, and I certainly didn't enjoy talking to non-coms on coke! Finally, by the grace of God, as the morning sunlight began to inflict pain on their bloodshot eyes, one by one they started to leave. But not the fucking Nebraskan girl with the glow-in-the-dark teeth. She looked like she'd just woken up from an afternoon nap in a bed of lilies.

Five A.M., another line! Was this girl a monster? He doesn't want you! You're a waitress. You think he wants to hear about how you got stiffed by the table of elementary school teachers? I'm a comic. I actually get him. We have things we can talk about. Of course, I communicated all this through a series of eye rolls and thumb gestures.

We both knew we were in competition. If the guy we were competing for was aware of our rivalry, he never acknowledged it. In fact, he never gave either of us the impression he liked one over the other. We both just knew in our hearts that each of us was "the one." At six thirty, twenty minutes after the only other person still hanging in finally left the apartment, the Nebraskan finally said, "I guess I should get going. I have to work at ten A.M. tomorrow. I mean, today." She said it with that kind of hesitant, "If you want me to stay, just say the word." I looked at him, my trophy, man-spreading almost the entire width of the sofa, wondering if he would say the word. I couldn't risk it. Before he even had a chance to respond, I took matters into my own hands and physically helped her through the door. She weighed about as much as a small pigeon, so it didn't take much effort on my part.

"Okay, bye! You better get some sleep." I kicked her foot out of the doorway and slammed it closed before she had a chance to try and barge back in. "It's almost seven. You'll get a cab no problem," I called through the door. Like everyone else on the planet, when I win something, I tend to celebrate with a victory lap. However, by the time I finished my end-zone dance, my man-prize was already curling up under his sheets. I removed my bra from my sleeve hole in an attempt to seem both sexy and playful and also, I have to admit, a little bit magician-y (I called out, "Voilà!" as I threw the beige front loader across the room), and slipped into bed next to him. Of course, I was hoping that I would have to gently fight him off, but unfortunately, neither of us had enough coke to fuel either part of a sexual power struggle and we fell asleep without consummating the relationship.

The next morning, we went for breakfast and I gave the comedian one final grasp at the brass ring that I was considering having pierced in my vagina. I shoved in another forkful of greasy hash browns. (Or maybe they were home fries. Has anyone ever ordered those without asking for a defining description?) I chewed and swallowed and asked, "Are we going to get married or not?"

"Probably," he answered. But I knew he meant not to each other.

THERE WERE ENTIRE DAYS WHERE I did not speak with anyone except the group of strangers who congregated in front of me at the end of the night, waiting for me to amuse them with clever turns of phrase otherwise known as dick jokes. During the day, I would play a game to see if I could slip through every social interaction without actually speaking. I allowed myself facial contortions, hand gestures, and on at least one occasion, the universal sign for choking, but absolutely no words.

It was only Ford Pineapple, an eighteen-year-old barista, who broke through my self-imposed muteness, and he did so by being rather rude.*

"Your face looks greasy," he told me one day as he handed me a latte with a stunning dollop of foam. I rolled my eyes. It was sunscreen. I might've shared this with him, but it was only four o'clock and I was still hours away from breaking a personal no-talking record. I just smiled and paid for my coffee.

"Is it sunscreen? Cause you could just wear a hat."

I gave him my best "noted" look and was about to leave.

"You'd be a lot prettier without a greasy face!"

"Fuck you, fuckface," I said, resting my hand on the door. Perhaps it was not up to my professional standards, but they were my first words of the day. Surprisingly, I heard not shocked-into-submission silence, as I'd hoped, but laughter. Not only laughter, but the best kind of laughter. That kind of youthful, no-holds-barred, bull-in-a-china-shop laughter, and it went right into my heart and warmed it. As we know, however, biology is sometimes complex, and I didn't feel it in my heart but rather my loins. He sealed the deal when he added, "You're fucking funny."

It was only a matter of time before I was all, "No, no, no, I shouldn't be doing this . . . no, no, no, don't stop."

Ford Pineapple had an older brother who was also named Ford Pineapple. I'm fuzzy on the details, but he might've also had a sister named Toyota. Besides not being old enough to rent a car, Ford was not an ideal candidate for a boyfriend. Yes,

* I've changed his name, but trust me when I tell you his actual name is as weird, if not more so, than the one I've invented for him.

he was the size and shape of a young rock star, and yes, he had thick black hair that flopped perfectly across his forehead, the kind that made both young girls and prematurely balding men swoon. Looks, however, held no appeal for me anymore. In fact, I didn't trust any man who didn't look several years older than he actually was and who didn't have a body shape caused by eating the majority of his meals after midnight.

Still, Ford was able to make my body react—sometimes several times in an afternoon!—but my mind, sadly, was never fulfilled. He was funny and kind but he still had that annoying, unflappable ignorant arrogance that only teenagers can possess. He couldn't make change if you gave him a five-dollar bill and a quarter for a coffee that cost $3.05, for example, but he'd be sure to look at you as if you were the dolt when he handed you back your nickel and then a handful of change.

The real killer was his earnestness. He hardly ever did anything ironically, and if he was watching *My Little Pony,* you can bet he was enjoying *My Little Pony.* On the plus side, he knew where to get Indian food for two dollars and how to carry a clipboard onto the set of a New York movie so he could meet Robin Williams and then brag about it for the next four years.

Ford Rollerbladed to my apartment every few days, usually with a bundle of daisies tucked under his arm, and I can only imagine the women who craned their necks to get a better look at this gem of a fellow and curse the lucky lady he was off to see. I was never that excited to see Ford. Sometimes, my protests were genuine. He seemed to be sexually insatiable. He told me about things he thought of doing and things he actually had done. If those were my thoughts or actions, I wouldn't have shared them quite so eagerly with the person I was intimate with. I rarely shared such private thoughts one-on-one because I felt these kinds of thoughts should only be shared publicly, preferably onstage in front of hundreds of people or as a Facebook update. Once, Ford shared this story with me: He was blow-drying his hair and the vibrations of the blow dryer started to turn him on, so he taped a drumstick to the shaft of the dryer and . . . well, I don't think I need to repeat the story in its entirety. If you don't get the point, you can stop reading now and hurry to your Bible-study group.

I never brought Ford to my shows. Not only because he wasn't old enough to drink, but also because I couldn't contain the shame I felt showing up with an attentive young model-looking fellow on my arm. It would be like letting the comedy community conclude that I had things on my agenda other than pure comedy. Ford momentarily satisfied my needs in the bedroom, various public bathrooms, and my apartment stairwell, but mentally, I was still looking for the guy who was going to get me excited, down there, with a well-placed callback.

There was no denying Ford was nice. He gave me an old pair of his Rollerblades that he'd outgrown the year before. That's right. I was fucking a guy who was still growing! I tossed Ford to the curb but kept the blades. Skating became my new passion and I got better quickly, since there was no possible way I could get worse. Day in and day out, I rolled through the streets of New York on my secondhand blades, getting slightly better every day, grabbing fewer and fewer innocent bystanders as I waited for a light, careening into fewer and fewer nannies and their charges as I attempted to stop. I had lost my Canadian accent very quickly, except for the word "sorry," which, as irony would have it, was a word I was saying up to forty times a day.

One night I Rollerbladed to my set at Stand Up NY, switched into my sneakers, and stuffed the blades into my backpack. After my show, a male comic, who was slightly cockeyed and had a large nose but who was attractive in the classic three-quarter pose, asked me if I wanted to take a spin on his motorcycle. At least, I think he was asking me. It's possible I was looking at the wrong eye and he was asking the girl behind me. In any case, later that night I found myself with my arms gripped tight around his midsection, wind in my face, cruising in and out of yellow cabs through Central Park, toward the World Famous Comic Strip. (I've often thought using the words "World Famous" when it actually is world famous seems unnecessary and redundant. Of course, until I moved to New York, I'd never heard of it.)

At one point, as we were stopped at a light, he turned to me and said, "Do you want to go out sometime?" Before I could answer, we were on the move again. I didn't want to go out with him but I also didn't want to scream over the hum of the motorcycle engine and the crosstown traffic that, as flattered as I was, I was still acclimating to the city and perhaps it was best to take things one step at a time before I started dating again, blah blah blah.

I thought a simple "NO!" yelled as loudly as I could manage would be more fitting under these awkward circumstances.

"What?"

I tried again. "No, thanks."

"WHAT?"

"NO!"

He didn't respond, so I attempted to clear it up for him.

"I DON'T WANT TO GO OUT WITH YOU!"

He pulled over in front of the Comic Strip. I got off the bike, removed my helmet, and shook out my hair. I could only imagine that I looked like an attractive ferret coming out of the water. Now that we could hear each other without straining our vocal cords, I kindly added, "I'd like to be friends." He took the spare helmet from me, restraddled his machine, and revved the engine a few times before putting it into first. "I have enough friends," he said, and zoomed off. I wondered briefly if one of them was a cool, Brooklyn comedian who liked thrift store shopping.

As I stood in the middle of Second Avenue on New York City's Upper East Side among the throngs of steady foot traffic, I suddenly thought of my cow Bessie, the good times we'd had, the secrets we'd shared, the laughs, the love. I looked into the sky and I made a promise to God. "God," I said, "this time if you let me make a friend, I promise I will not eat her!"

Chapter 10

ONCE YOU'VE SEEN ONE SUNRISE, YOU'RE TIRED ALL DAY

I wasn't one of those women who hated being alone. I actually enjoyed the time I spent in my own company. I just thought I was less likely to be committed to a psych ward under a 5150 if people could see that I was talking to an actual other person across the table from me when I went to a restaurant. Plus, it'd be nice if someone could split the bill once in a while. My prayers were answered when my best Canadian pal, Lynn Shawcroft, came to stay with me for a few weeks, which soon turned into a few months. To say that Lynn was outgoing was something of an understatement. For Lynn, making friends was as natural as slowing down to get a look at a car accident.

Lynn was able to talk to people in a way that I never could. After a few days, she was speaking a little Yiddish with the fellas at the bagel shop and rudimentary Spanish to the Asian ladies at the dry cleaner's. There was no one Lynn couldn't befriend. Even comedians. She immediately made friends with Todd Barry and went with him to tape his appearance on *Conan*. She got invited to perform on the coolest alternative shows and made a lifelong friend of Doug Stanhope. People were drawn to Lynn and soon we were hanging out with all kinds of comedians.

Lynn and I thought we were moderately cool and maybe even a little bit hipster but years later, Jim Gaffigan described us as flannel-jacketed Canadians who never took off our mittens after Labor Day. So maybe we were cooler and hipper than we even thought. But, as the world turns, all eras come to an easy end, with, of course, the exception of the Paleozoic and the Big Band Era. Lynn went back to Canada because she had a couple of Canadian loonies she was eager to unload and I was back to hanging out in my Harlem apartment wearing muumuus and sipping from tiny bottles of lemon gin.

It wasn't long after that when I had to find a new place. My manager's fiancée finally sold the place in Harlem, and even though I had plenty of notice, I waited until I had exactly forty-eight hours until I had to be out before I started filling a black garbage bag with my things and looking for a new place to live. After a series of this guy knows that guy who knows a guy who knows a guy, I found a place in the East Twenties, or Chelsea as it's known on the city maps, for only $650 a month. It was a tight one-bedroom, half bath, fully furnished, no roommates. It was a deal. A steal! A renter's dream. So what was the catch? No catch! Unless having to be out of the apartment every Wednesday from five P.M. until Thursday at nine A.M. was a catch. It wasn't for me. I mean, who doesn't enjoy walking around the streets of New York all night at least once a week? It was ideal.

The backstory of the apartment was this: The owner had gotten married, had a baby, and moved upstate. Unfortunately, his psychoanalyst wouldn't move with him and he was forced to return to the city once a week for sessions that I can only assume dealt with his insane codependency. Every Wednesday, he spent two hours driving to the city and then six hours looking for parking. He'd spend fifty minutes at his shrink's and then stay the night in Chelsea, shower and shave, and return upstate the following morning. I actually saw him only twice. Once when I was accepting the terms of the apartment and once on a Thursday morning as I was plodding up the sidewalk, a few blocks away from my "night, night, world" body slam onto the bed, and he was walking toward his car. I'm surprised he recognized me, what with the enormous dark crescent moons pillowing under my half-open eyes. He told me he'd read something in one of my notebooks that he thought was quite good. I didn't know whether to be (a) flattered that he liked it, or (b) pissed that he was snooping through my things. I chose (c) and stammered a needy, "Really?"

At first, I spent the ousted night at various diners writing diligently in my notebook, but by the third Wednesday night, I did what any girl would do if she needed a place to stay. I got a boyfriend. Lazy by nature, I mentally listed all the men I knew who already wanted to fuck me. I came up with one name: Mark. He was a comic on the rise. His wit was quick and he was quite manly in the sense that he could recall and recite any line of movie dialogue from any movie he had seen after the age of seven. This trait aside, he was exceptionally charming when he wanted to be, as most sociopaths are, but I wasn't completely convinced he was boyfriend material. However, forced by my apartment needs, I threw caution to the wind and began a close friendship. I showed up at his apartment and gave him a confusing talk about how much I liked him but mostly only on Wednesday nights and hopefully he could respect my boundaries because as much as I wanted to "be" with him, I was also overwhelmed by New York and this comedy scene and perhaps we should wait a while until we actually coitussed. Then we coitussed. I didn't particularly want to sleep with him. I just wasn't feeling it. Yes, back then, I had to be "feeling" it. Now of course, I'm married, if I did it only when I was "feeling it," I'd be having sex with everyone but my husband.

I slept with Mark because he showed a side of himself that most men would try to keep hidden as long as possible. The side I'm referring to is his back. Let me explain. After our "let's be friends" talk, Mark filled up the bong with some Super Silver Haze. I took a couple of hits and let the weed work its magic. I was getting to be a bong-smoking expert, save for the reckless coughing.

Through the hazy fog of the cannabis smoke I watched Mark take off his shirt and slowly turn around like a reluctant sex worker. Let me put this delicately; he had more hair on his back than anyone, ever, post- (maybe even pre-) Paleolithic era. It looked like a hundred caterpillars were trying to get up over a wall of mashed potatoes. I tried to think of something to say but nothing seemed appropriate. "Hey, want me to braid it?"

We sat for a few uncomfortable moments of silence, something Mark did not do very often. His default button was set on Robin Williams but with more manic energy. Finally, he looked at me and shrugged. "I just thought you should know," he said. Ahhhh . . .

That one small act of self-loathing made me swoon. It was the paradox of having enough self-esteem to show me his back and yet still having the realistic expectation that I might be grossed out. And I kinda was. For years I was forced to gain immeasurable control over my gag reflexes in order to make love to him with abandon. This training proved invaluable in later years, allowing me to have sex with an ever-expanding group of men who I'd previously thought were unfuckable.

They say we fall in love not with a person's assets but with their flaws, their vulnerabilities, and their pets. I did like his cats, but it was Mark's willingness to put it all on the line for me that was the key that opened the door to my heart and made me love him with everything I had. I ended up dating this fucker off and on for five goddamned years. As our relationship eventually moved to other nights of the week, however, it became crystal clear that we were not well-matched. For one thing, we didn't particularly like each other. Instead of dealing with this glitch in the relationship, we chose to ignore it. And his cats were so cute and cuddly.

ONE DAY MY MANAGER CALLED me to come to his office. I Rollerbladed into midtown right away and breathlessly asked what was so urgent.

"Remember how you auditioned for Montreal?"

"Yes." I remembered. Emotionally, we're more inclined to remember the bad stuff.

"They said you were awful. Called you green. Said you should become a dramatic actress."

"Yes. Yes, I remember."

"Remember how they told you you had a gift for making people weep? And comedy clubs were probably not your best venue with such a talent?"

"Yes. And?"

"And they said they might use you next year, but more likely, never?"

"Yes. Of course I remember."

"Well, looks like they've changed their minds."

I was booked to do the New Faces Showcase in two weeks.

It was Joe Bodolai, that supportive Torontonian producer who had taken it upon himself to show the head of the festival the raw footage of my Canadian special and convince him that

I had the talent necessary to be on the New Faces show. I think the game changer was that I wasn't wearing a bra.

New Faces was the show that everyone in the industry wanted to attend. It's where hot new talent was finally given a chance to perform for the most powerful industry types, or more likely, their assistants. These bigwigs traveled internationally to see talent they could see perform any night of the week in their own cities. These industry people would offer development deals to the talent they felt deserved it, or if they found out another network was offering someone a deal. Development deals were supposed to lead to television shows. After you got the deal, the network would hire a writer, who would write you a show that you thought was stupid and not in your voice at all, and you'd fight to write your own pilot but the network would refuse and if you didn't make too big a stink, you might actually get a pilot made that combined every cliché they could think of and then the network would keep you on pins and needles for a long time until they would finally assure you that after all you've been through, all the time and money that's been spent, your pilot would not be going to a series. Then, you'd spend the next fifteen years on the road in clubs like Chuckle Hut and Snappers talking about the deal you once got after two years in the business.

Or maybe, but probably not, your pilot would be green-lit for a series and then you'd have your very own television show, complete with loads of press and a launch date, and your life would change. At least, it would change for a little while, until it got canceled after two episodes. Or maybe it wouldn't. Maybe it would be a hit and you'd be a celebrity and everyone would talk about how overrated or underrated you were.

In any case, the New Faces Showcase at the Montreal Just for Laughs comedy festival was a big deal, which is why I contemplated "coming down" with something that week to get out of it. It was hard with everyone telling me how lucky I was because I didn't feel lucky. I felt like I was being set up for humiliation. I appreciated everything Joe Bodolai had done for me but at this point in my life, I was doing just fine bombing in clubs where no one of importance would see me. I wasn't sure I wanted to go global with my inadequacies just yet. Then I saw that the comedian I never was able to close the deal with was going to be there. Mark and I were in an "off" period and so, being of sound mind, I immediately started planning an amorous northern rendezvous with a comedian who had no romantic interest in me, and got busy packing all my underwear without holes.

The flight from LaGuardia to Quebec was only fifty minutes, but since the flight attendants had to do all the announcements in both English and French, we were forced to sit on the runway for an extra seventeen minutes until they were finished. Somewhere during the French stuff about seat backs, I overheard the Americans behind me worrying about how they might be disadvantaged in Montreal because they didn't speak French. Being Canadian, I was not worried at all. I had been immersed in French for one hour a week my entire school career and I knew that once I was in the midst of other Francophiles, it would all come rushing back in just one or two years. Since I was only going to be in Montreal for four days, I didn't try to dredge up any French from my childhood vaults, though I did get a kick out of cursing and then saying, "Pardon my French!" to literally every single person I encountered.

I arrived on a Wednesday night and the lobby of the hotel was already buzzing with activity from the festival. There were comedy fans mingling with industry types, of which you could easily tell the difference. The comedy fans were grown men in funny T-shirts that exposed the undeniable fact that they'd never in their lives seen the inside of a gym. They stood in sharp contrast with the television executives, who were wearing relaxed business attire and smiling uncomfortably, as if they were unsure of how to do it properly and in a way that made them appear from a distance to have recently had a stroke.

Within minutes of eying this crowd, I realized that schmoozing was not in my wheelhouse. I was not going to hit the ground networking. I wasn't able to incentivize or boil the ocean or throw things up a flagpole. It was too late to make business cards and my team-building skills lacked key insights. Personally, I was not a value add in this environment. So I left. I was only scheduled to do two shows the entire week: a warm-up show at nine on Thursday night at Club Soda and then my life-changing New Faces show at ten P.M. the following night. Wednesday and Saturday I was open. Sunday I was scheduled to fly home.

Thursday night rolled around and I did my practice show and it was fine but I was more interested in drinking and searching for cute boys. Not an easy task at a comedy festival! I set my sights on the same comedian who I never closed the deal with after the coke-fueled party. Late in the night, when I couldn't find him at the party in the lobby, I went to his hotel room. He was in there with a girl. I tried to wait her out but I could tell by the steely look in her eye that this time, it wasn't going to happen, so I left. These French-Canadian girls were not Nebraska.

I got back to my own hotel, where the lobby parties were in full swing. I got into the elevator at the unfortunate time my manager was also heading to his room.

"You're just getting back now? Where were you all night? I had people to introduce you to. You've got a very important day tomorrow. What are you going to wear? Did you bring a dress? Do you own a dress? Tomorrow, can you buy a dress?

Get your hair done? Can I convince you to take off your baseball hat? At least wear it backward so they can see your face. Are you okay?"

"Fine," I said, and then took out my driver's license and tried to open my hotel room with it.

The next night, in a T-shirt, jeans, no baseball cap, and, uncharacteristically, a bra, I sipped a beer as I was waiting in the wings. I tried to let go of all my anxieties about the show I was about to do. I wasn't sure why I wanted to be a comedian so badly. I don't know what drove me to try to get acceptance from the strangers that I refused to talk to during the day. I don't know why I wanted so desperately to be good at this. I did know, in that moment, that I couldn't do anything about it. I could only grunt and pause in the appropriate places and hope for the best. I watched as Todd Barry went on and did very well. This time I didn't allow myself the comfort of false confidence. I was prepared to bomb. I was ready to disappoint. It's just ten minutes of misery, I told myself. It'll be over in no time.

It was hot in the club and the audience was packed in tight, and as I sauntered out before 450 or so anxious audience members, I could almost feel the warmth of their breath wafting to the stage. I looked out at that audience and I smiled. Here we go, I thought. I looked into their eager faces. It made me smirk. I liked knowing something they did not know. This was not going to go well.

My first joke hung in the air for a minute and then dropped down into the crowd like Wiley Coyote going off a cliff. If people thought it was funny, they didn't respond with laughter. The second joke followed a very similar path. But the third joke dropped down and bounced around the audience for a minute. There was laughter. By the fifth joke, I was, and I don't want to overstate this because, as you might have gathered by now, I pride myself on being a straight shooter, but I was killing. Destroying. Bringing the house down. Murdering the set. Shitting the bed. Actually, shitting the bed might mean something negative. So let's go back to murdering. I ended as well as anyone could have wanted in that situation.

I sauntered into the greenroom where the other comedians sat, waiting to have career-changing sets of their own. They looked up from their beers and their set lists and nodded. I got a couple of "Nice"s. I tried to match their cool but my heart was pounding and my smile was fighting my face for real estate.

A young woman with sensible shoes burst into the greenroom. "Hey, Bonnie. Great set. I'm with ABC. Could I talk to you for a minute?" Then someone else: "Bonnie, I'm with NBC." "Bonnie, we're with *SNL*." Within a few minutes, I was surrounded by executives. I distinctly remember one woman with a business card at the end of an outstretched arm saying, "When I was watching you, I thought this is someone I could be friends with." I could've used you six months ago, I thought.

Jeff rounded the corner and started shouting, "I'm her manager. If you like what you saw, we can set up a meeting." I'm sure to this day he thinks I did well because I wasn't wearing a baseball cap. Then, the two guys with small pores and thin sweaters escorted me out of the greenroom. "Let your manager take care of this," they said. I was happy to. We walked out of the room and out of the building. "Wanna smoke?" they asked, and the one on the left pulled a perfectly rolled joint from his pocket. As a practice of habit, I checked them for cold sores. They were good. In fact, their skin was great.

"I guess," I said. "I don't have any other shows." I hadn't made plans with anyone. I was kind of open. After I had inhaled sufficiently, they talked about my set. "It was so fun to watch," they said. "You didn't get freaked out when your first two jokes didn't really work."

"Why would you bring up the shitty part of the set?" I said and playfully kicked him in the shin. He immediately brushed the microscopic dirt my foot had planted there. But he laughed. We all laughed. I was doing it. I was making friends.

"We're with the William Morris Agency," said the one on the left. "And we'd like to represent you."

Chapter 11

FOLLOW YOUR DREAMS, ESPECIALLY IF THEY TAKE GOWER

It wasn't long after the Montreal comedy festival and still just a year or so into my comedy career that I made a series of decisions that kept me stuck in a purgatory I like to call Hollywood for many, many years. First, I signed with the weed-smoking William Morris agents. They were convinced they could ride the buzz from my not-so-terrible showcase show at the festival and get me a development deal. In order to do this, though, I had to leave New York, fly to L.A., and take meetings with executives who claimed they wanted me on their network. I boarded my flight, located my middle seat near the back of the plane, and managed to make it through the entire flight without spilling anything on myself. Clearly, I was growing as a person.

Landing. Applause. Luggage. Taxi line.

In the back of the cab, my manager was going over what I should wear and what I should say and what part of my "story" I should tell. "And smile. Please." He practically begged me. "Don't get in one of your moods." I rolled my eyes and focused out the window as Los Angeles clipped by. It was the first time I'd seen the city not in movies or on postcards and it didn't look anything like the sunlit pictures with palm trees. It looked like an endless suburban parking lot with the odd patch of greenery. I figured the reason it was called the City of Angels was because everyone looked dead. The farther we traveled from the airport, the fewer people we saw with actual life in their eyes. There was little time for sightseeing, which was probably for the best. After just a few minutes of watching pin-thin girls in oversize sunglasses chugging Evian, I had an overwhelming urge to visit the Hollywood sign and jump to my death. Little did I know at the time, this suicidal feeling would be among my top-five best moments here.

It wasn't that bad, of course, but it wasn't that great, either. Being forced to talk almost exclusively to agents, managers, and executives for four days can make anyone reevaluate their lives. The meetings were, and probably still are, the best way for network executives to meet up-and-coming talent and decide if a sitcom with said aforementioned creative genius—in this case, yours truly—could produce a hit sitcom, or a hitcom, if you will, and make them loads of money. But because the outcome of these meetings was paramount to my career, I spent most of the time thinking stupid stuff that had nothing to do with the conversation going on around me. Like, for instance, why are olive jars so poorly designed? And do towels ever really have to be cleaned?

The meetings were almost carbon copies of one another. The faces, the phrases they used, the kind of shoes they wore all bore a remarkable resemblance to one another. There was always a young beautiful woman at reception who politely asked us (my manager, my West Coast William Morris agent, and me) to take a seat while she let "them" know we were here. She then offered to get us water, coffee, or soda. The meetings themselves were not nearly as exciting as deciding on what drink to get beforehand.

In one meeting, my manager fibbed about where we were staying. "We're at the Universal Hilton," he told them. But we weren't staying at the Universal Hilton. We were staying at a shithole near the airport. Without thinking about it, I said, "He might be staying at the Universal Hilton, but I'm at the Y." Everyone laughed so hard I thought my barn door was open. After the meeting Jeff and the agent conferred and decided, "That was good. Let's do that again." At the next meeting, without being asked, Jeff volunteered that we were staying at the Universal Hilton. I chimed in about the YMCA and another laugh ensued. By the time we ended our week of meetings, we had an entire act going on that included me singing a lullaby in French and Jeff jumping up on the coffee table and moonwalking. Not really, of course, as I'm pretty sure television executives have a very strict "no fun" policy when it comes to their meetings. I've never before used the term "abject bore," but it seems to apply here. If someone could bottle the energy in those executive offices, they'd put Lunesta out of business. It certainly didn't surprise me that every office had a couch.

On our way back East, while I was struggling over a *USA Today* crossword puzzle in coach, there was a bidding war between four of the networks that we'd met with. After careful consideration, after analyzing all the data, after going over what each network had to offer, after reading all the fine print, after conferring with lawyers and William Morris agents (both West and East Coast), my manager, Jeff, decided that $185,000 was the most money I was offered, and so we went with CBS.

I had agents, a development deal, and a new pillow that set me back one hundred dollars. My first big splurge. Up until this point, I had no idea you could even get a pillow that cost one hundred dollars. But you can. They're at Sears. Life was moving at such a fast pace I was barely able to take my new pillow for an eleven-hour test drive. I was nothing if not tenacious, and I managed to squeeze in eleven hours of sleep not once, but several times.

I MOVED TO LOS ANGELES. Properly this time. I shoved everything I owned into a suitcase, gave my landlord back his key, and took a taxi to the airport. I would have to be on call for CBS. I'd have to take more meetings with executives. I'd have to charm show runners and writers. I'd have to take lunches with producers. I was looking forward to it the way one looks forward to a colonoscopy or finding out you're on a revenge-porn Web site. After a few weeks, Mark joined me in Los Angeles. I was lonely and thought it'd be nice to have his cats around. Unfortunately, he wouldn't send them if he couldn't come along as a chaperone, so I shared my apartment with three hairy beasts, two of which I enjoyed sleeping with. We were officially "on" again.

I needed to get an American driver's license and I quickly realized I didn't know how to drive in America. In Canada, we drive on the same side of the road, but with less anger and aggression. If I was going to succeed on the roads here, I would have to learn how to signal with one hand while flipping the bird with the other. Freeways were also new to me. I learned how to merge from an on-ramp thanks to four hours of driving instruction from a tiny Mexican man who later stalked me for about a week and a half. It wasn't that I felt scared. I felt I could probably take him in a fair fight, since I was almost double his height. Most of the time, he just showed up at my apartment unannounced and asked if I needed any additional parking lessons. Gratis, of course. At this point, I already had my American driver's license, so I politely told him I had AIDS.

I bought a red, secondhand Honda Civic. It was the first car I tried on and it just felt right. I drove it off the lot. It was stolen twice and recovered twice. They didn't even take my music tapes, which I thought was rude. I like to think my taste in music spans all cultures and socioeconomic lines. I drove myself to auditions, but never without making ten to twenty U-turns. I had to give myself an extra hour and a half because I spent a lot of time at the side of the road, thumbing through a Thomas Guide, a book of maps for the greater Los Angeles area that weighed somewhere in the neighborhood of seventeen hundred pounds. Usually, it was easier to stop and ask someone for directions to the best way to kill yourself.

They say the two hardest things in life are moving and sneezing with your eyes closed. I was now fairly used to moving and adjusting to a new social scene. As you are probably well aware at this point, making new friends is not exactly my strong point. Learning from past experience, I tried to get out there and bully the less fortunate so the cool kids would like me. Mark knew lots of people because he was funny and outgoing and had started with most of the comics who had moved from New York to Los Angeles, so we went to lots of parties in those first months of getting to the coast. In L.A. there are really only two options: social climbing or mountain hiking. And while I didn't have the proper shoes for either, I thought I'd get fewer blisters by focusing my efforts on the first.

The L.A. alt comedy crowd was hard to keep up with. Everyone was always doing a bit. The key was to never look like you were doing a bit. Never do a voice. Doing a voice was a little too try-hard. The alt scene was all about *not* trying. Bits worked best when you used your real voice in a natural conversational tone that was perhaps just a touch more earnest than normal. Someone should not be able to ascertain that you are doing a bit. It's inside. Very inside. Deep-vagina mode.

Once, a friend from acting class was over at my house (yes,

I took an acting class!) and my boyfriend, Mark, and his friend Dave were fucking around, smoking pot, and playing video games. Mark kept asking him if he wouldn't prefer to be anywhere but in our apartment. A sort of passive-aggressive, "Get out." And Dave just kept saying, "No, this is great. Thanks." Mark would respond, "You sure? I thought you had to get to a thing?" And Dave would say, "It's fine. I'll go later." And then Mark would say, "You don't want to be late." And Dave would say, "It's cool to be late." This dumb bit went on and on and on and on and on. They might still be doing it if my acting-class friend hadn't finally yelled, "He doesn't want you here! Get out." Of course, we all laughed at her because she was an idiot for not getting that it was all just a "bit." She started sobbing. She was from the Midwest and the passive-aggressive energy that had been zipping around the room was bringing a lot of deep emotions to the surface. Her parents got divorced when she was eleven. I walked her to her car discussing how she should tap into that flawed psyche of hers in an audition. And that woman was Anne Hathaway.*

Hipster comedians used to show up at house parties carrying brown paper grocery bags filled with VHS tapes of unknown road comedians. Everyone would gather excitedly around the TV/VCR to watch and mock the content. Sometimes, the tapes came from something recorded straight off television, but most of the time these tapes were five or ten minutes of the road comedian's best stuff, shot themselves in front of brick backdrops from run-down comedy clubs or even in the comedian's basement. The tapes were then sent out to managers and agents in New York and L.A. with the hope that the comedian on the tape could secure representation and ride a wave of success to untold fortune. How exactly the tapes ended up in the hands of

---

* No, it wasn't.

the hipster elite isn't clear to me, but the collection was extensive, if not bottomless.

I couldn't sit through these sessions of hate-watching. I'd like to be able to report that morally, I was horrified by the group's behavior, and on some level I was, but I left mostly because I thought I could easily be one of the comedians on the tapes. "Now here's someone truly awful." Tape goes in. Play. "Uh, that's me. I should go." In another act of self-preservation, I pretended that I only *said* I liked the Dave Matthews Band *to be funny.* They agreed that it would be funny to say you liked the Dave Matthews Band. Because the Dave Matthews Band is horrible.

There were rules in the alt scene. Unwritten, of course. Yes, it is ironic that the jokes were all written down on little pieces of paper and placed on a stool during a set, but the real rules floated aimlessly in the ether. At parties, for example, everyone seemed to cheer the same MTV videos. This confounded me. I mean, everyone agreed every time? Surely, the chances of everyone agreeing all the time were astronomically low. Unable to work the precise probabilities ratio, I turned to my friend Karen and asked, "How does everyone like the same songs? How does everyone know?" "Watch Janeane," she said. I laughed, but then I realized she wasn't kidding. Everyone was watching for Garofalo's reaction. This advice in hand, I was on my way to the Promised Land, headed to Utopia. I cheered when everyone else cheered. I swiveled my hips when everyone else swiveled their hips. I made raspberry sound effects when everyone else did. We were one.

My grim mood was actually an asset when I performed at the alternative shows. My red-rimmed eyes and lopsided snarl gave off the impression that I was uncommonly cynical and maybe in the early stages of Bell's palsy, which garnered me some sympathy from the crowd. My bad attitude, though it won over the audience full of people who clearly had their own issues, was a total act—I really did want to be there and I really did want to do well. Not only did I love watching other great comics perform, like David Cross, Bob Odenkirk, Todd Glass, Kathy Griffin, Janeane Garofalo, Mary-Lynn Rajskub, and Karen Kilgariff, I loved performing that recreational style of comedy where you could take an idea to the stage and work it out. I didn't have to talk about the farm or knock out thirty-three jokes per minute. In fact, in the alternative scene, it was better if you weren't really funny in that way. Ideas were more important than jokes. This was, and is, one of the most important lessons to learn in comedy, so I will say it louder and with more feeling: original ideas are almost always better than jokes, unless the jokes pertain directly to the original idea, in which case, if you can make it work, you have truly accomplished something. You have birthed a comedy baby. Eat the placenta. You deserve it.

In addition to the alt scene, I also did sets at the Improv on Melrose, the Laugh Factory on Sunset, and any place they served coffee in greater Los Angeles. I performed at so many coffeehouses that for years, whenever I heard a cappuccino machine, I had a Pavlovian response and immediately started bombing. I also auditioned at the famed Comedy Store on Sunset. Many people believed the place was haunted. Like any comedian worth his salt, I was excited to see if the ghosts would enjoy my work. My audition spot was exactly three minutes long and I did quite well for at least two of those. When I got offstage, a bony hand shot out of the dark and grabbed me around the wrist. This is it, I thought. This is how it all ends, tortured and left for dead by a lifeless ghoul.

"I like you," said a raspy voice. It was Mitzi Shore, the brilliant legendary female owner of the Comedy Store. I immediately thought that if this was an episode of *Scooby-Doo*, she would later be discovered as the one behind the ghost sightings, done as a marketing ploy to drum up TMZ reports.

"Come back. Do another set. Next Tuesday," she managed to croak out.

"Thank you. Thank you," I said, trying to tug free. She continued to hold my wrist so tightly that I suspected rigor mortis was setting in on top of her rheumatoid arthritis. I eventually freed myself, but like the stupid girl in the horror movie, I went back the following Tuesday.

Since Mitzi had invited me back to perform, I was under the assumption that I would have a ten-minute set. I stretched beyond my seven-minute comfort zone and killed. When I got offstage though, I knew something was off. I was ushered to the entrance of the club, where the manager started barking at me. "You gotta respect the light! You gotta respect the light!"

"I didn't see the light."

It was true. I mean, I would've lied, but in this case, I didn't have to. I really didn't see it. Turns out the light was a star that lit up on the wall to the side of the stage, not a red light on the back wall like every other comedy club in the world. I'd performed for an extra five minutes, double the time I was allotted. I felt like such a dude. That was the start and the end of my career at the Comedy Store. I never saw Mitzi again. She died, but I'm not sure if it was before or after I met her.

IT WAS ACTUALLY AN INCREDIBLE time to be a comedian in the late '90's early 2000s. Comedians were getting development deals for their shows. The industry was looking to put comics in prime time. The alternative shows were packing out. It was the glory days of hipster comedy. It was cool to be a comedian, and I was right in the thick of it.

Then, something happened that nearly crushed my spirit. I

got cast in a sitcom. As the lead. A middle school teacher in a show called *Social Studies*. I mean, how bourgeois! It was heartbreaking. Of course, it was ridiculous to feel this way, but I was worried that it wasn't cool enough. I was worried that Janeane would boo it and then a nanosecond later so would everyone else. They'd have parties and hate-watch it, or worse, not watch it at all, because "I really only watch *Larry Sanders*. Sorry." So, to avoid any sitcom shaming, I didn't tell any of my friends. I told my family, but they didn't seem to know what to do with the information. "What are you going to do about your pet-grooming business?"

I was scared, and I refused to tell myself that I was scared. I had never acted outside auditions and a few classes. I actually liked preparing for the parts, breaking down the script, making my choices, and finding places to be funny. I liked performing in auditions, especially for a room of writers and producers because I knew that, no matter how bad they thought I was, they weren't going to heckle or drunkenly throw something at me. No matter how it went, they always said, "Thank you." This is something regular audiences should really start doing. But when I was auditioning for this sitcom, I never expected I'd actually get the part.

As the lead, or as I later asked to be called, the lynchpin of the series, I was treated like a queen from the moment I showed up at the first table read. It was more than a little different from the way I was treated at the clubs. No one yelled at me to get out of the aisle. No one shushed me or chewed me out because I didn't see the light. Everyone was incredibly accommodating and I felt that they laughed a little too easily at things I said that weren't particularly funny, like when I once mentioned I might have to leave midway through the read because I'd had some explosive diarrhea that morning. After the laughter died down,

I saw that someone's assistant had inconspicuously set a glass of Pepto-Bismol on the table. I managed to make it through the table read and I chatted with everyone for a while afterward, though I mixed up the female executive producer with the male gaffer, which didn't win me any points. Eventually I made it home, fell down facefirst on my bed, and zonked out.

I woke up to my phone ringing. It was my manager.

"They're going to fire you!"

"Huh?"

"They said you wore a hat to the table read." Guilty as charged. I didn't know it was going to be a big deal. That's just how I left the house.

"Well, you don't do that! You do your hair. You put on lipstick to go to a table read."

To my manager, the most important thing I could do for my career was to look good. "You have an audition for such and such. Look good." "You're meeting so and so. Do your hair." "You've got a spot at the Laugh-a-Lots. Wear makeup! A-Lots." I still didn't understand how wearing a hat could cost me the part.

"You got the job, but really, you don't. They could fire you at any time for any reason. Don't give them one. Wear lipstick every day. Do you promise? Do you promise?!"

"Can it be a gloss?"

ON THE FIRST DAY OF filming, I had my hair and makeup professionally done. I looked ready to anchor the midday news, but I was playing the part of social studies teacher looking for love—hence the clever title, *Social Studies*. Our first order of business was to film the opening credit sequence, which looks like it could be a lot of fun, but having a good time on cue is harder than it appears.

I don't know why I was so embarrassed by everything. It felt so silly locking arms back to back with other members of the show or pretending to dance on a spinning platform. I clearly suffer from an appalling case of self-consciousness. Once, headlining in Vegas, they put my face on a billboard and I cringed with horror. I felt humiliated. Why? I can't explain. I thought, Oh, God, now people will see me. I know it doesn't make a whole lot of sense. It's just too bad there was already a comedian who performed with a paper bag over his head and called himself the Unknown Comic. That was a genius move on his part. I wish I had thought of that.

As the cast and crew walked en masse to an outdoor location on the lot, I spotted Mary Lynn Rajskub, who had a recurring role on *Mr. Show,* walking to the set. I turtled, hoping she wouldn't see me. No such luck.

"Bonnie?"

"Hey, hi."

"What are you doing?"

"Nothing. Thought I saw something on the ground."

The creator of the sitcom sidled up next to me, beaming. "She's the lead of a new sitcom. *Social Studies.*"

"That's great." Mary Lynn looked at me and smiled. I rolled my eyes and shrugged like, "What are you going to do?" She eyed me suspiciously as I began filming, laughing, posing, dancing. After each time the director yelled, "Cut!" my shoulders sagged and I'd look over at her and shake my head like an idiot. Eventually, Mary Lynn left to film her scenes in the highly anticipated new season of *Mr. Show,* while I stuck it out on what would become the second-lowest-rated show on television. After they screened the pilot, they fired everyone except me and one other cast member. Just the night before, I had watched one of the producers hug a kid who was a cast member and tell them to get ready for a great season. An hour later, she had her assistant call the kid's agent and fire him. Maybe my manager was right. I started wearing lipstick.

On the set, I was constantly making rookie mistakes, like walking stage left when I was asked to move stage right, and casually telling the craft service guy that I liked vegetarian chili. One day I overheard a PA ask why there was always vegetarian chili on the set, and the craft service guy responded that I had demanded it. "It's her comfort food," he said, with more than a little hostility.

While I admit I was often moody and confused, I was not a diva. I did not demand chili or a closer parking space. I did not require white candles in my dressing room or ask that my hair be washed in dolphin pee. I did ask if I could wear unpadded bras. Every week, the bras seemed to get larger and pointier, and when I saw myself in the monitor, it looked like I was trying to smuggle two birthday hats out of the room.

Honestly, at that time, it felt like a lot of things were out of my control. Once, during a rehearsal, a PA asked me for the tenth time if he could get me anything. I finally asked him for some water just to be rid of him, and seconds later, I heard him yelling into his walkie: "Bonnie needs a water! STAT." There was a commotion over by the craft service and I could hear the order being passed on from one person to the next. "Water! Bonnie needs a water!" The director, who never really warmed up to me, took a deep breath. "Let's take a break so Bonnie can get a water." I wasn't even thirsty.

It's funny how wrong your instincts can be. I was convinced that being cast in a humorless sitcom would be the death of my social life in the alt comedy world, but in actuality it made me something of a VIP. The show was looking to cast a new gym teacher and almost every male comedian I knew auditioned for it. As a result, they were very respectful of me, unless you count the times they cornered me at the back of stand-up shows or called me in the middle of the night begging me to secure them the part. Looking back, I realize I could've used my power and influence to my advantage. I could have asked for extra stage time, or asked them to gift me a few vintage rock T-shirts. In the end, I just said I'd try my best, which meant that I didn't do anything.

After several auditions, the producers cast the comedian Adam Ferrara, who spent all his effort working on the part rather than working on getting the part. Watching him bounce around the set, smiling and hugging everyone from the script supervisor to the warm-up comic, I realized I needed to temper my attitude somewhat. I had an acting coach who tried to help me sort out the politics of the show, but I was unable to process everything in real time, and so I just walked around angry a lot. This anger and anxiety was compounded by the fact that my managers and agents called me every evening, begging me to not get fired.

Still, as low rated as the show was, for the first time in my life, people would come to my stand-up shows and recognize me not just as the girl who was doing shots at the bar, but as someone who had been on TV. It was terrifying. Sometimes they'd ask for my autograph and I'd literally break into a gig-gle fit and then write something nonsensical on a napkin next to my signature. Occasionally, people in the audience would cheer with recognition after I was introduced and I would practically fold in half knowing that I was just going to disap-point them. A few times I had panic attacks so strong that I could barely get a word out. Once, I stood onstage for nearly ten minutes saying, "I can't do this." It got about the same amount of laughs as my best set. My manager came to a show one night and stood at the back of the room while I tried to talk about things that were amusing to me. It wasn't killing like a panic attack, but it wasn't terrible. When I got offstage, he simply looked at me with an infuriated expression and said, "Your act makes me sick." And he walked out of the club. The next afternoon I fired him.

A few weeks later, *Social Studies* was canceled. I was relieved. The show was taking up a lot of time that I could've been using to keep up with the alt comedy crowd. Being cool required so much cramming. I had to learn exactly which television shows I should criticize and which bands were cool. I had to know which drinks my friends wanted me to put on my credit card (Jägermeister!) and I had to learn how to drive under the influence. I got invited to some pretty sweet parties if I agreed to take my car, drop off my fellow invitees, and spend a sizeable portion of the night looking for parking.

I was still represented by the William Morris Agency, and while they rarely took my calls, they still occasionally sent me on auditions. It wasn't long before I was cast in an HBO pilot created by and starring Christopher Guest and Eugene Levy. It was called *Dorkin Orkin Agency (DOA)* and it was a sharp comedy that satirized Hollywood talent agencies. It was cool and funny and I couldn't have been happier to spend all day joking with Eugene Levy, one of the all-time comedy greats who still had a Canadian accent. I found this particularly comforting.

I made a decision that I was not going to tell anyone about this pilot, but for very different reasons from the ones when I decided I wouldn't tell people about *Social Studies*. This pilot was brilliant and it was on HBO and it had Guest and Levy. It was sure to get picked up. My plan was to just let it hit the airwaves and wait for everyone to realize that I was in a show that would rate up there with *Mr. Show* and *Larry Sanders*. They'd say, "Why didn't you tell anyone?" I would shrug nonchalantly, maybe look at them over my dark Wayfarers. "I don't like to talk about my projects before they're on the air." But the show didn't get picked up, so I scrambled to tell everyone I was cast in a show on HBO with Guest and Levy but it only took a couple of follow-up questions for people to figure out that the show wasn't going to air. What should have been my happy moment became theirs.

"It didn't get picked up?" they'd say with their bottom lip jutting out in a fake pout. "That's too bad."

Chapter 12

NOWHERE TO GO
BUT UP YOURS

After easily getting cast on a couple of shows following my move to Los Angeles, I began making the rounds of casting directors with less and less success. Mark and I lived halfway up Beachwood Drive, the street that takes you up the mountain toward the famed Hollywood sign. As I drove home after auditions, an optical illusion made the sign appear to move farther away as I got closer. I'm sure God did that on purpose just to be an asshole.

Mark and I broke up every two weeks, but neither of us had anyone to turn to or anywhere to go. I knew I would miss his cats, so really, our breakups were an exercise in futility. This was the only exercise Mark ever got, by the way. He became something of a shut-in in Los Angeles. He hardly ever left the apartment. Even his weekly poker game had somehow relocated to our kitchen. He hadn't given up on his showbiz dreams, but I think he expected someone to walk by the window of our apartment and discover him. Until then, he pursued his other hobbies, one of which was reading computer programming books and the other was watching the television show *Cops* with his two lesbian, African-American drug dealers. "Hey, look! They're arresting a black drug dealer again!"

I should point something out. I know I've been hammering home the idea that Mark was to blame for the failure of the relationship, but I should tell you that everyone liked him. *Everyone.* Everyone but me. I mean, I liked him too, when we were out and he was being charming. When it was just him and me, we had nothing. We did not talk. We did not laugh. We did not connect. I couldn't even get him to engage when we were fighting. I would yell at him and he'd promptly go to sleep. In the middle of a fight, Mark would hit the hay and start a full REM cycle, snoring and drooling and all. You'd think I'd be more understanding, having my own issues with stress-induced sleeping, but I really think he just found the sound of my raised voice somewhat soothing.

One morning, while I was standing with my hand on the coffeepot waiting for enough black gold to filter through, Mark suddenly appeared in front of me with a small box in his hand. "It was my grandmother's," he said. I looked inside. A ring. I was pretty sure I knew what was going on, but to make sure, I clarified, "You want me to get a safety deposit box at the bank?"

"No," he said, picking up the bong for his morning hit. "It's for you. Like, for us. Wedding. Marriage. You know. Like people do."

"Oh," I said.

"Just wear it. We don't have to get married tomorrow."

I slid the ring on a finger and sat down. The romance was thick in the air and I suddenly couldn't breathe.

I met Lynn at the gym a few hours later and showed her the ring. She gushed, but not too much because she knew I had wanted to break up with him twelve hours earlier. She was playing it exactly right.

"Did you set a date?" she asked.

"We did not," I answered, still staring at my hand. "He just asked me out of the blue this morning. It's so weird. Can you believe I'm engaged?"

A girl with a rock-hard body and brightly colored workout tights was watching us. As she passed by, she said, "Why do you have it on the wrong hand?" Considering that Lynn and I are pretty guys by nature, I hadn't even realized I had the ring on my right hand. "I'm getting it sized," I said quickly, those improvisation classes suddenly coming in handy. "This finger's a little bigger." She didn't buy it. I didn't care.

Two weeks later, I delicately placed Mark's grandmother's heirloom on the table in front of him. I explained that the ring was something of a nuisance and sometimes made putting my hand in my front jeans pocket difficult. Without saying a word, he walked over to the couch and fell into a deep sleep.

The fact that I didn't want to be engaged to the man I was living with should've been a pretty big clue that we were done. Our relationship had so many red flags at this point that it resembled a used-car dealership, but we bravely soldiered on. We lived and occasionally ate together but we rarely spoke.

I STILL CRAVED MALE COMPANIONSHIP, and I found it one flight up and four doors down in my landlord's apartment. His walls were lined with eight-by-ten framed black-and-white photos of himself in full clown attire and makeup next to B-list movie stars, back when movies were still called "pictures." Hermann (I'm using a pseudonym here because there's a slim chance he might still be alive) was a seventy-something retired children's performer who began his life in Germany in the '20s or '30s and somehow ended up a clown in an even worse place than Nazi-occupied Germany. He was a tiny man, but he harbored the same amount of resentment as a full-size person who ends up alone in Hollywood, so his ratio of anger and bitterness to body weight was outrageous. I'd say Hermann was comprised of 70 or 80 percent resentment. That's probably why we got along so well. It was as if I'd found my soul mate.

My landlord/clown Hermann was my best friend in Los Angeles for a long time. When I look back on it though, I think he might've just been using me to do some light accounting and secretarial work for him. He would knock on my door almost every day, and the next thing I knew, I'd be over at his apartment organizing papers and labeling his videos. I typed up handwritten notes. I did a little dusting. I listened to his stories of back-lot birthday parties and kid friendly celebrations in the yards of the sort-of famous. I did him the courtesy of pretending to know who he was talking about and he returned the consideration by telling me I was an idiot. It was one of my healthiest relationships at the time.

Our friendship lasted for over a year, but when he must have realized I was never going to file his taxes topless and I realized I was never going to see a will, our visits became less and less frequent. One afternoon, I watched a younger, prettier actress leave his apartment carrying a few files, and I knew we were done. Hermann had moved on.

The building was definitely chockablock full of actors in various stages of success. Some had regular day jobs at coffee shops or the cupcake store, while others carried massage tables in and out of their apartments or were outright whores. Jenna Elfman, before she became the beloved star of *Dharma & Greg*, lived in the building with her charming husband, Bhodi. Both were actors, and they both took it very seriously. Jenna began her showbiz career as a backup dancer and it was clear that she applied the same discipline to her sitcom auditions. Her lines were always memorized. Her toes were always pointed. Her posture, perfect.

I saw Jenna at auditions all the time. We became friendly mostly because we never auditioned for the same roles. She was, after all, a blonde and I was a brunette, which is how the industry differentiates female characters. If a third female character is necessary (And are they, really? Talk about your estrogen fest...), the sitcom industry will employ a woman of color, a redhead, a short-haired woman, or someone with glasses.

One night as I was leaving the complex to walk to a party with my friends, already high and a little drunk, Jenna Elfman came out on her balcony.

"Hey!" she called to me.

"Hi."

"You ready for tomorrow?" We were both going to network on a project. This would be the last of several auditions before we auditioned for the higher-ups at the network and, hopefully, got the part. Or not.

"Yes, I think so."

Jenna raised an eyebrow.

"If you want to come up and run lines, you're more than welcome."

"Thanks, but I'm going to a party with my friends. You wanna come?"

Her face folded into a sour expression.

"No," she said flatly. "I'm going to work on the script."

She got the part. I didn't. The truth was, I wasn't getting any parts. My comedy was faltering. My boyfriend and I were wildly mismatched. I knew it was time to look closely at my life and make some changes. And then it occurred to me what the problem was. I was fat.

I didn't become anorexic living in Los Angeles, but I certainly tried. I began by cutting out cheese, then sugar. I stopped eating anything deep-fried. I had a sugar-free baked doughnut once and ate part of my sleeve before I realized the doughnut was gone and I'd moved on to my shirt. Still not happy with the results, I cut out carbs. I got a trainer. I bought a mountain bike. I did the Santa Monica stairs. I started eating vegetable broth. I took ephedrine. I drank nonfat, sugar-free iced blendeds and always took the stairs. All the hard work paid off. I lost two pounds and kept it off for several months.

This should come as no surprise to you, but my personal trainer was a comedian before he took a weekend course to become an accredited, though unenthusiastic, fitness specialist. "Ten more, nine more," he'd say, followed by, "You know what? That's fine." DumbleDoof (not his real name) was not muscular like a bodybuilder, but he was tall and fit. He wasn't a bad-looking guy, if you didn't look too long and hard at his nose. I always thought it lacked cartilage and just kind of clung to his face like a baby monkey trying not to slip off its mommy. He was an enthusiastic gambler and usually lost big at the track. I think it was an image thing. He felt it sounded better than "I lost my house because I'm addicted to scratch offs."

When DumbleDoof left comedy, he made a clean break. It was like he walked away saying, "That part of my life is over. I'll never be funny again." And he wasn't ever funny again. Trust me, I kept a keen eye on him, expecting his humor to bubble back up one day, but it never did. Worse, in my humble opinion, was the fact that he never acknowledged it if I told a joke. (My least favorite kind of person, incidentally. I once knew a girl who laughed at everything any man near her said, but when a woman said something witty, she would cock her head sideways and look quizzical. "I don't get it," she'd say, stopping the fun in its tracks. Evil bitch.) For this reason and several hundred others, my personal trainer and I hated each other so much that if our sessions were a romantic comedy, you would roll your eyes watching us, knowing that we were definitely going to end up sleeping together. Even he and I were quite sure that the only way to end the bickering would be to put our mouths on each other. And yet it never happened. Maybe we didn't really hate each other after all, but we were locked into a needy hopefest. He was looking to score the big payout at the track. I desperately wanted to lose weight. I didn't shed any pounds, but I did shed a lot of money, folks! I gave him so many advances that he owes me sessions well into my sixties.

Once, when he told me I should cut carbs, I yelled at him and stormed out of the gym, but I needed help with the door because my arms were so sore. I was living on just a few bagels a day, and the idea that I should stop eating those really sent me over the edge. I was a vegetarian. What was I going to eat? This is how badly I wanted to be thin, and I'm not proud of this, but it will make many readers happy. That night, that very fucking night, I stopped being a vegetarian. I started eating meat. I showed up at DumbleDoof's house and he made me a steak. There wasn't even a vegetable on the plate. Just a big, fat, delicious hunk of meat, and I ate every last piece of pink flesh. I went against my very belief system so I could fit into a size 0. Because, after all, if there's one thing we know, skinny people are the funniest!

THIS IS WHERE MY SAGA becomes tragic, where we leave the fun memoir behind and begin the dreaded cautionary tale. I may never have had a good grasp of who I was, but I appeared to be losing even the slightest grip on my authentic self. See, even the fact that I used the term "authentic self" should tell you that I am totally, utterly lost. If there is any truer sign of personality irresolution than using phrases popularized by Oprah, I can honestly say that I don't know what it is.

I am fully aware that old-timers in Hollywood have many stories of young, fresh-faced gals stepping off the bus from a state no one can remember the capital of—North Dakota? It's Bismarck. I just looked it up. You're welcome—dreaming of fame and fortune, only to find herself with a nom de porne that combines the name of her childhood cat and the first street she grew up on, and twenty adult titles to her name. (My porn name, by the way, would be Cat Rural Route 2.) By twenty-six, little Pussy Willow would be used up and spit out of the system. She'd wind up a star on a MILF Web site to support herself and the two kids that social services hadn't yet chucked into foster care.

For every one of these success stories though, there's one like mine: the story of a vegetarian farm girl/man who, after only a few months in Los Angeles, begins eating meat. I so easily fell into trying to become everything I hated that it's difficult to talk about these sordid days of driving over the canyon to auditions, saying lines out loud in my car, living on turkey jerky, and getting my head shots airbrushed so it looked like I had cleavage. (It was less expensive and had a faster recovery time than real breast augmentation, and I didn't have to pretend to my friends that of course I had done research on my doctor.) Remarkably, when I showed up at auditions, no one ever said, "Hey, you don't have tits, you lying sack of shit." Because everybody did it, and everybody included me, for once. I was finally fitting in. I put on my oversize sunglasses one leg at a time like every other wannabe actress in town. I discussed characters I was auditioning for like they were real people with backstories that would bring a tear to your eye. I let assholes in nice cars cut me off without laying on the horn and giving them a few choice hand signals in the slim chance it might be one of those rare Hollywood bigwigs. I told people I was blessed. I hiked Laurel Canyon. I was a shallow shell of a girl with no defined characteristics. "I can be whoever you want me to be!" Clichés and caricatures, it turns out, are my forte!

While being an empty vessel might work for acting, it's a real shitstorm if you want be a comedian. As we've discussed before, class, many audience members will be delighted by almost any banal premise or hackneyed portrayal of someone else, but you are not trying to get those people on your side. You're trying to reach the few who will come back to see another show of yours. To do that, you must be an original. If you have original thoughts and jokes, you must have a persona that can bear their weight.

In comedy, persona is *très* important, and I no longer had one. I had many. I could turn with the tide. When I was with my alt comedy friends, I tried to be like them, dress like them, sound like them. At auditions, I became whatever it was I thought the casting directors wanted. Onstage, I tried to please the comedians in the back of the room, but usually ended up not pleasing anyone. I got tongue-tied. I spoke too softly. I got drunk. I embarrassed myself.

As a stand-up comic, if your character is uncomplicated, it is in some ways much easier to put on a good show, at least in the beginning. When you start as a comedian, you generally begin with the most obvious thing about yourself. Fat people do jokes about the stage breaking, redheads make fire-crotch jokes. Women usually make jokes about being slutty, tomboyish, or dumb. If you wear glasses, I suppose you could start by saying men never make passes at girls who wear glasses and then explain who Dorothy Parker was.

But later, if you want to go beyond a four-and-a-half-minute television set, you have to start exploiting the incongruities of your personality and your nuanced ideas of the world. (Brace for an audience to hate you! Where are the dick jokes?) Eventually, the originality will pay off, and you'll have a persona that can sustain almost any idea you come up with. Whatever crazy thought you have, you can now filter it through the persona you've already established. Because that persona is not a one-trick pony. It's a complicated, real human being that the audience can relate to on many different levels. But please, as you read this, keep in mind, I have no fucking clue what I'm talking about most of the time.

I had the desire to be great, but maybe not the stomach for it. Whenever I tried to be "me" onstage, I failed outright and faster than you can say "airbrush tanning!" I had not established a persona that could tell jokes with complex ideas in them and so I went back to the jokes that worked. Little, tiny, bitty bon mots. It's not like these jokes worked brilliantly, but the audience seemed to get them. And for a while, at least, that satisfied me.

It didn't satisfy my "team." They felt I wasn't getting enough laughs. I wasn't "hooking" the audience. And so they arranged a meeting in the William Morris Agency L.A. offices. In the large corner office, surrounded by suits, one of the agents declared, "Smoke 'em if you got 'em!" His assistant closed the door and the whole brood lit up cigarettes and squinted through the thick smoke at each other.

"You need to hone your persona," they told me.

"I don't know what I am," I said, ashamed. "I miss my chain wallet."

"You need to go back to your roots," one agent said. "You need to talk about where you're from."

"You know what people love?" another agent asked as he inhaled on his cigarette and then blew the smoke out of the side of his mouth. "Fish out of water."

"You're the fish," the first agent explained. "And the farm is the water." At this point, I bore witness to a nonverbal discussion between the two agents as they made sure that yes, the farm was the water. They nodded and the one with seniority continued. "You need to talk about what it's like for a Canadian farm girl to be living in Los Angeles."

"I don't know," I said. It didn't feel right. I didn't want to talk about Canada. Or the farm. Those jokes seemed too complicated for the short sets I was doing. I was doing the equivalent of Twitter jokes at this point. Short, absurd observations about my life in Los Angeles. How was I going to explain what it was like growing up the way I did? I'd need to stage an hour-long one-woman show. And to do that I'd have to get started immediately making the flyers.

"You need to get a solid five minutes," a younger agent sagely pointed out.

"I had a client did five minutes on being a fireman on *The Tonight Show*," the old guy boasted. "Got a development deal with NBC the next day."

"Talk about the farm," said one of the agents.

"Talk about the farm," another agent repeated.

A COMEDIAN'S BREAD AND BUTTER is her crummy childhood, so I thought I'd give it a shot. I tried talking about hating to work from sunup to sundown, but it came off as ungrateful. I complained about not having television as kid, but this childhood woe paled in comparison with the funny things other comedians were talking about. One guy had a bit about getting hit with a roller skate as a kid. My sister Lynn, who was a great source of amusement in our home, was a difficult sell to audiences who, when offered stories about a person with a mental disability responded with either derisive laughter or, even worse, pity. My ironic observations about playing the board game FARM after working on one all day didn't get the laughs I needed. Still, I forged ahead, trying to please my team.

"I used to cut the heads off chickens," I began. This elicited a couple of groans. "Not just for fun," I said. "I grew up on a farm." I couldn't see how uncomfortable people looked, since I was blinded by the spotlight, but I could hear them shifting in their seats. I kept going. "So black people could eat." Booo.

Weirdly enough, doing jokes about growing up on a farm and being a fish out of water made my stories seem inauthentic. The audience's own ideas about what it would have been like growing up on a farm in Canada were massively different from the reality of growing up on a farm in Canada—though we both agreed that it was as cold as a witch's tit. I didn't have the skills to close the gap between the two views, much less in under ten minutes, which was how long my spots in the city were. If I couldn't bring some kind of truth to the topic, I wanted to avoid it. I wanted to, but I didn't because nifty men in expensive suits told me to talk about it. So I did.

ONE NIGHT, A FEW OF these nifty men from the WMA came to the Improv to see me perform. There are three big clubs in Hollywood, the Comedy Store on Sunset, the Laugh Factory on Sunset, and the Improv on Melrose. Of the three, I liked the Improv the best, probably because they liked me more than the other two did. I spent my days auditioning and my nights performing at any number of clubs in the city but I often ended up at the long bar in the Improv, drinking with the other comedians who were hanging out bragging about our lack of success. That's a comedian thing. We love to outdo one another with tales of catastrophic misfortune. It was a game I was good at.

On this particular night, I did my "farm" set and afterward, one of the boy geniuses from William Morris asked me if I really grew up on a farm. I looked at him for a long time, trying to understand how someone with such limited brain activity could function without round-the-clock nursing care. Why would anyone lie about growing up on a farm in Canada? What could possibly be the benefit? And didn't he get the interoffice memo? It was their idea that I talk about the farm.

"No, it's my cover story for my covert CIA operation. Unfortunately, now that I've told you, I'll have to kill you."

My team was annoying, but that didn't stop me from taking advantage of the WMA corporate card. I knocked back a few beers and probably a couple of shots of tequila while I regaled them with charming tales of life in the McFast Lane. I was showing them I was likeable. Castable. A star who could hold her liquor. I wasn't winning anyone over with my comedy and so I knew I needed them to send me out for something big so I could succeed in this town in some way. I smiled with both sides of my mouth instead of just curling up the left corner in a sarcastic sneer, as was my habit. It was rare, this full smile. I only pulled it out for special occasions, like an expensive pair of pumps or a dry-clean-only blouse. I was willing to stop at nothing to win over these suits. I even covered my mouth when I burped.

And then DumbleDoof walked in. DumbleDoof! Remember DumbleDoof? My old trainer, the one who'd left the comedy scene behind and owed me at least three hundred dollars and the deed to his house? That DumbleDoof! He was suddenly standing just a few feet away from me, looking like tragedy and smelling like a gym. At first, I thought nothing of it. I even gave him the nod (also known as the lesbian hello) to assure him there were no hard feelings. I didn't need him breaking up my agent-bonding party, not when I was so close to the finish line. But when I glanced his way again, he was staring at me with a look in his eye that told me things were about to go south.

I smiled very slightly, the way one smiles at a rabid dog that looks like it might attack. "There, there, boy. It's all going to be okay." He dug his hand deep into his pocket, pulled out a handful of crumpled bills, and threw them on the floor in front of me. My agents looked at me and then at him. Was this going to be a scene? No, no, it wasn't. I swooped down and picked up the money, shoved it into my pocket, and turned to them and laughed. "Comedians. So funny," I said.

I'm not sure what DumbleDoof thought I was going to do, but stuffing money into my pocket was clearly not what he expected. He started yelling at the top of his lungs. The word he chose to yell, not once, not twice, but repeatedly, was "cunt." The bartender asked him to stop. He would not. The customers asked him to stop. He ignored them. Emily Post popped her head in and warned him that yelling "Cunt!" at a woman in public more than three times in a row was just plain rude. He would not relent. I just stood there like a deer in the headlights. My agents chivalrously ditched me for the valet. They zoomed away, one after another, in their fully loaded Lexuses. Except for their assistant, who drove a Saturn.

Shortly afterward, DumbleDoof was escorted off the premises. He promptly started banging on the window and yelling something, probably at me. Maybe it was the word "cunt." It could've been "can't," but that doesn't make much sense. And if past experiences are the best predictors of future ones, he was probably asking for money. But he wasn't finished. Dumble-Doof then used the pay phone outside the club to call my home phone and yell, "Cunt!" into my machine. He left twelve messages in total.

Mark arrived home from a poker game after I had already gone to bed, but hadn't fallen asleep. I sat up and told him about DumbleDoof.

"Oh, who cares?" he said, climbing into bed. "Let it go."

"Let it go? One cunt, okay. Two, I could forget. But this was like twenty-five cunts! I'm supposed to just let that go?"

"Can we talk about this in the morning? I'm just so tir . . ." And he was out.

I fumed all night. In the morning, I pressed the issue with Mark. "You're not mad? He called your girlfriend a cunt. In public. In front of my agents. Repeatedly."

"What are you going to do?" Mark said, blowing it off. "It's DumbleDoof. You know, he's DumbleDoof."

I wouldn't let it go, and eventually, seeing no other way out, Mark finally dialed DumbleDoof's number. He motioned that he had gotten his machine. I motioned for him to leave a message. "Hey, buddy," he began. "Give me a call." Hey, buddy?!

It was just the briefest interlude before William Morris informed me that they were going to stop representing me. "Good luck with everything!"

It wasn't Mark's fault, but I was definitely pissed at him. That was it. We were done. This time, we were really done. I'd just tell him later.

A FEW AFTERNOONS LATER, AS I jogged up the hill toward the Hollywood sign, I saw a cute apartment with a little For Rent sign in the window. I broke left and ran up to take a closer look. The landlord was standing in front of the building. She wasn't doing anything, just standing. "You here to see the apartment?" she asked. I nodded.

Two nights later I had my own apartment. Now I just had to tell Mark I was moving out. After five deep breaths, a couple of deep knee bends, and half a bagel, I walked into the living room and stood in front of him. As I cleared my throat, the phone rang. It was Mark's sister, calling to tell Mark that his father had died. Well, even I could see this was not a good time to tell him I was leaving.

I booked us flights back to Springfield, Massachusetts, where he grew up and his mom and sister still lived. We had only a couple of hours to get to the airport. I was ferociously throwing items into a suitcase when, eyes red with tears and cannabis, Mark shoved the ring in my face. "I never told anyone we weren't still engaged. Would you?" I put the ring on the correct finger. Then I wriggled that hand into my front jeans pocket and fingered the keys to my new apartment, which was waiting for me just down the street.

At the funeral, there was a lot of "Next time we all get together, it'll be for a good reason" and "When are you guys going to have the wedding?" I fielded questions with the ease of a sociopath. Maybe I was a better actor than I gave myself credit for. It felt awful. As we flew back home, I knew I had some moral questions to answer. How long after someone loses a parent can you break up with him? I settled on two months. For sixty days, I continued to live with Mark, occasionally slipping away to sit alone in my empty apartment.

Eventually, the big day arrived and I ended my relationship with Mark quickly and efficiently. I'm not even sure he was aware of what was actually happening until I grabbed a backpack and headed for the door saying, "I'll come back and get the rest of my stuff tonight." I have to hand it to Mark, he did something I never expected him to do. He left the apartment. He ran after me down the street in his bare feet, yelling, "Don't do this!" As I power-walked toward my apartment, I was starting to think I was going to have to lose him by running and hiding, lest he discover where I'd be living. It wasn't that I thought he was going to stalk me or break in and have his way with me. I was ashamed that the best I could do was move two blocks away. I wasn't exactly going to win any awards for achievements in breakups.

Mark gave up after a few feet and I made it to my new place undetected. I stood in the middle of the empty room. I had no furniture, no television, no money, no boyfriend, no friends, no manager, and no agent.

There was nowhere to go but up. Which is a saying that is not really true. Technically, you could stay at the bottom forever.

Chapter 13

LAUGHTER IS THE BEST MEDICINE, UNLESS YOU HAVE ACTUAL MEDICINE

I might have been living in the smallest known residence in North America, but at least I was happy. I had broken up with Mark, at least in my head, months earlier, had already mourned the loss of the relationship, privately though it was, and was now moving through acceptance and into bliss at a frightening pace. I was writing easily. That is to say, I was writing without my usual negotiations with God that always ended with me screaming the word "Forsaken!" to my ceiling at full volume. I filled stacks of notebooks in a matter of weeks. I looked forward to going onstage. I was enjoying stand-up. I talked to people after shows. I spoke to strangers on the street. I made the people in line behind me at the grocery store laugh. On purpose! Without tripping. I found myself smiling before I had my second venti morning coffee. Despite the fact that I could open my fridge from my bed, I lost ten pounds.

I liked me. I really liked me—which was a pretty big red flag that I was in the throes of a major manic upswing. I was shooting off like a T-shirt cannon during the commercial break at a daytime TV talk show. I was well aware it was happening. One afternoon, I was riding my bike during a rare Los Angeles thunderstorm, laughing and squealing as the sheets of rain washed over me. I said to myself, This is not normal. You are going to crash. And I didn't mean my bicycle. I knew at some point, I would come floating down somewhere in the Hollywood Hills, where the coyotes would tear me into bite-size pieces and eat me during a power lunch.

I picked up smoking again because I'd read that smoking can prolong an upswing and stave off depression. In a further attempt to stay manic, I quit drinking, quit pot, quit sleeping, and quit eating. I limited myself to just a few activities, which included jogging up the side of a mountain, doing stand-up, and chain-smoking until the sun came up. At any given moment, you could probably find me laughing uproariously at anything anyone said to me. I was truly a delight.

I was performing regularly at the Improv and even started getting the coveted weekend sets. I was also getting booked at most of the alternative hotspots, including Largo. My panic attacks onstage subsided dramatically, which made me think that taking short breaks before nailing the punch line to inhale into a paper bag had been hampering my ability to get laughs in the past. This side of mental instability was much better for stand-up.

I radiated confidence, which is a perfume from The Limited, and it wasn't long before my odor caught the attention of a bartender at an alternative comedy hotspot, a Tom Cruise look-alike who would've towered over the real Tom Cruise by at least two and a half inches. He was intent on becoming an actor, a serious actor. But he was willing to start anywhere, even in a comedy *if he had to*.

He took every kind of acting class, and even took jazz and tap dance. He went semiregularly to a shooting range, drove a taxicab, jumped out of an airplane, got his motorcycle license, took a typing class, and, although I didn't read all the way to the bottom of the document, probably even had a threesome to fatten up the Special Attributes section on his resumé. Looking like Tom Cruise, though, appeared to be his most prized accomplishment. It's unclear if he was obsessed with Tom because they looked alike and it was actually a kind of narcissism, which would've at least given him a hint of personality, or if Tom Cruise really was his idea of the greatest living actor and it was merely a fantastic coincidence that they actually looked alike. Whichever the case, he had the box set of all Tom's movies in mint condition. If you would like to borrow one, you cannot.

Unfortunately, all his hard work went largely unnoticed. His resumé went vastly underviewed by anyone other than the people who dropped by his apartment. He displayed his acting resumé neatly on his coffee table next to his head shot. I was more impressed, as I believe many of his friends were at the time, that he had both the room and the means to have a coffee table.

He exhibited no bitterness. Come to think of it, he lacked other personality traits, including the comedy staples, irony and sarcasm. He didn't even have much of a sense of humor. When I suggested, since he was a staggering five seven, that he refer to himself as the tall Tom Cruise, he simply furrowed his brow and asked, "Why?" Initially, I thought he took a shine to me because of my comedy prowess, but after dating for a few weeks, it became pretty obvious that my wit was less of a turn-on and more of an irritant. I was in denial at the time, but in retrospect, I think he noticed me because I tipped rather heavily on my Diet Cokes.

To add to the cons column, he also had the small problem of getting and maintaining an erection. Cynic that I am, I assumed that he'd heard a rumor that Tom Cruise had ED and he wanted to have it, too. In an effort to work the system, we started using the female condom. Female condoms are nice because you can use the packaging as an overnight bag. The female condom is fairly similar to the male condom, except it's 220 percent bigger and gets paid 23 percent less than its male counterpart. It has a ring at the bottom so you can anchor it inside your vagina, a process that is, as I'm sure you can imagine, very comforting. After kissing and fondling, we'd call in an ob-gyn to insert it, which tended to dampen the mood somewhat, mostly because the doctor needed so much light.

I loved being the Nicole to his Tom. (This was before that *Dawson's Creek* actress turned him into a couch-jumping loon.) Like those two lovebirds, we had no idea about the challenges that we would face together. We embarked on a relationship the way that I almost always embark on a relationship: I said no an unreasonable number of times, and then I "reluctantly" agreed to a dinner invitation. He was low on funds, so we went to that cute, modestly priced Scottish restaurant, McDonald's Drive Thru. I suggested we take the booty to my place and watch a movie. I was interested to see if two people could comfortably fit inside my apartment.

As we parked the car, I saw a hirsute figure standing in the middle of the road. I almost didn't recognize him without the couch attached to his side. It was Mark. His face registered actual horror as he watched my date and me emerge from the hatchback with our colorful takeout bags.

"It's my ex-boyfriend," I warned Tom 2 in a tight whisper. I moved forward with extreme caution. "Mark . . ." I said gently, as though talking down a wild animal. I didn't want to get OJ'd.

Mark shook his head in disgust. "McDonald's, Bonnie? McDonald's?" I suppose he expected that I'd find a new lover, but he hadn't worked through the idea that I might share

Mickey D's with another man. This betrayal was almost more than he could handle. When Mark and I lived together, I not only refused to eat the nutritionally vacant foodstuffs, I often berated him after finding empty bags and cartons in his car. I loudly accused him of being addicted to chicken nuggets and told him he was going to die. Looking back, I realize I might not have been the best girlfriend, either.

As a peace offering, I gave Mark my French fries and he took them, munching on them as he stumbled down my driveway. Tom 2 and I went up to my apartment and watched *The Fourth of July* a couple of times. In the dates that followed, we managed to make it through about half of his Tom Cruise box set. Ultimately, it wasn't his inability to keep an erection or pay for Viagra that was his undoing. It was his earnestness. Dealing with someone so boring practically amounted to abuse for me. I require levity every three or four seconds in a relationship, or I start researching women's shelters and planning my escape route. I quickly went back to my own people: unattractive funny dudes.

I FELL PRETTY HARD FOR a New York–based comedian who was half of a comedy team and was thus well versed in give-and-take. He wasn't just impressed that I understood him. He also expected any partner of his to add something of her own, which made me feel like I was a necessary part of his comedy process. He's married now and I'll bet my nana that being part of a comedic duo makes him an outstanding mate. I highly recommend anyone who wants to be a good husband to spend a few formative years in the back rooms of restaurants and the basements of bars being the straight man in a comedy duo. No one will respect you at the time, of course, but later, when you're married, your wife will be pleasantly impressed. Say what you want about Jerry Lewis but I bet he can pillow-talk like nobody's business.

I enjoyed our time together but, just like in *Grease 2*, summer ended and so did the relationship. Full disclosure: I never saw *Grease 2*.

The end of this relationship was hard because I liked him a lot and it was a difficult transition to make to doing comedy bits solo in my apartment. I was lonely. I missed having someone around that I actually enjoyed being with. We liked being silly and dissecting comedy and coming up with new bits to try onstage. He was the comedy girlfriend I had been searching for my entire comedy career. And I felt a distinct void after he was gone. Before long, I began to feel that nasty old tingling in my frontal lobes.

The dreaded crash that I had managed to keep at bay for so long finally caught up with me. Before I knew it, I was lying facedown in a pile of cigarette butts, waiting for the world to swallow me whole. Up, down, up, down: my moods were locked in an ongoing game of tug-of-war. I would call my mom crying and say, "I can't do this anymore." She would always say the same thing: "Uh-huh." My sister Andrea was forced to deal with most of my depression-era phone calls. I would be crying so hard that I couldn't talk, and I could hear the pain in her voice too, as she was trying to convince three boys under the age of five to eat their dinners while talking me off my proverbial ledge. She'd always find the time to call me back a few days later to find out how I was doing, and I'd already be breaking the ceiling on another new upswing. "I'm great!" I'd answer, almost stunned that she was worried. "I just had the hiccups," I'd say.

My swings began moving at the speed of light. I'd be lying on the floor, lamenting my existence to a friend, who was usually someone who grew up with an alcoholic mother and needed to get off maternally. The friend would stroke my head and tell me, "No, Bonnie, you're a good person . . ." I'd sit up and look at them dry-eyed. "Good?" I'd say, jumping up off the floor, "I'm great!" And I'd be out the door heading for a nice jog up Runyon Canyon.

Eventually, the downswings eclipsed the upswings, and I settled in for a long, terrible hibernation in my apartment. After several weeks, I stuck my head out from under the covers to see if I could see my shadow. During those few weeks, I had responded to only two e-mails. One was to confirm a set that night at Largo. Even the deepest, darkest depression couldn't keep me from performing at the best comedy night in the city. The other e-mail was from Joe Bodolai, my producer friend from Canada. He was in Los Angeles for a couple of nights and wanted to know if we could meet up. I forced myself out of bed and into the shower. I quietly urged myself not to cut my own bangs and then cut my own bangs the minute I got out of the shower. I don't know why depression makes you want to trim your hair, but let's just say I went through a period of baby bangs and I burned all photo evidence of that time.

Performing felt good, the approval of the audience lifted my spirits, and afterward Joe took me out for dinner. I was feeling better, still riding the adrenaline from a good stand-up set, but he knew I was struggling. His advice was simple: service the creative, he said, however that needed to happen. Up until this point, I had been schooled in the cliché that your personal relationships are the most important thing at the end of the day, but Joe's philosophy was that relationships come and go and it's jokes that last forever. I don't know that it was good advice—he had been drinking, after all—but he said it with conviction. And I believed him.

I went back to my apartment and wrote. I wrote every thought I ever had, and Joe was right. It helped. I wasn't cured, but I was awake and able to leave the house. People who have suffered from depression know what it feels like. It feels sleepy and slow and unbalanced. You can never get your shirt to stay tucked in and everyone is always doing their best to irritate you. It's being in a constant state of hyper-self-awareness. It's awful. I chose to ride it out, but if you feel like this, it's probably best to talk to someone. To get help. And also take magnesium!

A few weeks later, still fighting the despair, I ran into Mark at a party, and he did something for which I might never forgive him. He made me laugh. Just like that, we started it up all over again. In hindsight, of course, I can see how pathetic this is. But when I woke up at his apartment the next morning, I mistook that awful sinking feeling in the pit of my stomach for hunger. After we ate egg-white Spanish omelets, we decided to move in together.

WE RENTED THE CUTEST LITTLE two-bedroom house in Burbank, complete with a guesthouse, full bath, and shag carpet. I'm not sure I was in love with Mark, but I was head over heels for my new writing office that was twice or maybe even thrice the size of my current apartment. If that wasn't enough, smack in the middle of the backyard sat the most gorgeous plum tree anyone had ever seen. Mark and I weren't without our problems, but they all paled in comparison to that goddamn plum tree.

Maybe you've never had a plum tree in your backyard, so let me tell you what it's like. First, the fucking thing makes plums, lots and lots of plums. Imagine a plum tree with a plum hanging from every branch. Now, add four thousand more plums to that image. First, it's exciting. You naively point them out to friends. "Look! We're going to have plums. Fresh plums!" And you excitedly wait for them to ripen. One day, the plums do ripen, all of them, all at once. They fall to the ground. You walk outside one morning and your backyard is literally carpeted with the dark blue orbs. You can't step around them, so you step on them and as they squish under your weight, the pits embed themselves in the bottom of your shoes and the juice squirts onto your pants legs. Once you're safely back inside your house, you track plum juice throughout your home. You stain socks and shirts and curtains with it. The gardeners won't remove them because it isn't in their contract, or . . . I don't know why, exactly. I don't speak Spanish. I mean, you can't live in Los Angeles without picking up a few phrases, but "Why the fuck won't you do something about these plums?" isn't one of them. It was like a horror movie: *Plums: This Summer Runs Red.*

I didn't spend all my time in my office writing, as I'd hoped I would when I signed the lease. No, I spent the majority of my time outdoors picking up the fruit and filling pails and baskets and bags with them. I had moved 1,102 miles into another country to basically do what I did my entire childhood. Friends would call and say, "We're all going to the Smokehouse tonight to drink extra-wet martinis! Come down." And I'd have to say, "I can't tonight. I've got these plums." I began making jams and jellies and giving them to friends, but that hardly put a dent in the massive amount of fruit I had acquired. I made bread pudding and plum upside-down cake, plum dumplings and plum sorbet. But still, I was drowning in plums. I should've called this tree Lindsay Lohan because this was a tree that would not quit. At night, I lay awake in bed, trying to formulate a plan to get rid of the fruit. I envisioned starting a microbrewery and making plum beer or sweet plum liquor. I thought about standing near the on-ramp of the 405 and trying to cut in on the orange-seller's market, but being that I was Canadian and not Mexican, I wasn't sure I could handle the heat that would inevitably come off the blacktop. I thought about starting a Pick Your Own Plums Garden, but the plums were already on the ground and most of them were overripe. By the time I got the word out, it would be too late for most of the fruit and I didn't have time to respond to the number of complaint letters I would inevitably get. I thumbed through Martha Stewart magazines, looking for a solution, but using the fruit to tie-dye a head scarf required only five plums. It was a joke. I had a recurring fantasy of myself dressed in a black catsuit, sneaking bags of fruit into the grocery store and emptying them into their bins, mixing my plums with their plums, but the thought of getting caught off-loading the stash—the opposite of stealing, you could say—was too embarrassing. I decided to let them rot on the ground, allowing the nutrients to flow through the earth back to the tree, making it bigger and stronger and healthier for the next year.

Plums 2: This Time It's Worse. Pruning Shears Terror.

ONE NIGHT WHILE WALKING THROUGH my neighborhood, I spotted a tiny kitten peeking out of an overgrown weed garden next to an insurance place. Maybe it was all the plum juice, or the full moon, or a combination of the two, but I knew I had to save this fragile little thing. Several scratches and two twisted ankles later, I was holding the miniature kitten in my arms. He had no collar and was so skinny that I was worried he wouldn't last more than a few more days in the wilds of that strip mall. I carried him home in the hammock of cloth at the front of my T-shirt. Mark's cats did not exactly turn up in a welcome wagon, so I slept with my new guest in my office.

It took only a few days before my little kitty and I had agreed to an unwritten trade-off. I kept him safe from Mark's cats, and he kept me from turning into a bitter spinster. I got him all his shots but was told that he was tremendously malnourished and was much older than he looked. He sounded like a lot of stars in Hollywood, so that's what I named him, Hollywood, despite the fact that we lived in Burbank. Little Hollywood was sicker than I realized. After a few months, he started stumbling around like a tiny drunk when he walked. It was as though something as small as a kitten couldn't escape the inevitable route of a Hollywood starlet. I took him to one vet after another, and they all said the same thing: he had a neurological disorder that would only worsen. The humane thing, they all assured me, would be to put him to sleep. The idea ripped a hole in my heart, but after a lot of contemplation, I decided I didn't want Hollywood to suffer. I held him in my arms as the vet injected a lethal cocktail into his veins, and I watched the light slowly, peacefully fade from his eyes. I cried so hard I couldn't see. "Mark," I begged, "please take care of things. I just can't." I meant pay the fee. And he did. Thankfully, he did.

Later that night at dinner, we tried to make jokes about it. Some I laughed at, some I couldn't. I was glad Mark was there for me. The love of a pet is powerful, and even now, when I think about Hollywood, I tear up. I try to comfort myself with the thought that for at least three months of his life, he had food and a warm bed and unconditional love. And I did, too.

My birthday was around the corner. I wanted a new kitten but I didn't dare ask. Instead, I talked a lot about how lumpy my old pillow had gotten. I sensed that my mood would crash again, and I felt that the best thing to do was get a new pillow to soften the blow of the inevitable slump. Mark wasn't so easily manipulated by my not-so-subtle hints. He told me to cut it out because he was getting me something better than a pillow.

Elated, I prepared myself for a new kitten. I spent a little time at a nearby PetSmart filling up a basket with toys and food. I was impressed with Mark. This was a newer, more thoughtful boyfriend and I was grateful that he'd finally turned the corner. My Mark was growing up. The morning of my birthday,

I gave Mark a kiss and a flirty wink as I left the house on my bike. I whistled all the way to work. I was writing for a game show and I wrote my quota of questions in a matter of minutes and then made a list of kitten names. I ended the day playing several hours of solitaire on the computer, keeping my eye out the window, wondering if the kitten was wandering around his new home yet.

The minute my supervisor let me go, I got on my bike and pedaled home as fast as I could. Breathless, I opened the door. Mark was on the couch, a bowl of dried oatmeal partially tucked under it.

"Hey," I said.

"Hey," he answered, not bothering to turn off *Entertainment Tonight*. He was playing it cool. I assumed he wanted my new feline to be a surprise, so I played along.

"Just going into the kitchen . . ."

I looked around for signs of a new kitty but didn't see one.

"Going out to my office . . ." I walked out to the guesthouse. No kitten.

I returned and stood between Mark and the TV but he didn't break character.

"I can't find it," I said.

"Huh?" Maybe he'd forgotten today was the day.

"It's my birthday," I said.

"I know," he answered.

"Where's my . . . present?"

"I didn't get you one."

"You didn't get me one? But I thought . . ."

Mark looked at me like I was the biggest diva in the world. "I had your cat put to sleep. You know how expensive that is?"

I made a decision right then and there that I had to get out before Christmas.

I MOVED BACK TO BEACHWOOD Drive. This time, though, I didn't have as much money, so I moved lower on the hill. Mark didn't have the time to stalk me right away, since he had secured a gig as the host of *Make Me Laugh* on Comedy Central. It took up a lot of his free time. He replaced the host from the first season, who, in a twist of fate, also became a friend of mine.

One night, this first host, Ken, showed up for a visit at my new bungalow. We were talking and laughing at the kitchen table when suddenly there was a pounding at the window. It was my ex-boyfriend, Mark. I'd never seen him so aggressive. As a man who had posters of pot plants in his bedroom, I didn't expect him to move so quickly or yell so loudly. But yell he did. All the bungalow apartments faced each other. There was a courtyard garden in the middle of the complex with a few concrete benches arranged in a semicircle, just in case you wanted to look at dandelions and overgrown weeds while you drank your morning coffee. Suddenly, I could feel everyone clicking on their lights and peering out their windows to see what was going on. My Canadian side needed to put a damper on the public dramatics and so, against the judgment of my sane side, I let Mark into my apartment with Ken. Introductions weren't necessary. They knew each other well. They skipped the pleasantries and started yelling loud insults at each other, though my ex was the one doing most of the shouting. I could not get him to leave. I begged him to go. I negotiated, pleaded, conned, and sang a lullaby, but he was not swayed. I even pretended to call the police and instead called my friend Stefanie. She immediately knew what was happening and told me to call the actual police. Mark didn't buy that I was on the phone with 911, probably because I had said "dude" too many times. I hung up and really did call the police. When they asked me what the perp looked like, I said, "He's Jewish looking." After nearly half an hour of yelling, Mark finally left to drink a cup of soothing hot tea with lemon. A few minutes later, Ken, loaded up with nerves and anxiety, decided the coast was clear and made a dash for his car. But Mark wasn't finished yet. He jumped out of the bushes and there, in the middle of the modest group of bungalows, a fight broke out between two Jewish-looking fellows who had both, at one time, hosted the game show *Make Me Laugh*. Maybe "fight" is too strong a word. "Confrontation" is more accurate. It was a confrontation consisting of hoarse whispers and a little finger pointing.

I imagined my neighbors looking out their windows as the events unfolded. "Isn't that the host of *Make Me Laugh*? Wait. I think they both are." The fight ended the way all fights with Hollywood Jews end. One of them yelled, "You need therapy!" and then they both stormed to their cars, which were parked closer to each other than they would have liked. There was the *bleep, bleep* of their electronic door openers, followed by two doors slamming in quick succession. Ken's car pulled out and then Mark's car pulled behind him. They followed each other to the stop sign, where they both turned right.

About twenty minutes later, the police arrived. The younger cop took the statement and raised his eyebrows so high that his face looked like the tragic result of a gunshot wound to the forehead. Then, as he looked around my barely furnished apartment, he asked, "What do you do?"

"I'm a comedian," I answered.

He closed the small, top-ringed notebook and smiled. "Well, it's fifteen minutes of new material, right?"

The cop said that to me. Hollywood.

Chapter 14

WORKING 10:00 TO 10:15, WHAT A WAY TO MAKE A LIVING

In interviews, people often ask me what I'd be doing if I wasn't a comedian. I always shout out excitedly, "Molly Maid!" because I'm very good at cleaning off my desk if I'm supposed to be writing. I hear a lot of comedians say, "I can't do anything else!" but I think what they really mean is, "I can't do anything else that would allow me to drink on the job." However, judging by the way those blue and pink cars zip in and out of traffic, you might need to be slightly buzzed in order to be a Molly Maid.

Though it's hard to become a comedian, you can do most of the writing while you're doing almost anything else. (With the exception of your place of business. Despite your passionate pronouncements, your place of work is not "exactly like a hilarious sitcom.") Even a trip to the dry cleaner's can yield a lengthy bit about getting a funny stain out of a funny item. If there's a comedian out there who hasn't written a joke about getting blood out of a bedspread, I'd like to meet him. Not really.

I write jokes everywhere I go. My brain is always churning, looking for a joke or two. That said, while multitasking certainly has its merits, filling up a bank account doesn't seem to be one of them. Unfortunately, my mother and father, though good moral people, failed to give me or any of their other children the one thing all kids really crave from their parents: a trust fund. Lacking the necessary reserves to live a leisurely life watching television as I thumb through glossy magazines drinking iced beverages through a crazy straw, I was forced, as I had been so many times over the years, to do the unthinkable: work.

I was thirty. I was single. I was beyond broke. I was nowhere near where I thought I should be in my career. Had I really been honing and practicing my Academy Award acceptance speech all this time for nothing? To add salt on the wound, my new managers trimmed their roster and cut me. I needed a new visa, but I didn't have anyone to sponsor me. Then, William Morris, who I can only assume had been monitoring my bank account so that when it finally hit zero, they could call me and capitalize on the sting of my insufficient means, told me that I owed them nearly $40,000 in back commissions. I had no idea that I hadn't been paying them, because I'm an idiot. I was slipping into debt at an alarming rate. Actually, "slipping" is a little like saying, "I slipped in the snow," when, instead, you're falling ass over teakettle in the middle of an avalanche. Things were bad. I was in no mood to be happy. A friend was concerned enough to give me his leftover Wellbutrin. It didn't cheer me up, but I did quit cigarettes, which was great because I could no longer afford to smoke.

I needed a job. Molly Maid was no longer hiring English-speaking women with a current driver's license, so I was thrust into the less exciting world of writing for television. I found a new agent willing to sign the paperwork for my visa, but it never occurred to either of us to include him in my job search. I just assumed he was too busy expensing lunches with more successful clients. Instead, I called or e-mailed everyone I had ever worked with and said, "I'm looking for a writing job, if you know of anything!" Usually, I'd get one, maybe two e-mails back that read, "Here's a fast, inexpensive way to enlarge your penis."

Showbiz isn't good at finding suitable talent for its projects. Despite the massive amount of time and money executives spend on auditions and talent searches, it's still really all a crapshoot. The same is true for finding writers for TV shows. Television executives organize exhaustive searches for the perfect scribe for their shows and the searches almost never work out the way they want them to. Executives almost always insist that applicants submit a lengthy writing sample that includes several entire episodes, half a dozen sketches, twenty jokes, a local congressman's campaign speech, and your own obituary. These "spec packs," or samples, are mostly a formality. Writers do get hired from their samples, but it's rare. They usually wind up hiring someone who had a marginally funny tweet about Obama. Most writers are hired based on recommendations from other writers. That's how I got most of my writing jobs. I also got one by using a fart machine in the interview. The executive thought it was funny.

In the early stages of my television writing career, I got most of my jobs thanks to an already established television writer, Stefanie Wilder (now Wilder-Taylor), whose recommendations got me my first, third, fifth, sixth, and seventh jobs. Stefanie was the first friend I had who actually made a living by working in the business. She is still the best joke writer I know.

In the beginning, I mostly worked on game shows that required writers to churn out a certain quota of questions by the end of the day. I loved it! I was good at it. This shouldn't be considered bragging, since it's like saying I was good at going down stairs or blowing kisses. The job afforded me a lot of free time to write jokes for myself and spec scripts for other shows. For those of you who've never had an office job and need a little time to catch up on personal correspondence or just hone your mahjong skills, I recommend it. Also, if you don't think you've spent enough of your life in heated discussions about lunch, this might be the change you're looking for. Also, I was paid every two weeks.

I may have had to spend my days behind a desk, but my nights belonged to comedy. I had become completely obsessed with finding the perfect setup punch. I was convinced every new joke would set me on a path to fame and fortune, or at least a car with a working gas gauge. At the time, I had a Jeep with a gauge that showed my gas tank as always full. When it started to jerk and sputter, I had exactly four hundred feet to get it to a pump. It wasn't as fun as it sounds.

While I was writing for the comedy show, any thought I had was filtered through my frontal lobe, parietal lobe, and Wernicke's area—not necessarily in that order—and organized into actual jokes that I would say out loud in my car as I drove through the streets of Los Angeles looking for places that hosted stand-up shows after hours. I was looking at the usual suspects: bookstores, laundromats, or art galleries that turned into boxing gyms at five A.M. To this day, the best sets I've ever had, bar none, have taken place en route to the show. Turns out, I really get me.

My writing jobs never lasted long enough. The writing season for game shows is maybe six weeks at best. It seemed I was always in search of a new gig. I needed a day job so I could pursue my night follies. I got hired writing on a hidden camera show for NBC. A week after getting my parking pass, the boss came into the office and went on a firing rampage and told almost every employee to hit the road. In a proverb I'd like to entitle "Early Bird Gets the Shaft," I showed up late, after my boss had calmed down by secretly smoking some weed, and I escaped the pink-slip massacre. I took the good desk by the window, and later that afternoon, I got a pay raise that tripled my salary, which still gave me only a slight edge on a Walmart employee. Things were finally going my way.

The show, *Spy TV*, was a high-stakes hidden camera show on NBC. High stakes simply meant we scared the fucking crap out of people or made them cry. All in good fun! It was hosted by Michael Ian Black the first season and a pretty lady the second. Television, even the comedy kind, often requires a push-up bra and hair extensions to get the masses interested. We aired during the great hidden camera era, which was sandwiched between the trivia game show renaissance and the reality show competition epoch. At that great time in history, every network had a prank show. There were shows that pranked your boss, pranked your parents, pranked a celebrity. There were scary pranks and funny pranks and, of course, that short-lived but loveable hidden camera dynamo, "The Prank a Baby Show." There were so many prank shows that I was convinced at some point during our hidden camera filming, actors would unintentionally try to prank another network's hidden camera actors. "You're on *Spy TV*!" "Uh, no, you're on 'Skanks Love Pranks'!"

While I was working at *Spy TV*, I became so obsessed with hidden camera prank shows that one night at the World Famous Improv on Melrose, a group of three guys came in wearing trucker caps and black horned-rimmed glasses. I knew immediately they were actors on a hidden camera show. As an expert on the genus, I knew that their hats housed little cameras that captured wide shots and their glasses shot close-ups. I felt it was my job to let everyone know these guys were hidden camera actors and to steer clear of them. I don't know why I thought it was my job to alert the masses, but chances are I was just being a know-it-all killjoy, which is a hobby I still relish on the weekends. I tipped off the bartender, who told the patrons, who told the kitchen staff, who told the waiters. I didn't tell the comedians because they would obviously act like fools trying to get some camera time, and I wasn't going to let them embarrass themselves on an inferior hidden camera show for a competing network. Thanks to my efforts, the trio was ignored, or treated like pariahs, given a wide berth and watered-down cocktails.

When they went onstage, it became fairly clear that I had not unearthed a sly hidden camera operative but had instead turned everyone away from an up-and-coming comedy group who'd flown in from Kansas or somewhere to audition at the club. When I look back on my bully tactics, I like to think that though I was wrong about their objective at the club, my behavior likely brought the group closer together and stronger as comedians. I've never seen or heard about them again.

Paranoia aside, I learned a lot about making television by working on that show. The writers were credited as producers so the show wouldn't have to pay us as much as the Writers Guild insisted. We saw an idea through from its inception to its completion. We learned every part of the process, from getting an idea green-lit to hiring the cast, producing the bit in the field, and then hanging with the editor while it was assembled. I also learned a few rudimentary expressions in the fine art of passive-aggressiveness, which, if you ever really want to excel in this business, is something that is instrumental. If you can find "Rosetta Stone: Passive-Aggressive Speak," get it.

On Friday nights, all the writers gathered at a nearby bar after work and immediately started to drink heavily. After a few pints of Guinness, the head writer relaxed his odd and uptight attitude into an odder and looser attitude. He spoke too loudly. He slurred his words. He stood too close. I liked him. He was exactly the kind of weird that made me happy. I once very nearly convinced him to start wearing a cape to work. "It'll give you that added bit of panache," I told him. One day he showed me a cape, still in its package, in the drawer of his desk. If he wore it, he did so in the privacy of his office with the door closed, Nana Mouskouri blaring.

One Friday night from across the bar I heard him say in a tone that was a mix of disappointment, frustration, and tequila, "The girl is the best writer we have!" I should've been livid. How dare he be so surprised by my talent just because I'm a female? But I wasn't mad. I was thrilled. Sadly, I still am.

Chapter 15

EQUALITY IS FOR UNDERACHIEVERS, AM I RIGHT, LADIES?

For most of my career, I have ignored sexism and the possibility that it exists. I admit, I put on blinders, but only ones that match my outfit. I think it's important not to focus on the things that could potentially limit you. I try to go through the doors that are open instead of standing in front of the ones that are closed. And sometimes, believe it or not, being a woman has its benefits.

At one of my many writing jobs, the men I worked with were mandated to go to a half-day seminar on "political correctness in the office place." Because I was born a woman, I was not required to attend, since I think we all know women are amazing and superior when it comes to this stuff. I didn't squander my time alone, however. While they were at their meeting, I mustered up all the artistic will I could to draw something of a masterpiece on the big office whiteboard. It was a detailed depiction of my coworkers blowing and sodomizing the boss. I'm a pretty good caricature artist, and I think everyone was duly impressed. I heard a lot of "Oh my God!" as they walked in and bore witness to my work of art. Despite the NC-17 nature of the mural, I wasn't fired, reprimanded, or even asked to erase the artwork. I think that was because of my XX chromosome.

I WAS ONCE HIRED TO write jokes for a female-driven talk show on the lady-friendly network Oxygen. One day, two of the female executives asked me to stop writing the funny stuff, since their research showed women found comedy "abrasive and distracting." As a woman, this confused me, since I always felt great when I heard a good joke. Thankfully, they let me know that enjoying jokes was inappropriate. I was demoted from punch-up writer to setup writer, which was a less exciting job but much easier by a long shot.

This was the same show that featured two female hosts who seemed to have very limited life experience. The fact that they made it to the set every day was astonishing to me. I always greeted them with, "Well, isn't this a pleasant surprise!" At a table read for the executives, one of the hosts continually read the stage directions as part of her monologue. (This is by no means meant to suggest that she was the dumber of the two hosts.) When she finally read the words, "End Credits," the executives fawned over her and insisted on telling her how talented she was. They shamelessly beamed with pride until the energy in the room was so awkward that I started biting my hand in an effort to feel something less painful. The hosts were politely asked to leave the room so we could discuss some problems with the writing. Turns out, stage directions, like comedy, were abrasive and distracting to some women. Even before the door closed behind them, the male executive bellowed, "Are we going to fire one or both?"

They fired neither of the hosts, which caused the bellowing executive a lot of frustration. At the very least, he confided in me at one point, the show should have "hired someone with better boobs." It didn't seem to matter. The pilot was never picked up, which, as I am sure you can imagine, was a huge mistake. An earnest talk show with hosts whose reading abilities were capped at two syllables? Who wouldn't want to watch that? Later, of course, ABC stole the idea and called it *The View*. Ahem.

I WAS ALSO HIRED TO write on a movie directed by Penny Marshall's daughter, Tracy Reiner. Tracy had her own way of doing things. For example, inspired by a stroke of genius, she locked the script, which meant no scenes or pages could be changed, and started filming before the script was completed. I was asked to rewrite and drum up an ending to a script without changing any of the locations or its current cast of characters, regardless of whether any of it made sense or not. This made a page-one rewrite challenging, to say the least. I turned in the first twenty pages and got a phone call from the producers the next day. "We love it!" they told me. "This is funny. This is much better. Thank you. You are a godsend." This, if you're unclear, *is* bragging.

I went to the studio the next day and sat proudly behind my desk. A few techs popped their heads in. "We love it!" they said, holding up the new pages. I began to swivel cockily in my chair, thinking of the best place to display my Golden Globe. People love to say they keep it in the bathroom, but do they really? If you care that little about the award, why did you hire a publicist and buy a dress and write an acceptance speech that you pretended not to write? No, I'd keep mine on a chain around my neck and wear it everywhere. And I'd have a personal chiropractor come to my house every morning to help me get out of bed.

Then Tracy walked in. I snapped out of my daydream as she dropped the pages in front of me on my desk. "It's funny," she said, without the accompanying complimentary tone that usually goes with that phrase. Was this going to be like that iconic Mary Tyler Moore/Ed Asner scene where he calls her spunky and then says, "I hate spunk"?

"I hate funny," she said. Turns out, yes, we were rehearsing that iconic scene. To be fair, I don't think she realized she was regurgitating dialogue from *The Mary Tyler Moore Show*. Obviously she wouldn't have seen the show because she hates anything funny. "I hate it. HATE IT. Hate it." On the off chance I might've misinterpreted where she stood on comedy, she added, "Everyone thinks because my mom is Penny Marshall and my dad is Rob Reiner that I'm going to love comedy. I don't. I hate it."

"Okay," I said. "So this is not a romantic comedy?"

"No," she countered. "It's just a romantic. No comedy."

So there I was hard at work writing my first romantic nothing.

Tracy was able to convince successful actors to be in her movie because of who her parents were, but she wasn't a stickler for details (what good director is?) and often didn't really have a part for them to play. She'd leave them waiting in her corner office while she dashed into my windowless workplace and start flipping through the pages of the script and breathlessly say things like, "Can you give this cabdriver a few lines?" Or maybe, "Can we have a waiter start a conversation with the lead?" "On page fifty-four there's a corpse. Can we give him a five-minute soliloquy?" All right, I'm exaggerating for effect, but not by much.

After I dashed off a couple of lines for a security guard in the middle of a mall montage, Tracy came running back into my office.

"Please," she begged me. "You've got to go talk to an actor! He's upstairs and he's pissed."

Oh, he's angry, is he? Stomping mad? Well, you don't have to ask me twice!

"I'm a real actor!" he yelled at me as I was still walking toward him down the hallway. I didn't know his name, but he was certainly recognizable. One of those actors who has been in 287 movies but never quite achieves name recognition. "I didn't agree to be in a movie as a bit player. This is bullshit. I made time for this!"

"Well," I said scrambling, "I could flesh it out a little more, try to give you some more lines."

"You don't pad a part for someone like me! Fuck you!" And then he threw the script at me and it cut my hand. I bled. Being a comedy writer isn't for the faint of heart.

Back in my office, as I attached a Band-Aid to an important typing finger, Tracy came out from her hiding spot behind the door. "Thank you!" she said. "I owe you one." A "one" turned out to be an enormous gift bag with crackers and salsa and chocolate and wine. I was thrilled. Perhaps I could get another actor to throw something at me. I could get used to this. One of Tracy's assistants handed the large basket to me as I was on my way to ask one of the producers why our checks were two weeks late. By the time I arrived at the producer's office, I'd forgotten all about the original reason for tracking her down and was prattling on about the gift basket. "It's a nice thing to do," I said. "It's a gesture that lets an employee know you really care about them." The producer cocked an eyebrow and then told me something I'm only slightly embarrassed to admit that I think about all the time:

Penny Marshall has a gift-bag room.

According to legend, when Penny gets a gift bag, gift basket, or goes to an event with goodie bags, she simply puts them all in a dedicated room of her home. I wondered if this was where Tracy had gotten my southwestern basket. If it was, to be fair, though, she picked a good one. It's the thought that counts.

Now, I don't know if Tracy liked me, but she seemed to like talking at me. It seemed like she spent more time in my office talking to me than directing her films, but since I had to keep on top of the production schedule, I kept my head down, tapping away at the script and nodding occasionally. She told me her whole life story, the people who would just hang out at her house: Albert Brooks, Tony Danza, John Belushi, Art Garfunkel, and on and on. She told me having to be around these crazy, funny, talented people wasn't fun at all. The poor thing. It was really a tough way to grow up. All that laughter and nonsense. I think we can all think back to our own childhoods when we just wanted everyone to be somber and thoughtful once in a while.

As so often is the case with visionaries, Tracy's efforts were cut short. Gift bags just weren't paying the bills anymore and those grips and gaffers and camera operators demanded pay in U.S. dollars. They all walked out one afternoon and that was that. The dream of starting a romantic nothing genre was dead. I was able to get a portion of what was owed to me since I actually lived just a few blocks from her house. I sporadically showed up on her doorstep and threatened to be funny until she gave me money.

BEING A WRITER FOR TELEVISION meant hanging out with other real television writers. Through friends of friends, I met a writer named Scott Buck, and we became very close pals. He helped me write a spec sitcom script and it was like getting a master class in TV writing. He introduced me to his circle of writer friends: Jill Soloway, John Levenstein, Ron Zimmerman, Jim Vallely, Jonathan Schmock, Claudia Lenow, along with so many other talented people. They were insightful and witty and had the appropriate resentment toward justifiable targets. The women were thought of just as highly as the men. It was different from stand-up in that way.

As a female stand-up comedian, you hear male comedians and club owners say all the time that women aren't funny. People write articles about it. There's a persistence to this opinion that's kind of remarkable. As a result, as a female in the business, there's a constant low-grade need to prove yourself. Even with blinders on, you can feel the pressure. I'd tell myself, They're not talking about you, but sometimes it was hard to believe myself. I didn't feel that pressure with the writers I was now hanging out with. It wasn't that they were always kind to each other—they weren't—but tensions between people didn't have so much to do with gender. The anger they exhibited was just your run-of-the-mill backbiting and jealousy.

Jill Soloway started a show for writers called "Sit N Spin." Scott wrote a piece for the first show and asked if I would perform it. I did. The next week, Jill asked if I could read a piece of my own, which I did. I wrote and performed my own stuff on a fairly regular basis, along with other talented writers and performers I admired. I was as proud to be a part of this show as I was not losing my Quiznos loyalty card until I scored a free sandwich.

Over the course of a few months, Jill and I became friends and she let me read everything she was working on. She wrote a book, a screenplay, and was at that time a writer on the exceptionally well-written show *Six Feet Under*. Her writing was easy and unpretentious, funny and addictive. I pretended to give her notes but really I just burbled out compliments in list form. There was no denying that Jill was brilliant and I was eager to be just like her. Once, when we were rehearsing a "Sit N Spin" show, she looked at me and said, "Hey, I was wearing that exact same outfit yesterday." I scoffed and rolled my eyes and said,

"Oh, no one else is allowed to wear blue corduroys with a yellow T-shirt? I wasn't aware you owned this sartorial combination." But really, I was just buying time. I knew it wouldn't be long before she noticed the new way I parted my hair, or that I had circled the name "Jill" in my Name Your Own Baby Book.

Jill wanted to try her hand at stand-up. One night, she called me and asked me to take her to an open mic. It had to be somewhere where she could get on without saying she was a writer on *Six Feet Under*. She wanted no special treatment. In my experience, if you can get special treatment in stand-up, you take it. Hell, if you can get special treatment anywhere in life, take it. For me, not bragging to everyone that I was hanging with a writer from HBO was something of a setback, but this is what friends do for one another.

I found a place that purported to have a "true" open mic in the basement of a restaurant on the Sunset Strip. This meant we wouldn't have to pay to go on or bring a certain number of paid audience members with us to watch the shaming. After the sun set, we descended into the basement of a well-known tourist-trap restaurant and told a guy with a clipboard that we wanted to go on. He nodded. Then, we waited while comic after comic went up and performed for the animals. The place was tragic. There were very few actual audience members and by very few, I mean none. The audience was comprised entirely of comedians. Or worse, poets turned comedians. Or worse still, lawyers turned comedians. It would be an understatement to say no one was laughing. No one was listening. Jill turned to me and I was sure she was going to say, "Maybe this is a bad idea," and we'd both ditch the idea, but instead she asked, "When am I going to get to go on?" I reluctantly found the show's producer and he asked if we'd signed up. "No," I said, going on the defensive, "no one told us to do that." "Well," he said, "it's past the cut-off time." I was thrilled that we finally had our excuse to leave, but then he added, "I can only fit one of you in." I looked at Jill and she looked back at me, pleading with her eyes. "Oh, all right," I said, playing the hero. "You take the spot."

I was relieved, and Jill's face didn't show a trace of concern. In fact, she actually looked excited. She didn't seem to realize how horrible this was going to be. I even felt a little guilty giving her the spot, since I knew in my heart that she was going to crash and burn and I'd possibly have to hug her awkwardly in the car afterward. I tried to tell the emcee that she was a real fucking writer. "Don't let them destroy her!" I shouted, but he couldn't hear me over the hum of small talk in the audience. The emcee stepped onto the riser, looked at a list, and said, "Our next act is Jill Soloway." She hopped up from her seat and bounded to the stage. Looking out into the "audience," smiling like a Lotto winner, she told a joke. People began quieting down. The audience listened. And then they laughed. They listened. They laughed. Listened. Laughed. She knocked that set out of the park.

I learned a valuable lesson that night about naiveté. Jill had never bombed before, and so she didn't expect to bomb now. She couldn't know what she didn't know. I knew how bad it could be. I would have expected it. The point is, your past experiences can ruin your present ones. Even though conventional comedy wisdom says to always do every show you can, to perform at every shit place that will let you near a mic, I think there might actually be a tipping point where it works against you. It's like being in a bad relationship. You become wary of every man. You start to project failure before you even get to the second date. The same is true if you do enough crappy rooms. It is possible that only (or at least mostly) doing rooms where you feel safe creatively will make you a better comic. So I say this: If it looks like you're not going to get anything out of it artistically and you're not getting paid, go home, write four pages of jokes, and do them to your teddy bear. It's probably going to benefit you in the same way. Maybe it will benefit you more. Or if you're Jill Soloway, do whatever you want.

I certainly benefited from the workshops we had with the other writers for the "Sit N Spin" shows. We would find a spot on the floor or in the first few seats of the theater and one by one read our pieces to the group. No matter where you were on the literary spectrum, we all pretended we were equals, which felt nice. Suggestions were given, argued about, refined, and dismissed as a group. This couldn't have been more enlightening and helpful. In fact, this is exactly when I started to really find my voice as a writer and performer. I say "find," but really, I was given my voice. The other writers would say to me, "This is your voice," or, "This is something you would say." It was fascinating and great because (1) it was about me; (2) I had no idea at that point that I had a voice; and (3) it was about me.

The "Sit N Spin" shows were all meat and potato intellectuals both onstage and in the audience. The performers, who were mostly writers, wanted to write and discuss things they couldn't bring up at their day jobs on their network shows. As a comedian, murdering good taste was something that I was already doing quite effortlessly. I talked about rape, race, weight, religion, and vegetarianism, the last of which I discovered people find the most repugnant. I joked about pedophiles, I made light of cancer, I rolled offensive ideas around in comedy and pinned them up for ridicule. At "Sit N Spin," these ideas were more than tolerated. They were encouraged. When I took the same ideas onstage at comedy clubs, the audiences often reacted in shock. They were offended. They wanted comedians to talk about sex and drugs but certainly not offensive topics like eating disorders or euthanasia. For whatever reason, I didn't care. I was invigorated by my success at Jill's shows, and eventually, the jokes started working in the clubs.

MY LIFE MIGHT HAVE LACKED romance, but certainly not male companionship. Most of my encounters with men were longer than one night stands but shorter than an Academy Awards season. Not one to let anything but cottage cheese go to waste, I made a short film about all the men I dated during that period and cast my friends, Doug Benson and Patton Oswalt among them. Without doing any research at all, I'm going to go ahead and say it is the first film in which Patton strips down naked. He looks just like a baby with his clothes off and it took everything I had not to let him suckle at my breast.

The film, *Sushi Whore,* was reluctantly shot and directed by my friend Scott Buck. As a writer, he hated having to get up from behind his desk, hold a camera, and ask people to do whatever they did in the last shot again and again. Justin Roiland and Sevan Najarian, barely twenty-one at the time and now big shots at the cartoon network, did the artwork and editing. Between making fart jokes and drinking Welch's, we finished the movie, showed it once, then put it away in a drawer and eventually lost all the copies. I later made another short film with Zach Galifianakis and Eddie Pepitone, and again, showed it once and moved on to the next project. I did this again and again. I wrote, cast, filmed, edited, packed up the finished product in a box, and labeled it "Obscurity." My motto was lights, camera, action, desertion. It turns out that my art and my love life are not that different. I enjoyed the process, but after I was finished, I wasn't willing to put in any more effort.

ONE DAY, MY MANAGER DU jour called me and said the words I'd been dying to hear since I'd started this little comedy experiment nine years earlier.

"You got *Letterman*."

I was ecstatic. I couldn't believe it. I could finally let my parents know what I'd been doing with my life. The secret would be out. I'm a comedian!

I was tired of the passive rejection that showbiz loves to dole out. Contrary to popular belief, no's in the entertainment industry are pretty rare. Executives don't reject you so much as go in a different direction. They love you, but you're not a good fit for them right now. I've had some no's that have felt better than yesses. Most of the time, though, you just don't hear anything at all. The old saying "no news is good news" is wrong. No news probably means no. So when my manager called, I picked up the phone with a hopeful, "Hello?" But this time, after I hung up, I didn't have to give myself the "Next time you'll get 'em." pep talk. This time I got a definitive yes. Which brings out its own need for a pep talk. "You can do this." "You are good enough." "You don't look fat."

Any comic will tell you that Letterman was the guy. You wanted to be on his show. *The Tonight Show* might've been the pinnacle when Johnny was behind the desk, but after Leno took over, Letterman was the gold standard for comics. Not that *The Tonight Show* was something to scoff at, of course, but given the choice, most comedians would rather make their debut on the *Letterman* stage. (This survey consisted of four of my friends. I actually asked six people, but two of them said Conan and it got a little too complicated for me.)

Comics come into the public consciousness differently from before. Families don't hover around the television, waiting to watch the latest comedic discovery on channel 2 or 4. Comedy sets from late shows are no longer recorded on VHS and passed around in the back rooms of accounting offices. Shows are Tivo'd and then play in the background while the viewer is dressing for work. The sets are distributed by social media and watched at the office or on the train. If anyone is still watching television as a family, they need to stop. It's embarrassing. That's just not how it's done anymore.

Unfortunately, I was doing *Letterman* during the dead years of television, before social media but after family watching stopped being a "thing." Not as many people watched, so not as many people cared. That's not why I wanted the show. I wanted it because that's what all comedians dream about. Being on *Letterman*.

Before I got the show, I fantasized about it endlessly. Though Letterman rarely called people over to the couch, in my version, he stands and frantically waves for me to come sit down. After a lot of earnest compliments, which I brush off with a few, "Oh, you . . ."s, we have a long funny, interesting, and deep conversation. Our chemistry together is undeniable. In some versions of my fantasy, I become his cohost, while in others I am the guest host. I know this is ridiculous. Letterman never has a guest host. He shows up consistently night after night after night.

The show was not easy to get. I auditioned for it many times without sticking the landing. The first time I was slated to audition for Letterman, a producer from the show called me and we went over exactly what jokes I should prepare. I was a shoe-in. Everyone, including me, thought I would get it. During a softball game a couple of days before the audition, though, I broke my wrist. I had lots of last-minute meetings with my manager about my cast: Should I mention it? Should I play it cool? Several hundred conference calls later, we all agreed that I would not mention the cast.

I ate it start to finish. Although to this day I blame it on the cast, it probably had more to do with my nervous, stilted performance. It was so bad no one even pretended there was a chance I got the show. We just all agreed that I should've mentioned the cast. Hindsight, it's 20/20.

I had a few more auditions over the years that produced no results, and then a friend told me that I would never get *Letterman*.

"Why not?" It seemed like a shitty thing to say.

"Because Letterman doesn't like women comics. He's old school. They're all like that. They are all misogynistic assholes."

I was shocked. It sounds crazy, but I had no idea sexism was still an issue. Gender inequality seemed like something from the past that women didn't have to deal with anymore, like corsets and ironing. Any obstruction I experienced that I might've chalked up to sexism, I very quickly reframed as an industry-wide problem.

Over the course of what I will call "my career," I'd heard all kinds of people complain about all kinds of prejudice they suffered. I'd even heard white guys talking about how hard it was being a white guy, which led me to conclude that perhaps feeling discriminated against was, for most of us anyway, merely a disorder of the mind. And so, when I felt it, I usually just pushed it out of my conscious mind, down into the depths of my psyche and waited for it to rise up as uncontrollable, misplaced anger.

There were a few instances, however, that I had trouble categorizing as anything other than, "This is bullshit! This is because I'm a girl." For your scrutiny, I include the following two stories because they combine the two best things necessary to tell an unjust story about yourself. They paint me as a victim in a terribly unfair world, and they also remind you that at one time people thought I was hot. Not just hot, but *too* hot.

Horribly unjust story in which I am too hot number 1:

My friend Stefanie and I had written a spec packet to submit to the MTV Movie Awards. We'd worked hard on it, but that didn't mean that we weren't also guzzling both red and white wine in her living room. By the time I left her home in the wee hours of the morning, we were convinced it was the funniest thing ever written. Sure enough, a few days later, we were called in for a meeting. We were less drunk at the meeting and had combed our hair. This turned out to be our undoing. The executive took one look at us and said that we'd never be able to write for the MTV Movie Awards because the guys would not be able to stay focused with us around.

"Why?" we asked, though I think we knew what he was getting at, since he was smiling in a really creepy way.

"You're too pretty," he said, "I can't hire you as writers. None of the guys would ever get anything done."

Too pretty! We were too pretty to work in Hollywood. We called TMZ, but they didn't seem to realize how big and important this story was. Hollywood, which prides itself on hiring only the most beautiful people in the world, had finally met its match! We were Angelina Jolie and Jennifer Aniston combined, times a thousand. We had broken a ceiling of some kind but not the kind that gets you hired. We were the tipping point in prettiness. We were too, too, *too* pretty. And it was so very challenging for us.

Horribly unjust story in which I am too hot number 2:

Again, I wrote a submission to work on a television program. Again, I was called in for an interview. This time I wasn't told to my face I was too pretty. Instead, the executive e-mailed me later in the day to tell me he could not hire me because if his wife found out I was working for him, he'd have to get a divorce.

Again, this story emphasizes something important. My

beauty. In retrospect, it's pretty surprising that I was able to work at all.

MY FRIEND AND COMEDIAN SUZY, the self-appointed expert on misogyny in late night, had been reading a book about how to dress so that men would still find you attractive even if you were being a ballbuster in a bosslike position. Anything with lace. Frills. Pink. Sexy but tasteful. I was skeptical, but she was nothing if not compelling and maybe even a little bossy (and I'm sorry, I know you're not supposed to use that word to describe other women, but I have a limited vocabulary and saying "someone who tells you what to do all the time" seems like an extraordinarily long way to say "bossy"). With Suzy as my guide, I showed up at my second *Letterman* audition in a pink blouse and tea skirt. I felt terrible. I hated it. But if this was going to get me the show, then put a ribbon in my hair and call me Bethany.

It didn't get me the show. Please stop calling me Bethany.

I started noticing the dearth of anyone other than white males in late night. There they were, one after another, across the networks, with only slight variations in the material. Even the hosts' desks were all angled in the same direction. I'd always thought I'd be on those shows, but it became harder for me to ignore the fact that I was different from them. The landscape of late-night television, the place where I was supposed to start my rise to fame, was including very, very few women. I couldn't ignore it, and it was depressing. But I still couldn't shake the hope that maybe someday, I'd be on one of those shows.

A few months later, I was in New York and the opportunity to audition for the Letterman program presented itself again. As luck would have it, the night before I had the temerity to lose my wallet, and so the following day I was unable, as I normally would have, to spend my whole day obsessing about what jokes I would do, the order in which I would do them, what I would wear. Hair up? Hair down? Lipstick? Nail polish? Banjo?

Instead, I spent the better part of the day and early evening retracing my steps uptown, downtown, and even, appallingly, crosstown. When it became clear that I was going to be late for my audition if I didn't begin my trek to midtown, I gave up the search and set my internal GPS for Caroline's Comedy Club on Broadway, where the auditions were being held. I had no money, no identification, and this time, no cinnamon buns.

The showcase for Letterman's booker was at the same comedy club where I colossally bombed on my television debut so many years before. I had performed here many times over the years, of course, but I could never shake the feeling of inferiority that had settled deep into the osseous tissues of my bones after I bombed that first time. I didn't have time to reflect on any of that. I was late, I was sweaty, and I wasn't wearing a belt. I would have to hike up my pants every third joke.

I dumped my backpack in the corner and hit the stage. I didn't even have time to satisfy my preshow ritual of deeming the audience too well dressed, too white, or too Jersey. I was convinced that, if an audience member was wearing a T-shirt with the sleeves cut off, they were from the Garden State. I can also pick out Europeans because they wear their shirts so tight. Canadian women have short, high hair, and people from China look Asian. It's just something I'm good at.

Without time to overthink things, I just did my jokes. I fired them at the audience while pulling at the belt loop in my pants, like a hobo running to catch a train. When it was over, I got applause. I left the stage and hit the streets to look for my wallet and I found it. It was at a bar that I had already gone to and was told it wasn't there. Well, it was!

What is the moral of this story? If you lose your wallet, it's always in the last place you already looked.

The *Letterman* booker called my manager the next day and told him I got the show. But there was a catch. They weren't going to give me a date, but they would let me know when a spot opened up. Be ready, they said. Sure enough, five months later they called on a Wednesday and told me I'd be doing the show on a Friday. I was to fly out the next morning. Haha! I had beat sexism! I sat on its face.

In the meantime, my manager knew about an open mic that very night where I could run the set if I felt the need. I certainly felt the need. I wanted to do it as many times as possible before stepping out onto the *Letterman* stage. The open mic was located in a Mexican restaurant on Sunset and Gower. I walked in and was confronted by the smell of refried beans and fresh-off-the-boat beginners writing in their notebooks, doing a series of tequila shots, or shadowboxing in the corner.

I ambled over to the guy who appeared to be running the event. "Hey, hi, I'm Bonnie. Did my manager call you?"

"I don't know."

"I'm doing *Letterman* on Friday. He said you might let me run my set."

The guy looked me up and down and then walked over to the mic. "Hey, this girl says she's doing *Letterman* on Friday. You be the judge. Her name is Bonnie or something."

This was a puzzling thing for him to do, since the show hadn't started yet. People were still standing by their tables, patrons were ordering food and drink at full volume, the house lights were still up. I wasn't sure what to do, but I felt that, with all my years of experience, an answer would soon float into my head. It did not, so I walked over to the mic and stared at the confused faces of everyone staring back at me. I smiled, but this did not warm their cold demeanors. I acknowledged that while this situation was a bit odd, I was grateful to them for letting me run the set. My impromptu speech did not engender kindness. I think, and I could see all their faces very clearly with all the lights on, it actually made them more hostile. As I ran my set, I got almost zero response. I say almost zero because, to be fair, there were a couple of groans.

When it was over, I left the stage, picked up my bag, and tore ass to the exit as quickly as I could without looking like I was running for my life. As I neared my evacuation point, I heard the guy who introduced me say into the mic, "I guess we know how she got the *Letterman* show." Then I heard just a bit of cocksucking noises followed by raucous laughter before the door thankfully shut out the rest of the insults. I guess I hadn't quite silenced sexism just yet.

Normally, I would've cried, but I hadn't started drinking yet. Instead, I reminded myself that I was doing *Letterman* and they were not. Incidentally, this is how I now cope with any situation that puts me in a bad mood. For example, when I am informed that my Chase account is overdrawn, I say, "I did *Letterman*." When I spill an entire bag of popcorn kernels on my kitchen floor, I say, "I did *Letterman*." When someone cuts me off in traffic I yell, "I did *Letterman*, asswipe!" And then pretend-reach for a firearm.

With the Mexican-restaurant episode behind me, I flew to New York the next night and met up with Eddie Brill, who was the *Letterman* booker at the time. He and I went from club to club and I ran the set for him. This is standard operating procedure. Most late-night shows are very specific about the material they want you to do on their shows. Sometimes they even make you change a word that seems completely innocuous. Eddie was very hands-on in this process. He gave me notes after each time

I did the set. Some comedians complain that this stifles their creativity. I thought I would be one of those comics, since I've never been good with authority, getting notes, or working after ten P.M. without copious amounts of alcohol, but the truth was, Eddie made my set better. He took out words and phrases that didn't need to be there. Sometimes, you set up a joke in a particular way and it works, so you never revisit it. You just keep doing it the same way every time without realizing there is a better way to set it up. Sometimes, you do a certain gesture the first time you try a joke and without even thinking about it, you repeat the gesture every time you do that same joke. Two years later, you think, what am I doing with that arm? You don't even know what the mime was supposed to be anymore.

That night, as I lay my head down on an eight-thousand-thread-count pillowcase in a five-star hotel, I knew I was ready. The next day, I'd meet my comedy idol. I'd check off one of my most sought-after goals. I'd be able to tell my parents, "See? I did make the right choice." I ran my set in my head 208 more times and fell asleep as the sun was coming up.

The next morning, I had breakfast in the hotel with a journalist who was writing a little blurb about me for *Marie Claire* or *Glamour,* I can't remember which. It's interesting to point out that the rarity of a female doing stand-up on late-night television attracted the attention of a national publication. The journo dashed my dreams in a single sentence. He told it to me as casually as he was telling me I had a little egg on the side of my mouth. Letterman was not doing the show that night. I nearly spilled my orange juice (though I'd only ordered a small, so it had almost all evaporated anyway). A quick call to my manager confirmed it. Letterman was sick. This could not be happening. He never missed a show. Never. Now, suddenly, when I had finally jumped through all the hoops to appear on the program, he was going to take a sick day? How dare he? I could barely finish my mile-high stack of pancakes. I chewed angrily for a few bites and then asked if the show was going to be canceled.

"Apparently there's going to be a guest host," the journalist told me. That guest host was Megan Mullally who, at the time, was starring on *Will & Grace*. She was kind of the perfect guest host. She was silly and funny and every gay man in America would be watching.

When I made it to the studio that night, there was very little drama backstage. This was old hat to everyone on the show. They did my hair and makeup while the first guest, Molly Shannon, was onstage. While I watched her and Megan on the monitor in the hair and makeup room, it suddenly dawned on me that this was exceptionally uncommon. Two very funny women were holding court on late-night television. I was about to be a part of something special. If they got my fucking hair done in time. The two women in charge of my head were talking about a birthday party, for God's sake. I was about to make my *Letterman* debut!

I stood backstage while a very recognizable Biff Henderson put a mic on me and told me where to stand. All the while I couldn't stop thinking, Oh my God! He actually works here.

"I'll tell you when to go out," he said as Megan was announcing my name. Now? He shook his head. Now? Nope. Now? Not yet. Good lord, the show is going to be over by the time you tell me to walk out!

Finally, he nodded. Now. I stepped through the curtains.

Jim Gaffigan, who'd already done *Letterman* a number of times, told me to walk out onto the stage and say to myself, I'm on *Letterman*. I thought this was terrible advice. I assumed the best thing to do was pretend that you were just doing comedy in *any venue, any town*. But the minute I hit my mark, an *X* on the stage, and saw Paul Shaffer to my right, I reminded myself, You're doing *Letterman!* And a huge smile spread across my face. Jim was right. Live in the moment. The set couldn't have gone better. I even got called over to the couch, and despite the fact that it wasn't Letterman, I was thrilled to be sitting there talking to Megan before she signed off.

THE SECOND TIME I DID the show, he was there in the flesh.

A little over a year later, I was packing for a lovely summer week in hot, sweaty North Carolina where the crowds are great but the weather is draining. I was shoving every tank top I had into my carry-on, even though I knew I could never do stand-up with exposed arms. I've seen women do it, but they are clearly on some kind of antianxiety medication. I was folding a cargo jacket that I hoped was thick enough that I wouldn't sweat through it but thin enough that I wouldn't faint mid punch line when Eddie called me. Could I have a set prepped for next Tuesday? It was less than a week away. I assured him I could. I stopped packing long enough to type out a complete transcription of my jokes. It's odd to write out your comedy like that. You wonder if the person reading the joke is going to understand how to hit the punch line. If they're going to understand your timing. If you should write PAUSE or use ellipses every seven words. Should you write out the hand gestures? "Hey, Eddie, I wave here coyly, not dramatically. Each finger going down before the other one starts. Like an audience of five doing the wave."

When you're tapping away at a keyboard, you have the tendency to edit and to add. Suddenly, as you're writing out the joke you've done seven hundred times, you realize the word "contemplate" might work better than the word "think," and if you said, "Horses are like that," after the last tag, you might be able to squeeze out another laugh. Before you know it, you have seventeen extra minutes of material. *Letterman* sets run exactly 4.5 minutes, or between twelve and fourteen jokes in the classic setup, punch line, tag, tag formula. Economy of words is vital.

With the set approved, I left North Carolina on Sunday morning and flew to New York. I checked into my five-star New York hotel and paced until sundown. Then, in a montage of taxicabs and comedy clubs, I ran the set a half dozen times as Eddie looked on. After some of the sets, he offered suggestions, like using "with" instead of "and." In television, no word is above reproach.

I could not believe I was getting another shot at this. The last time was exciting, but this time Letterman would finally see me. The night of the show, I pulled on the same pair of jeans I'd worn my first time on *Letterman*. I stood backstage. I waited for the "Now." When I got it, I hit the stage, said to myself, "I'm doing *Letterman*!" and began the set. Again, the audience was warm and receptive.

And then, just like in my fantasies—well, not exactly, because in my fantasies I get waved over to the couch, but still, this is pretty good—Mr. Letterman himself walked over to where I was standing at the mic and shook my hand. "Nice set," he said. This was it. This is why I do it, I thought. This makes all the heartaches and headaches worth it.

I smiled my best smile, the one I reserve for heads of state and three-week-old babies. "Thanks for having me," I said, with as much magnetism as I could conjure up. Then I dropped the mic at my feet. Not like a rapper drops the mic after free-styling some sick beats, but like a comedian with sweaty palms. I bent down, picked it up, and put it back into the stand. And then, because words are my business, my God-given talent, I turned to Letterman and repeated the exact thing I'd already said, but this time with less magnetism, "Thanks for having me."

Dave looked down at me. He was not smiling. He was not magnetic. What I saw was a slightly annoyed face full of heavy pancake makeup, which is not how one thinks of the King of Late Night. I finally had the chance to meet the coolest, funniest man in the world and all I could think was, I prefer a more natural look on a man of a certain age. And then he spoke to me like an annoyed teenager: "Okayyyyy, byeeee." Whatever. I did *Letterman* and you—well, you are Letterman, but still. Whatever.

I put my designer blinders back on. This business is tough for everyone.

Chapter 16

THE B TEAM

By this point, I'm sure you've noticed I've run through a lot of managers and agents. And you might be thinking, What do they do exactly? Why are they necessary? Is it not their job to take your creations and do something with them? Cue polite laughter. It's a common misconception. An agent is a very busy man or mannish woman who spends an enormous amount of time trying to get other people to think they're successful, and that can involve an endless amount of shoe shopping. It's harder than you think finding the most expensive pair of Italian leather loafers. As for managers, no one knows *what* they do exactly.

In most cases it's difficult to ascertain if an agent or a manager is useless or if the work is subpar. First, you must realize both points are moot. The agent's opinion of the client's work is inconsequential, since no one in a sales position seems to know if comedy is good, except by accident. What the agent is selling is the client, not the work. That means the client must have a "cool factor" and this is where it gets complicated. Sometimes, having a cool factor means not being cool at all. Sometimes it means lacking charisma and being unable to maintain eye contact or an erection. Being cool is that *je ne sais quoi* that makes other people think that you know what you're doing when really, you're pretending not to care if they think you know what you're doing. The wardrobe for being cool changes, but the sentiment is always the same: "I don't care what you think." More often than not, a lot of thought has gone into promoting this illusion of indifference.

When the industry embraces an agent's client, sometimes for reasons that are hard for the layperson to understand, it makes the agent's job considerably less time consuming. They no longer have to "sell" the client based on actual past triumphs. Now they can show a picture of their client standing with a top-forty rapper and wearing a frayed flannel button-down and skinny jeans and get back to shoe shopping.

I've never been cool, but as long as I can remember, I've really wanted to be. I think I am physically unable to be cool because my desire to be cool is outweighed by my inability to follow the "rules of cool." I hate conformity, which has made it practically impossible for me to fake being cool with industry types.

My list of past representatives range from tough guys to pot-heads, scatterbrains, the uptight, and dandies, to white women with cornrows and a juggler-turned-executive. I had one manager who only dated women who were physically perfect in every way, meaning that they were intimately familiar with the wonders of modern plastic surgery and hair extensions. Being that kind of beautiful has always impressed me. The spray tanning alone would eat up a good portion of your week. Anyway, Martin (his name has been changed because I can't remember his real one) himself was very meticulous about his personal appearance, and I couldn't shake the feeling that I smelled of garlic whenever I was within ten feet of him, possibly because of the way he curled up his nose whenever I approached. Appearance was very important to him. One day, I made fun of his socks in front of other agents and forty-eight hours later, I was looking for a new manager.

I also had a female manager who resembled Meg Ryan pre lip and cheek enhancement. She was dizzy and scattered but wasn't charming like Meg Ryan, unless you count that movie where she played an alcoholic. (Why do movies depict female alcoholics as so much more interesting and fun when they're drunks?) She would sometimes call and give some information and then say, "Shirley? Wait, who'd I call? Oh, hahahahahahaha I think I called the wrong number. Shirley? This message is for Shirley. If this is not Shirley, disregard." Shirley was clearly working more than I was and so the relationship didn't work out.

I had a lawyer/manager who would accuse me of throwing auditions if I didn't get the part. You know what? Maybe I did throw a few. I had a tendency to mock the material in front of the producers if I didn't think it was very good. It's amazing, given my propensity for working all the angles, that I'm not a bigger star of stage and screen. This particular manager had a real nasty side to him and that's probably why I stayed with him longer than I should have.

As varied as my representatives were, there was one thing they all had in common: the ability to avoid me.

When I could get them on the horn, I felt an enormous pressure to not waste their time, and so I dispensed with the formalities and the small talk and launched right into the nature of my call. "Why aren't I working?" The direct approach had limited appeal and people—wrongly, I'd like to think—thought of me as difficult. Thus, time after time, I was told that "This isn't a good fit" or "We're moving in a different direction," and I'd be thrown back into the big, blue ocean to fight over agent bait with all the other unrepresented fish.

If I wanted to keep an agent, I needed to learn the fine art of being passive-aggressive. It wasn't going to be easy. My brain had already made most of the neurological connections it was ever going to make and it would take a tremendous amount of effort to rewire it. Once, when an agent asked me to go with him to his mother's for dinner, I responded, "No, thank you." This is, as I'm sure most of you are aware, completely unacceptable. When you don't want to do something, you must always say, "Of course, I'd love to! I wouldn't miss it for the world." And then, when the day in question rolls around, come down with what you think might be Ebola and despite being utterly disappointed, decide that it's probably safer for everyone if you just stay home. In Hollywood, you must learn to use extra words. Smile when you're saying something nasty. Start gossip with the phrase, "I absolutely love her like a sister but . . ." It's not uncommon in showbiz circles to see two people embrace and remark on how insane it is that it's been so long and "Good lord! We must do cocktails soon!" and then later, out of earshot, watch one of them asking a third party who the hell it was they just hugged. Los Angeles is so gripped by the plague of passive-aggressiveness, I once saw my neighbor say to his dog, "No rush, it's not like I've got a billion other things to do."

THE THING I'D LIKE PEOPLE to remember when they hear the story I'm about to tell is that though I am not a cool person, I'm not really a bad person. Not really. Of course, I'm not proud of everything I've ever done. I have regrets. I've pretended to send gifts that I claimed later must have gotten lost in the mail. I've worn stuff and then returned it. I've said hurtful things when it wasn't in the heat of the moment. But I want to make this perfectly clear: I have never, ever killed anybody. Not intentionally.

One time, though, and I'm not proud of this—in fact, it's pretty shameful and when I don't have other more pressing reasons to hate myself, I will conjure up this memory in the middle of the night and will toss and turn until the sun comes up. Anyway. One time I almost, *almost*, let an agent of mine die during lunch.

Now, I had had this particular agent for only a few weeks—thus our lunch. I don't know how it works in New York, but in L.A. every agent comes with one free meal, a lunch, usually at the beginning of the relationship. Later, when you start making them money, you get a dinner. Let's put it this way: I'd cashed in on several thousand lunches but had rarely valeted at a posh eatery after dark.

If I was going to succeed in L.A., I needed to get with the program. More important, I needed to get an agent. I found one young, well-dressed upstart willing to take a risk on me at a small boutique agency owned by his father. He'd been preparing for this his whole life, he told me. Since he was a young boy, uh, er, younger boy, he was taught at the knee of his father, one of the greats in representing moderately successful actors.

Our first meeting went well. It was fun, almost flirty. We discussed all the big things I would do with my career. My magazine covers. My movie franchise. My fashion line. I brought up my idea for a series of stand-up shows in dry-cleaning venues across the country. He looked confused. "They already have everyone's pictures on the wall," I told him. You could tell it wasn't something he could conceptualize. I was too out of the box. Too ahead of my time. Still, I didn't call him an idiot. I didn't throw up my hands and yell, "Why am I smarter than everyone?" No, I just crossed and uncrossed my legs several times and smiled without showing too much teeth.

This time, I thought to myself, I'm going to add a little passive to my aggressive. I'm going to do it right. A few days later when I called for my free lunch, I didn't say, "You promised we would go for lunch." I said, "Hi, how are you? How's the family? How's your dad? I was just thinking about how lucky I am to be represented by you and maybe, if you're not busy, if you can find the time, if you are in the country next week, we should have a lemonade together and just make sure we're both on the same page." "Yes," he said. "Let's do lunch. I'll have my assistant set it up." Nailed it.

I practiced my passive-aggressiveness all weekend. I told my neighbor I would love to go to her one-woman show called "Love and Penises" and then never even found out when or where it was. I told my landlord that he could definitely fix my sink at seven A.M. if he really needed to. That was probably more important than me sleeping anyway, and I might have told him that I was a few months' pregnant. I made a date with a guy to go to the movies and then brought a few of my friends along. I also might have told him I was pregnant. I had progressed leaps and bounds. By the time Monday rolled around, I was ready. "I'm ready," I said to myself as I walked into the upscale diner.

I made small talk, brought up the velocity of the breeze, and clucked about the latest political snafu. When the waitress arrived, I said, "I'm not really very hungry," and then ordered the lumberjack breakfast. My new agent ordered the chopped tuna-topped salad and asked her to hold the onions and the peppers. "I've got a big meeting after this," he explained after the waitress had left.

"I love big meetings," I said. "The bigger the better."

We talked about the shows we liked and even though he didn't understand television at all, I managed to like everything he did. He did me the same courtesy, which was nice. It couldn't have been going better.

And then, he started choking.

I politely looked the other way. He choked for a long time, but I didn't do anything. I scanned the other patrons in the restaurant and focused on the bustle of the lunchtime rush.

He grabbed at his water. He gurgled and chugged and clawed at his throat. I just waited for it to be over. He was turning blue. This is getting awkward, I thought. But I just kept sitting there, sipping my iced coffee.

When he finally dislodged the chunk of not-so-chopped tuna from his airway and sucked in several lungfuls of upscale diner air, he turned to me, his face drained of any goodwill that I had built up during the first half of our lunch, and said, "Why didn't you help me?" I really didn't know why not, but I had to think of something. I couldn't very well let it go at "I don't really like agents."

I came up with "I didn't want to embarrass you."

"You didn't want to embarrass me?" he repeated. He must have been really mad because he did something I had never seen any agent do: he completely dropped the passive from his passive-aggressive. "You are not a nice person," he said as he waved to the waitress for his bill. He slammed a couple of twenties between the billfolds and stormed out. I finished my eggs, making sure to chew each bite carefully. Our working relationship ended shortly after and so I was never able to cash in on my free dinner.

THE UNIVERSE KEEPS GIVING YOU the lessons you need to learn until you finally get it right. I was soon faced with another opportunity to save the life of an agent. It's still not clear to me though whether I'm supposed to help them live or let them die.

I got a manager I would stay with for a long time. This manager was the one who paved the way for my *Letterman* spots and later my HBO and Comedy Central specials. We liked each other. We got each other. I trusted him. He had a pool and a Wiffle ball court and liked to use sports analogies, many of which I didn't understand. He told me that I needed a team, an agent and a publicist, but since I had nothing to publicize, I'd best first get an agent. The agent he wanted me to meet had once been a performer himself and so, according to my manager, would understand me. The agent was a very small man with a very big personality and by that I mean he consumed a lot of coke. The first meeting we had, he sat behind his desk and pointed a remote at a television on the other side of his office. He wanted me to see him at his finest, as a child actor. As I watched a twenty-years-younger version of my agent cracking jokes in a mid-Atlantic accent, I heard a snort and turned around. My agent wiped his hand across the top of the desk, brushing off a bit of dust, and pinched his nose with the other. Then he waved his hand back toward the TV. "Watch," he insisted, "watch."

He liked hanging out at comedy clubs, and one night, he showed up at the Improv on Melrose and attempted to ply me with cocaine. I told him I preferred pot and, within a few minutes, we were in his car. He took off the middle section of the steering wheel and gave me one of the half dozen joints he had stashed there. "I don't like pot," he explained. "I just keep a few for the ladies." I liked that he thought of me as female, and he always had one for me after that.

He developed something of a crush on me and often told me I was "uncommonly" beautiful, a compliment no girl can quite understand or deny. I don't like to generalize, but short men find me attractive and I'm pretty sure it has something to do with my lack of nose hairs. I look good if you're looking up at my head, which is weird because once, I accidentally turned on FaceTime and saw myself from that angle and immediately took thirty sleeping pills. When I woke up forty-six hours later, the bags had disappeared from beneath my eyes and I looked better.

Though it might surprise you to hear that this agent was fired from his agency, I am told he lost his temper and yelled obscenities at a female colleague. I'm sure that had nothing to do with his infatuation with a certain white powder. He returned to his first profession, performing, and I often got late-night phone calls from him, begging me to marry him or at least come by for a visit.

One night, he called me to say good-bye. I asked him what he meant by that. At first, he told me he just meant he wasn't going to call me anymore. That he was "giving me up." "Oh," I said, breathing a sigh of relief, "I thought you were suicidal. I didn't want to have to rush over there." To his credit, he immediately homed in on my weakness and started blurting out clichéd suicidal patter. "This is it," he said. "This is the end. I just can't do it anymore."

I knew I was going to have to go over there. Still, I tried to get myself off the hook. "Promise me you're not going to do anything stupid," I pleaded, but he knew he had me. "I can't promise you anything except that this is the last time you'll ever hear from me," he told me. I yelled at him to stop fucking around and he told me he had a belt over a door. "It'll all be over soon," he said quietly.

What if he isn't hoaxing me? I thought. On the one hand, I knew he was, but on the other hand, I'd promised myself that I'd never again look the other way if an agent was dying. Even though I really did not want to get out of bed, I got out of bed, pulled on a pair of jeans, and got in my Jeep.

When I got to his apartment, he was downright jovial as he answered the door. "Welcome!" he said, ushering me in. "You're an asshole," I responded, and he grinned from ear to ear. His place was spotless, because wouldn't you spend your last few minutes alive tidying up your place? I saw a belt hanging over a closet door. A prop he hung, no doubt, moments after hanging up the phone.

He opened the fridge. "Do you want some chicken parm from the Palms? I had dinner there tonight and brought home my leftovers." I took the chicken parm and ate it cold, standing at his counter with my coat on.

"Your apartment is so clean," I said.

"A cluttered home is a cluttered mind," he answered without irony. I finished the parm, used the bathroom, declined the joint, and drove home.

JOE BODOLAI WAS NOT AN agent or a manager but a friend who guided me throughout my comedy career. Although I hadn't seen him for a couple of years, we did continue to e-mail each other, albeit sporadically. Most recently, I had sent him a story outline for a screenplay that my friend and writing partner Stefanie and I were planning to write. Joe sent back scene after scene of hilarious dialogue. We'd read the scenes aloud, crack up, and then e-mail him back: "Hilarious!" Encouraged by our enthusiasm, he just kept sending more. "Prolific" isn't the right word for it. When he wrote three pages of dialogue for a character called Quiet Guy, we suspected he might be going off the deep end.

One day, I got an e-mail from Joe's wife. I was curious as I clicked it open and then shocked by what she wrote. She was certain that I was having an affair with her husband. Let me be very clear before we continue with this story: I was not.

The e-mail was accusatory, and full of blunt claims, but was surprisingly well written and I liked her, despite the fact that she called me bad names and was so wrong about the nature of my relationship with her husband.

Near the end of the note she included a bit of interesting advice. I'm paraphrasing, of course, but it was along the lines of: "You're sleeping with the wrong guy. You think he can help your career," she wrote, "but he can't even help himself." I know she must have been angry with Joe if she thought he was cheating on her, but it's kind of a funny thing to write to some-one who you suspect is sleeping with your husband, essentially saying, "Hey listen, slut, I'm going to save you from this piece of shit." Again, it made me like her. Under different circum-stances, we might even have been good friends.

I gently explained in my return e-mail that I hadn't even laid eyes on him in two years. He lived in Toronto and I was here in Los Angeles. Even when I was in his actual presence, Joe and I had never exchanged anything more than a brotherly hug. We were in no way entangled in a sexual relationship. Perhaps I was unwittingly involved in an emotional affair, but I'm not sure it was one worthy of suspicion. We only talked about writ-ing and comedy. Besides, to me, cheating is the old-fashioned, time-honored dick in the mouth.

But her e-mails kept coming. She wanted me to never e-mail him again. I agreed but the accusations would not cease. Joe's wife was a good writer, deeply intelligent and unintentionally funny. She was so angry and so far off base it was literally com-ical. Because I was not very mature, and because I myself had not been through rocky times in a marriage, perhaps I wasn't as sensitive to her heartbreak as I could have been. I chose to read our e-mail exchanges on stage one night. It turned out that Angry Wife and I were a hit. I read them at another show, and again, the response was what every comedian hopes for when they're accused of sleeping with someone else's spouse: raucous laughter. So the letters went into the act. I explained to my new comedy partner in one of my e-mails that I was reading the letters in front of a live comedy club audience, which gave the letters a meta vibe when I got to this particular part in the show. Maybe she thought I was kidding. In any case, she kept writing them and I kept reading them.

In the meantime, Joe e-mailed me under a pseudonym and from a new e-mail account. I felt fine exploiting the correspondence from his wife, but I was more reluctant to throw a wrench into his relationship. Still, he was my friend and my loyalty did lie with him, so I felt compelled to answer every third or fourth e-mail. But the fun had to end at some point. One night, I arrived home to a ringing phone. I answered it. It was her. Her voice was strong but feminine, with a slight French accent. She sounded pretty. "I know you still write him!" she said. In the background I heard Joe yell out, "I'm sorry, Bonnie!" I imagined him duct-taped to a chair, in the middle of a warehouse, one lightbulb dangling over his head, creating long, stark shadows. "I'm sorry! Bonnie!" Slap. There was no slap, but it wouldn't have surprised me if there had been.

His wife ignored him and continued pleading with me. "You are ruining our marriage!" she said, her French accent turning the word "marriage" into "mirage." The situation was no longer funny. Maybe it had never been. Whatever had been amusing me before had turned tragic. I could hear the pain in her voice. She told me he was sick. "Seeek," she said, which at the time I took to mean depraved. Years later, when I looked back on this conversation, I'm pretty sure she meant it as actually sick. Bipolar, probably.

I felt awful, even though I had very little to do with the problems in their "mirage." This time, when she asked me to never contact him again, I agreed. "Sorry, Joe!" I yelled, unsure that he ever heard me. And I never contacted him again.

Never.

He tried to e-mail a few times under different names with

different e-mail addresses, but I never wrote him back. I made a promise and I kept the promise. It was a pact that never sat well with me. Joe had never been anything but encouraging, and for that, I abandoned him.

Ten years later, soon after I had been bullied by society into opening an account on Twitter (it's sooo amazing!), Joe tweeted at my Twitter handle. I didn't respond, out of habit, but something in me started wondering, Why am I still doing this? He e-mailed a few days before Christmas 2011. Again, I didn't respond, but I thought to myself, Why am I still upholding a promise to a woman he's probably not even married to anymore?

Christmas morning, 2011, I opened a new iPad from my husband and began surfing the Web, testing it out. On the HuffPo Web site there was a headline, EX *SNL* WRITER KILLS HIMSELF, LEAVES SUICIDE LETTER. I clicked on it, wondering in a very minor way if I might know this person.

I did.

It was Joe Bodolai.

He drank antifreeze and vodka as he penned a suicide note. A very long suicide note. In it, among many other things, were some very nice thoughts about me and one slightly disturbing memory about me not wearing a bra on my first special.

Joe also took the time to highly recommend the podcast I do with my husband, *My Wife Hates Me* (available on iTunes).

Joe and his wife had been divorced for some time, something I don't think anyone saw coming. In retrospect, of course, I wish I had responded to his tweets and his e-mails. Joe never stopped encouraging me, even as his world closed in around him. He even managed to give me a pat on the back after his death.

I'm not sure I would have continued in the early days of my career if it hadn't been for Joe, and for that, I'll never forgive him. He gave me good advice and he gave me bad advice, but having someone care enough to give any advice at all is invaluable. If you get someone in your corner, do whatever you can to keep them there. Behind every successful person is someone stabbing them in the back. It helps to have allies who can reach the wound for you and put a little Band-Aid on it.

I regret many things in my life, most of which I did while drinking on an empty stomach, but letting this relationship fade into the ether is something I really wish I'd handled differently. Joe was sick, obviously, and I don't know that I could've changed his final decision, but maybe I could've given him a pep talk after all the ones he'd given me.

Chapter 17

MIDSEASON PROGRAMMING IN THE GARDEN OF GOOD AND EVIL

I don't mind when men call me sweetheart. I guess when you've been called a cunt as many times as I have, "sweetheart" doesn't really have much of a sting.

I SAID "CUNT" ON THE second season of *Last Comic Standing*. Yes, that was me. (All this reading and you finally figure out who I am.) It'd be a better story if I had screamed it at someone during a heated moment in a reality show and then discussed it ad nauseam for six more episodes, taking individuals aside at dinner parties to defend my choice of verbiage. I did the less sensational thing. I premeditated it. I wrote it as the punch line of a joke.

Now hear me out. I thought the joke would be a great way to open my set in the semifinals. I didn't do it to be provocative. (I didn't!) I really thought it was a good, clever joke. I still do. My concern was that I would turn the audience off before I really got rolling. I wasn't oblivious to the power of that word, at least in this country. Across the pond, Europeans spit it out at an alarming rate, sometimes in the middle of the afternoon or in the presence of their children! That's the funny thing about words. The impact they have is completely, utterly dependent on whether or not you have an accent.

Here in the U.S., where everyone speaks normal English real good, the word "cunt" can cut like a knife. On a prime-time network show where the audience votes for the contestants, I probably would've been better off to choose a joke that used words that didn't make an absurdly high percentage of women seethe with anger. But I did it because I thought it would make Brett Butler laugh. She was one of the judges on the show and not only did she laugh, she nearly fell out of her chair. Mission accomplished.

I was secure in the knowledge that the joke would never reach the purported eight million people watching at home. Not only is NBC extremely curse adverse, *LCS* didn't have time to use the entirety of everyone's act. Each comedian did somewhere in the neighborhood of five minutes' worth of material, but the show only had time to televise ten to thirty seconds of each person's set. They had four and a half other minutes to choose from.

While calculating the success rate of this joke, however, I had failed to factor in the Hockey Principle, which has trickled into nearly every other form of entertainment, most notably reality shows and Fox News. The Hockey Principle clearly asserts that, despite people's claims that they watch hockey for the passing and scoring, what they really want to see are the fights. In one fell bleep, I became something of the villain on the show. Even my family was stunned that I had resorted to the ludicrously low tactic of shocking the audience. "I understand that you had to do something to stand out, Bonnie, but the *C* word?" wailed my oldest sister, Audrey, when I spoke to her on the phone. "I'm not sure what to say." Rendering my oldest sister speechless was something I'd been attempting and failing at for a lifetime, so maybe this could be considered something of a win.

Some of the other contestants, who were more schooled than I in the machinations of the reality show juggernaut, used my expletive transgression as a reason to rally against me. There were times when I would walk into a room where several of the comedians had gathered and they would suspiciously disperse, taking out notebooks or digging through their pockets for things they could not seem to find. I made a few jokes about coalitions to alleviate some of the tension, but I'd find myself laughing alone. It's hard to believe, since I have now watched enough reality TV to consider myself an expert, that I really didn't believe they were establishing alliances. We were professional comedians, for God's sake. I thought we were going to be funny. Hell, I was there to make friends.

Before I starred on the second season of the show, I was grunting my way through life in oversize T-shirts and absurdly low-cut jeans. I was driving a dirty Jeep with a faulty gas gauge and a roof that I didn't know how to put back on. My most prized possession was a red and black backpack that I took with me everywhere. I couldn't leave it in the Jeep. It didn't have a roof.

My home was furnished in a neomodern minimalist scheme that hadn't yet caught on and, honestly, still hasn't. In my apartment, I had four coffee cups, a George Foreman grill, and no TV. While I agree that not having a TV was a good move, since at this point we're all aware of the fact that it is an imagination-depriving, brain-rotting, intellectually-diminishing technology, I really didn't have any books, either. I'd paid off all my credit card debts and was living the grand life of a newly immigrated single mother with all of the off-brand kids' cereal but none of the kids.

I watched the entire first season of *Last Comic Standing* at my job as a writer on *The Man Show*. This was the season Doug Stanhope and Joe Rogan were the hosts. We stood around the TV in Doug's office and watched the show, as all comics did, with horror and revulsion. We were appalled at the comedians they'd passed over and equally sickened by some of the talent they'd green-lighted. I was nervous for the people I knew and delighted when the audience got behind them.

When the top-ten comics were chosen and moved into a house to live together for the remainder of the competition, I was truly rooting for all of them. Except for one guy, Rich Vos. I'd never met him and, in my opinion, he was a fucking asshole. Everyone who's ever encountered Vos has a story about how much they hated him when they first met him. He turns people off immediately, but later can somehow carve out a relationship with people based on deep affection while still maintaining his complete and utter dickishness. I followed the same trajectory as everyone else. At first exposure, I found him to be arrogant and unpleasant. As the episodes progressed, however, I looked forward to seeing this asshole's face fill the frame. I was happy when he was onscreen. He was irreverent and disrespectful and irrepressibly mischievous. Just my type. Two years later we would be married.

The first time I met Vos in person, I was feeling pretty good about myself, since I was wearing both a dress and deodorant, which only happens once every seventeen years. I was in New York for a week to do stand-up and attend Jim Gaffigan's wedding. (I still haven't gotten him a gift. You have up to ten years, right?) Jim's reception was a block and a half from the Village's Comedy Cellar, and comedian Ian Bagg, who was also attending the wedding, was smart enough to book himself several spots at the club that night. I tagged along as we voyaged back and forth between the venues.

As I walked down the stairs toward the show room, I saw Vos standing in the doorway, waiting to go on.

"Hey," I said, holding out my good hand, "I like you on the show. I'm a big fan."

"You're that comic broad," he said. I perked up at this. I was recognized! Then he continued, "I'd hit on you, but I'm on a date." The emcee introduced him and he made his way through the crowd onto the stage. I left before he was done. I had to get back to Jim's wedding before they shut down the cheese station.

After that, Vos stalked me for a few more nights. When I found out he drove a Mercedes, we ended up going for pizza the night before he was scheduled to leave for Las Vegas to film the finale of *Last Comic Standing*. For about two hours, he ran through everything he said and did that didn't make it on to the show, then he spent a few minutes trying to convince me that I'd be an idiot not to audition for the second season.

"No, no, no," I assured him. "It's not for me. I'm not that kind of comedian."

Cut to me standing frozen before the two *Tonight Show* bookers who were the judges for *Last Comic Standing*, season two. (I signed a five-million-dollar gag order to prevent me from talking about this, but since I no longer have credit card debt, I think I can afford to risk it.) It was daytime. There was no audience. The houselights were on as high as they could go. It's amazing that I was struggling to stammer out a set, since this is the exact environment where a comedian can really shine. "That's enough," said one of the judges. And that's that, I thought, but it wasn't. "Come back tonight for the live show." I had made it through the first round without telling a joke. Maybe I would make it to the finals without using up any of my material. "And wear a dress. Show your legs," the lispy one called out as I left the show room.

I dug out my one and only skirt for the live show and moved on to the semifinals. I prepared for my future network television appearances by buying as many skirts as I could afford: two. This brought my total to a whopping three skirts. (I haven't fact-checked this, but I'm confident it's right. I'm pretty good at math.) I got mustard on the khaki one before I made it to the stage. No one seemed to notice that I wore it backward. I wore one of those three skirts every time I performed on *Last Comic Standing.* The producers didn't tell me that I had to wear a skirt, but they didn't yell "whore" when I did, either.

There's a lot of discussion among the female comedy community about what one should wear onstage. Joan Rivers told me you should dress well out of respect for the audience, which I took to mean that comics should match their sports socks. On *The Howard Stern Show,* Amy Schumer said looking sexy onstage makes men pay more attention. I test-drove this theory at home while my husband was watching the U.S. Open and ended up using my tube top to blow my nose and dry my eyes. In my humble opinion, a woman comic should look as though she very recently escaped a cult by passing herself off as a local fifteen-year-old farm boy. It works for me. I don't want the audience to think about my sexuality, not until I've figured it out for myself.

Above all else, I want the audience to think I'm funny and I want to lead with that. While I was on *Last Comic Standing,* I also wanted to make it as far as I could on a show that valued "type-casts" as much as or more than comedy. They needed diversity. I was white and mostly straight, so if I wanted to be a type, I'd have to try for the part of "girl." That's why I wore the skirt. Actually, three. If you think that's selling out, go fuck yourself.

Skirted up, I made it to the top ten, and then I was the first one sent home after the individual, sudden-death, head-to-head challenge. The comedian I competed against sent me a note before we hit the stage in our head-to-head comedy battle that said, "I will destroy you." That felt a little overboard for a comedy contest. I think "I'll barely best you!" might've done the trick. In any case, he didn't need to be so heavy handed. He won easily. If we believe the producers, who are second to only politicians and pedophiles in trustworthiness, the winners were chosen by the studio audience. I was told that I got 4 percent of the vote and the opposing comedian won with a whopping 96 percent. I'm not sure I believe it. No undecideds? (You might think it's just another wacky conspiracy theory, but I think we all know the undecideds make all the decisions in this country.)

To lose on such a big scale was humiliating, but I'd been humiliated publicly many times before. I once took out several kids and the DJ booth during a particularly bad spill at the roller rink when I was a kid. The memory still burns inside me to this day. In any case, I'd gotten over my public disgraces in the past and I knew I would again, but I sank into one of my worst depressions after the show. I spent a lot of days not getting out of bed, which didn't raise any red flags for anyone I knew, which I guess is a sign that your regular life might need upgrading.

I knew that the best thing you can do for yourself when you're depressed is to get up and get moving! Join a gym, get a smoothie, talk with friends about lowering your carb intake. I tried. I attempted to eke some serotonin out of my brain by jogging throughout the neighborhood. If you lived on a nearby block, you might've caught a glimpse of me. I was the one sobbing as I sprinted past you in a pair of Nike cross trainers.

I felt a huge wave of negativity wash over me. I'm sure I exaggerated much of it, but some of the pessimism was bolstered by actual e-mails and message board comments. I never searched out anything, never Googled, never set up an alert, but people will, for some ungodly reason, send you links to comments about yourself that are terribly unflattering. People who considered themselves my friends did this. My sister did this. My parents, less technically adept, simply relayed the negative comments they overheard while at the hardware store. Then they tried to comfort me by telling me that everyone else on the show was really, really funny and truthfully, I didn't stand a chance.

I was forced by my contract and my own need to prove my comedic worth to the public to participate as a "wild card" in the finals. My mother and my sisters decided to buy plane tickets to Los Angeles and sit in the front row for the final show, a live taping in which I, once again, came in tenth place, dead last. The five of us squeezed into a midsize rental car, and my sister Andrea drove us back to my apartment without so much as a word. I cried and sniffled sporadically in what appears now to be an enormous overreaction to the loss.

A few weeks later, as I cheerily chatted on the phone with my sweet sister Lynn, she casually asked about the *Last Comic Standing* experience. "I heard you lost, eh?" Apparently, crying in the car all the way to my apartment after the show didn't tip her off to my loss. She was probably on the plane home, wondering when she would find out who won. When I think of *Last Comic Standing,* I always think of her saying, "I heard you lost, eh?" And it always makes me laugh.

When the show asked me to participate in season three of *Last Comic Standing,* I declined. Then the calls started coming. NBC wanted to broadcast a season one versus season two special, and they wanted everyone to agree to it. And everyone did, everyone except me. The producers were not happy about it. I complained to everyone I had ever known, and several people I had just met at Trader Joe's, that the show had left me in a state of abject depression. I couldn't just happily agree to return. It felt too battered-wife syndrome. I was afraid it might all end in a murder/suicide.

The executives from NBC were relentless. I stopped answering my phone. One of the show's producers called me and left a lengthy message that started with him telling me how talented I was and quickly devolved into him angrily shouting that I'd never work again. It was kind of an empty threat, since that's exactly the kind of intimidation my brain yells at me all day long anyway. They ended up using another comedian. The host Jay Mohr cleared up any confusion by telling the audience I had AIDS. I don't want to get that again.

I DID WORK AGAIN, AND I did not have to wait long. I did *The Tonight Show*. I sat in on *The Howard Stern Show*. I did the TV gala for Montreal's Just for Laughs comedy festival. During that festival, I got one review that said I was among the best of the fest and another that declared me among the worst. Another reviewer, in an example of the worst tiebreaker ever, said she didn't know if I was good or bad, or even if she liked me or not. Maybe that person shouldn't be reviewing things.

With the help of my infamous *C*-word joke, I was now considered an "edgy" performer. I was someone who could be counted on to be cleverly fearless or repulsively thoughtless, depending on what you thought about my work. As much anguish as it caused me to be so polarizing, I had become the kind of unsettling performer that apparently HBO likes to champion. They asked me if I would be interested in doing a special for them. I said no, thank you. Because I was scared but also polite. I didn't think I was ready. My managers were still Messina Baker, who I'd been with for a couple of years now, and Melanie Truhett, a smart, wonderful woman with the softest telephone voice in the business, was my day-to-day contact. She tried to convince me that I should send HBO a tape of the set I would do for my special and let them decide. I told her that I'd submit the following year when I was convinced that I could better withstand the booing.

After *Last Comic Standing*, I hit the road, and the material that had been working in the L.A. and NY clubs was falling flat in clubs from Texas to Minneapolis. After a show in Indiana, someone gave me the number of a suicide hotline. I was bombing. My confidence was shaken. I had the emotional stability of a drowning cat.

I was opening for Rich Vos, both onstage and in the hotel room (ahem). I didn't really tell anyone we were dating until after we got married. I am nothing if not discreet. Without my knowledge, Rich taped my set while we were performing in Atlanta and sent the tape to Melanie, who then sent it to HBO.

One day Melanie whispered into the phone that HBO was giving me a special. I was confused. Rich had sent her the tape, she told me. I had to wonder if he taped me anywhere else without my knowledge. When I asked him about it, he just shrugged and walked away looking guilty. I don't know if Rich taped my set because he really believed in me or because he couldn't bear to see an opportunity wasted, but it certainly made me fall more deeply in love with him. I dedicated every set from that point forward to working on the special, and somewhere, somehow, my stand-up turned the corner. I went from giving the audience low-grade anxiety to genuinely entertaining them. By the time the HBO taping rolled around, I was as ready as I could possibly have been. I wore pants.

Like everything else I do, once it was done, it was done. I used it as a credit, but I didn't promote it. My family never asked about it and I never brought it up. In an attempt to avoid having to defend it, I just never talked about it. For some reason, I watched it myself for the first time just a few months ago and I barely cringed. This happens when I look at old photos of myself now. I seem to have a seven-year delay on self-appreciation. "Hey, why did I think I looked fat back then? Why didn't I wear spandex when I had the chance?!" Why didn't I feel proud of this accomplishment when it was fresh? Beside the fact that it's kind of creepy to be proud of yourself, I'm actually glad I don't waste time patting myself on the back. Never thinking I'm good enough is my superpower. It's what keeps me trying harder, working longer, and showering on a regular basis.

Chapter 18

F*** CENSORSHIP!

Let me be clear. I have killed. I have slaughtered. I have murdered. I mean this mostly figuratively, but there was that one time, after witnessing a young lady smile with her tongue in her teeth while baby-waving with both hands that I, blind with rage, snuffed out her last breath using just my thumbs and her own oversize feather necklace. The judge declared a mistrial and then high-fived me in the hallway. I am able to walk free today because no one likes people like that. But killing isn't the thing that people want to know about if you're a comedian. This is what regular people want to know: what if you bomb?

When people pose this question to me, I always shrug and say something like, "I guess I'll have to wait until it happens." Because fuck people and their stupid questions. I have been at this for a long time so I am aware that this is only the first question in a long line of pointless questions that I'll have to answer on the subject of stand-up comedy, which includes but is not limited to, "Who writes your material?" "Do you get free food?" and "Can I see your tits?"

I have bombed. Of course I have. I have bombed in front of friends, family, industry executives, and I even died a horrible death on television on a few occasions. Not to sound incredibly defensive, but dying and death are an integral part of the comedy process. After a set it's always, "I died." Or "I killed." Or "It was okay." But let's ignore that last one because it doesn't really serve the analogy about death. In comedy, it's kill or be killed. In the beginning, for the first five years, it's pretty much exclusively about getting your ass handed to you, over and over again. Eventually, hopefully, the ratio of bombs to kills tips in your favor, but you never stop bombing. At least, I didn't. Of course, I'll deny this if you ask me face-to-face at a cocktail party or, more likely, from the middle seat in coach.

Comedians bomb because they have to stand onstage and tell their jokes to strangers who may or may not have a sense of humor. There are studies showing that some people really do not understand comedy. Their minds are unable to make the necessary abstract connections in their frontal lobes that link understanding to laughter. These people are often referred to as tax auditors.

There's no shortcut for a comedian. There's no magic trick. There's no book or teacher who can help them. Comedy classes are bullshit. Standing in front of a mirror holding a hairbrush doesn't count. To be good at comedy, a comedian must practice onstage in front of an audience. This is hardly ideal, since an audience that is tired, drunk, or, worse, full of people straight from their place of work is almost always the worst judge of comedy. But there's no other way.

Imagine if you were learning to play an instrument, say . . . the bagpipes, but you could only practice in front of groups of strangers who were not entirely well versed in the nuanced art of bagpiping. After struggling through a few notes, the bagpiper would watch those strangers rush the stage and tear his bagpipes to pieces. I guess, using that perspective, comedians have it lucky. We are often humiliated, but are generally not hurt. The reason comedians can only practice in front of a crowd is because the audience is the instrument the comedian is learning to play. I'd say that the audience is our bagpipe except that the truth is, one night, the audience is a bagpipe, and the next night, it's an accordion, and the next night, it's a pocket piccolo, and, well, you get the idea. The audience is a different instrument every time a comedian sets foot onstage, so they have to make adjustments every night. Sometimes these adjustments are subtle, and sometimes they're very big and dramatic. For example, sometimes the audience doesn't get your perfectly crafted pop-culture references because they're mostly sports guys, or they've just watched a documentary about bullying and they are sensitive to every joke you make about little people. Sometimes the audience is predominately bald, which is why you won't get as many laughs during your genius hair stylist bit. You have to figure it all out as you go.

Becoming a good comedian, even if you're naturally gifted, takes practice. Lots and lots of practice. As the author of *Outliers,* Malcolm Gladwell, points out, to truly master something, you need to practice it for at least ten thousand hours. That's a problem with stand-up, because when you start out, you're only doing three-to-five-minute shows. Even when you graduate to doing thirty-minute shows and then become a headliner and do sets that are over an hour long . . . let's see, multiply by seven, carry the one . . . by my calculations, you'll start to master the art of comedy at around seventy-five years of age. Just right for the Comedy Central demographic. Turns out, Gladwell is a dream-crushing asshole. Don't read his book. You just don't have time! If you want to master the art of telling dick jokes, you have to get onstage!

Even becoming a mediocre comedian takes a very long time. A good one, even longer. That's why comedians are terrible for weeks, months, and in many cases—in my case—years and years. I did do well on occasion too, against all odds. Those sets were what kept me going in the beginning. Killing is the drug, the dragon that I cannot stop chasing.

Once, after only a few months of performing comedy, I got a standing ovation. It wasn't magical or awe inspiring. I was so green that I didn't even know I was doing well. I was mystified by the applause break at the end of my bit about the mating habits of carrier pigeons. They mate for life, but it's not like they're going to find one that's better looking or who makes more money. A funny premise, definitely, but applause worthy? The audience chuckled and chortled and clapped and stomped after every joke. Then, when I was fumbling to put the mic in the stand at the end of my set, they all stood up and cheered. I don't remember much else about the set, but I do recall that I was more shocked than pleased. The headliner, who had to have been horrified by the audience's enthusiasm for me, was actually very nice about it. "Enjoy it," he said when I came off-stage. "That isn't supposed to happen."

It's not supposed to happen because even if you can think up a couple of good jokes, which obviously I could (see above: pigeon joke), it takes time to perform them well. It takes time to get your timing. There's a saying in comedy that I'm sure you're aware of: Timing is everything. It's not one of the things. It's everything.

About seven years into my career, I was at a casino, opening for a comedian who'd gotten a lot of heat at the time. He had done several *Tonight Show*s and had just signed with a new big-shot manager. Before every show, he'd kneel down and have a little one-on-one convo with the lord above. It's possible he was apologizing in advance for all the sexual shit he was going to talk about onstage, but I'll never know because we never talked. He zipped past me backstage and in the greenroom. He never said hello. He didn't look in my direction. He never gave me so much as a nod of the head before my show the third night, right before I stepped onstage. I was waiting in the wings, doing my last-minute mental preparations, the same ones I do before every show, which consist mostly of hating the act on right before me. In this case, I was directing my anger toward the emcee. He was a jovial guitar act who was wrapping up his last "joke" that detailed, in a catchy song, how he preferred women to groom their nether regions. "Shave it, wax it, pluck it, if you want us to fuck it!" Or something equally toe-tappy. However it went, it was a great way to bring a woman comedian to the stage. This guy was a gem. While the audience was crowing and applauding the final stanza of the emcee's song, the headliner sauntered over to me as I grimaced.

"Hey," said the headliner, apropos of nothing. "You ever hear that timing is everything?"

I gave him a side glance but didn't turn my head. The emcee was asking the audience if they were ready to start the show and I was on high alert. Next, he'd list my credits, which wouldn't take a lot of time, and then he'd say my name and, for better or for worse, I would hit the stage. Probably for worse, but never prejudge an audience because you just never know. And this is when the headliner was going to engage me in a conversation?

"Uh, yeah," I answered. I had heard that "timing is everything" but I didn't elaborate. Instead, I remained crouched in my waiting-to-be-introduced stance, kind of like a track star waiting for a "Ready, set, go."

"Well, I've been watching you the last two nights and, uh . . ."

The emcee was done with my credits and on to my name. Let's go, dude. Spit it out.

"Timing is everything, but, you know, your timing is terrible."

" . . . Bonnie McFarlane!"

I stood there for a moment, in shock, then crossed the stage, nodded at the emcee and looked out into the audience of degenerate gamblers and short-haired Midwestern women.

"Great," I said into the mic, shaken slightly by the comment. I took a deep breath. . . . "to be here."

Maybe he had a point. But to be fair, his timing wasn't so terrific, either.

If timing is everything and getting stage time is paramount, then confidence comes in third. Likeability is right behind it, and the quality of actual jokes is probably somewhere near the bottom. None of it matters if you never have the balls to go onstage that first time. Every single comedian you've ever watched and admired has convinced themselves to do what is, for most people, their number-one fear: getting stuck in an elevator with Nancy Grace. Maybe that's just me. For most people, it's public speaking. As the famous Seinfeld joke goes: Public speaking is, according to most studies, people's number-one fear. Number two is death, so that means for most people, when they have to go to a funeral, they'd rather be the one in the casket than giving the eulogy.

And that's because even at a funeral, people will judge you. The tone of your charming story about the dead guy has to be just right. Appropriate, yet amusing.

THERE HAVE BEEN MANY ARGUMENTS on both sides of the offensive joke issue. Is it okay to make offensive jokes? Of course it is. We can joke about anything we want. Can the audience react any way they want? Of course they can. Is it annoying to listen to someone pose questions and answer those questions themselves? Yes, it's insufferable.

Audience members sometimes get passionate about opposing the things a comedian says even if, as is often the case, the comedian is actually saying the offensive thing to enlighten the audience to society's hypocrisies, or to simply mock a bigoted person by spouting their rhetoric. Aided by alcohol and a sense of righteousness, an audience member will occasionally try to argue with the comedian from his darkened seat among the crowd. This is something I recommend against, simply because the comedian is probably a gifted orator and comfortable discussing sensitive subject matter in public. Also, it's worth mentioning that, even though it's pretty obvious, the comedian has an unfair advantage. The comedian is standing, is higher than you (likely both in terms of elevation and drug use), is awash in a flattering light, and has a microphone. They can easily talk over you at any time and can usually win any quarrel by making you look like a raving lunatic. In the same way that rightwing radio hosts hang up on someone who has a valid opposing argument, within no time, a bouncer will likely tell you to shut the fuck up. This is not the time or the place to add your two cents. So don't be a dum-dum.

Sometimes a comedian really is saying racist, sexist, or homophobic things. We often put up with these comedians "if they are funny." I hear that a lot. "As long as it's funny!" Let's put aside for a moment the fact that funny is subjective. (And it's so subjective that the same joke might be funny in the first show and not in the second.) The "if it's funny" argument relies on the assumption that a comedian tells a fully formed joke. I'm aware that this happens occasionally, but really, telling fully formed jokes is the exception, saved mostly for television, and not the rule. Being funny is a process. I usually write my jokes out longhand on a yellow pad and then type a better version on my computer. Days or even weeks later, when I'm sure the joke will not only work but be the best of anything I've ever written, I will jot down bullet points in the smaller notebook that I take with me to gigs so I can have easy access to the brilliance I worked on all day. Then, I go onstage and try it out. Let me point out that I always think it's going to work. I always think it's going to be funny. I think this, despite the fact that it almost never is. Very often, I'd say 75 percent of the time, it gets little to nothing from the audience. Coming up with new jokes is a numbers game. So, I revamp, rework, and try again. And again. And again, until it starts to work, which it does sometimes. Not often, but sometimes, you really do work it into a gem.

This is why a comedian should be allowed to attempt being funny, fail at funny, and try again, even if the subject matter is dark and twisted and deeply offensive. Otherwise, we will become a group of narrow-minded philosophers who can only talk about food. Then, when you want to sit in a darkened room and hear things you'd be fired for talking about at work, you can't. When you want to really laugh and release your tensions, you won't be able to. You'll have to kill a hooker instead. So let a comedian offend you. Save a hooker.

WRITING AN OFFENSIVE JOKE THAT people laugh at is still my favorite form of entertainment. Sure, it increases my odds of getting stabbed by a dinner fork, but those are the stakes and it wouldn't be as fun without them being so high. I've been chewed out by comedy club managers, a waitress or two, and, of course, the occasional half-sauced patron. After shows, I'll watch a woman with blue smoke escaping out her ears stride cartoonishly in my direction and I'll think, Which joke pushed her button? Was it rape? Race? Diabetes? And she'll say something like: "I can't believe you tell people not to get organ transplants! An organ transplant could've saved my grandfather!"

Sometimes I apologize, sometimes I don't. It mostly depends on how much I want to engage. If I want to get rid of the angry protester so I can resume discussing the pros and cons of T-shirt merch with another comedian, I just apologize. I don't care. I'm Canadian. I say I'm sorry all the time. Even to inanimate objects. Yesterday I banged my knee on a coffee table and managed to eke out a heartfelt apology even as I rolled around on the carpet.

Lately, apologizing has become very, very important. We now have a contingent of vigilante watchdogs whose sole purpose in life it seems is to catch celebrities saying (in their opinion) inappropriate things either in jest or in anger, and forcing them to publicly apologize or lose their jobs, their fans, and their frequent-flier status. It all started with Kramer. Remember how uncomfortable it was when Michael Richards went on *Letterman* to apologize for his racist meltdown and everyone kept laughing? That's because it was still fairly new to see a celebrity openly begging for absolution from regular people like myself who say crazy horseshit all the time. But by the time Tracy Morgan (who wasn't melting down but was doing his actual shtick) performed his comedy piece "I'd kill my gay son," Americans were not only used to celebrities pleading for forgiveness, they were demanding it. They didn't care if it was supposed to be funny. They made it clear they wouldn't tolerate intolerance.

This intolerance of intolerance has carried over to social media as well. Death by Twitter is a phenomenon that has ruined more showbiz careers than the talkie. It's incredible to me that people can fully interpret the actual personal politics of an individual based on a single joke that contains less than 140 characters. From this sliver of information, we think we can determine if someone is racist, sexist, or not funny, the latter being the worst crime, apparently. When it comes to Twitter jokes, celebrities are expected to bat a thousand.

With the threat of punishment so high, why do celebrities,

newscasters, and actors continue to attempt to tell jokes about sensitive subjects? If you're protecting a big paycheck, I'd think a good Twitter rule of thumb would be to heed the same warning as Billy Peltzer should have about his gremlin: whatever you do, never, never feed it after midnight. Comedians, however, *have* to make jokes. Not because it's their job, but because it's in their DNA. The idea that this thought, terrible as it might be, might make someone laugh will almost always encourage me to share it. No risk, no reward.

It's interesting to me that people will sit and laugh as a comedian rolls through eighteen topics that could be classified as immoral, obscene, and even traitorous, but when the nineteenth topic is something that affects their sensibilities, that's when they lock and load their weapons and engage in battle. What offends people, personally, is the most important thing ever in the history of the world. Each group and subgroup and subsection feels they are being unfairly maligned. Animal rights activists could care less if you use the word "midget," but make a joke about clubbing baby seals and you'll get a vegan shoe thrown at you.

Nothing scares me more than backlash from a feminist organization, and I consider myself to be a feminist. It's no wonder they scare the shit out of men. First of all, men aren't used to being scared all the time the way we are. Women have a lot of challenges in life that I identify and sympathize with, which is why I feel I've earned the right to joke about all the things I joke about, including but not limited to rape and a funny autocorrected text. There are more people than you'd think who like to deal with the uglier aspects of life by using comedy. I'm sorry if that upsets you. (That was sincere, though by no means a retraction.) I will not be bullied into being politically correct. Bullying is wrong, by the way. I know this because it's been hammered home in unrelenting blog posts written by the same people who don't seem to realize that they are doing it.

AND SO, WHILE IT'S TRUE that I might be offensive, inappropriate, and possess a few troubling similarities to a serial killer, let's be clear that I have never actually killed anyone.

I started out on a farm without television and ended up writing and performing on it. I began this life not knowing if I'd ever find anyone who shared my belligerent take on the world and I did. And I married him. I hang out with the most offensive, hilarious, original thinkers on this planet. I got lucky.

Some of my favorite memories involve sitting around with other comedians, joking about things that are of highly questionable taste, laughing until my stomach muscles ache. There's something so soothing about saying your worst thought out loud and having people laugh at it instead of judging it. It's probably on the top of the list of why I am a comedian. Next on the list is writing the jokes. And third, though it took me a while to be able to enjoy it as I do now, is performing those jokes. Fourth, of course, without question, are the free drinks.

How to Deal with a Heckler

1. First, calculate the collateral damage the heckler might cause. For instance, if the heckler is in the back and everyone can hear him, you address him differently than you would a heckler who is right up front and who you can reach with your boot.

2. Always wear a boot with a reinforced toe.

3. If the heckler is not within kicking distance, you must respond as quickly as you can. The longer it takes you to say, "Can someone throw him out?" the harder it will be to have him removed.

4. If you are working a club without security, then you are probably not very successful, i.e., funny, and it's possible the heckler is correct. As a last-ditch resort, you should order the heckler several shots of tequila and hope he passes out.

5. Distinguish between the hecklers who are trying to be mean and those who feel they are helping you by yelling out stock tips.

6. If you are forced to engage with a heckler, always repeat what he or she says so that you can have a little extra time to think of a clever rejoinder. If the heckler is particularly cutting, then just keep saying, "What?" until he gets tired of repeating himself.

7. Get the audience on your side. Crying will almost always guarantee a portion of the audience will start sporting TEAM COMEDIAN T-shirts. If you can't muster up the tears, be sure to let people know you've had chemo earlier in the day.

8. After the heckler leaves, dry your eyes, blow your nose, and spend ten or fifteen minutes tearing apart his character. Without the heckler around to respond, you'll almost certainly win.

How to Get Representation

"How do I get a manager?" It's the first thing young comedians want to know after, "Can doing stand-up get me sex?" Before we can effectively answer the how, we must first understand the "what." What is a manager, exactly? The word itself holds the clue to its meaning. The root word "manage" is easy enough to understand. But to manage what? Sometime in sixteenth-century France, when mimes were de rigueur, a young managerial upstart with Machiavellian charisma started a rumor that a comedy manager managed one's comedy career. Due in large part to an indefatigable wind that kept many of the mimes from meeting up to discuss the fiction by means of precise hand gestures, this delusion soared uncontested throughout Europe, and eventually, along with the pox blankets gifted to the Indians, arrived intact on the shores of North America. This unfortunate misinterpretation has plagued the comedy community for centuries, befuddling even the most ingenious of talents, and it's high time to set the record straight.

A comedy manager, to be quite clear, manages not one's career, but rather, one's expectations.

It has been my experience that a manager loves to wax on about his many efficiencies but remains discreet about his one true gift, which lies in his ability to dampen your spirit. If he is worth his salt, he will let you down before you even get a foot up. It is, after all, in his best interest, if not yours, to assure you that despite his charm, his connections, his unflagging work ethic, and his salesmanship, you are effectively persona non grata in the business you have chosen for your life's work.

The only thing a manager does better than making you feel shame about your own lackluster talents is avoiding culpability and laying all the blame for past, present, and future failures at your clumsy feet.

Now, if this is something that appeals to you, we can move on to the how.

How to get a comedy manager:

Eager as you are to get started convincing a middleman that you have talent, the first thing you need to do is wait. Just wait. If you've never read a book on the patience necessary for hunting a deer then now is the time, since you've got nothing better to do. Catching a manager takes a minute. (I'm using the urban vernacular, which translates loosely to "a rather long stretch.")

You can never approach a comedy manager and ask them to represent you unless you are about to sign a five-figure development deal with a major network. Without a check to hand over, they will simply inflate their egos until you are forced out of the room with your vestigial tail between your legs.

At the risk of sharing trade secrets, becoming a comedy manager is pretty easy stuff. To get started, one simply needs a business card and a client. Parents of child actors become their managers all the time. That's how easy the job is. You can go from being a Waffle Hut waitress in rural Arkansas to a successful Hollywood manager just by upgrading your BlackBerry. If you can effectively set up an outgoing voice-mail message, you are 90 percent there.

Still, everyone knows that anything worth having is difficult to find. That's why the best way to entice a comedy manager is to make them work for it. Act like you don't want a comedy manager. It's classic reverse psychology and it works. (*Jumanji*, anyone?) Put a joke in your act about how you think comedy managers arc worthlcss. Update your Facebook with claims of "Managerless and happy." Tell people, "I need a manager like a fish needs a bicycle," often. This is a riff on an old feminist slogan about women not needing men and it worked like a charm. Studies showed that any woman wearing this T-shirt without a bra got married within the year.

However, should a manager approach you after a show and give you his business card, by all means take the business card. And then rip it up in his face. Scream at him to leave you alone and shout, "I don't need you, scum! I already have big things going on. Very big things."

Now you've given the comedy manager a reason to get up in the morning. You've infected him with a zest for life he hasn't felt since he picked up his stack of business cards from the kiosk at the mall. The manager is now pursuing you with all the passion of a forty-two-year-old businesswoman intent on finding a way to fertilize one of her last three eggs.

Here's where things get interesting. If one manager aspires to pinch 10 to 15 percent of your future net profits, then other managers will feel an intense desire to do the same. Unfortunately, this has very little to do with you and is actually a psychological condition clinical therapists refer to as "grabby-toddler response." The thing to remember, and managers know this all too well, is that this is just a game. Sure, your entire life is riding on it, but do try to have fun.

Now that you've got everyone charging through your door, which manager do you pick? The key is, it doesn't matter. They will all stop returning your phone calls the minute you sign over power of attorney.

Good luck!

How to Properly Give a Compliment to a Working Comedian

While it might sound outrageously simple, the best way to show appreciation for a comedian is to laugh while they are onstage. Many times, I've looked down at an audience member and was convinced that they were either hating my show or suffering through day three of a constipation marathon, only to be shocked after the show when they asked for a hug. To set the record straight, a hug is not something a comedian wants from a stranger after the show, unless that hug also involves coke and a stripper. Hugs are big-ticket issues for a comedian. The reason a comedian is a comedian has a lot to do with "the hug" or, more accurately, the lack of it. Two more hugs as a child and many of us wouldn't be comedians at all. But as adults, we've come to disdain the thing we could not have as children. Simply put, we hate hugs. Please don't put me through a kind of psychological torture just so you can later tell your Facebook friends, "I hugged her!"

If you're interested in letting the comedian know you enjoyed their show, there are several simple ways to do this.

1. Say, "I enjoyed your show."

2. Say, "Great show."

3. Say, "You crack me up!"

4. Say, "That was fun!"

5. Say, "I had a good time, thank you."

The key to using these accolades is to be brief. Keep moving. There's no need to stand around, hoping the comedian will give you more comedy in a face-to-face setting. The comedian's talent is performing onstage. Offstage, they will only disappoint you, and that good feeling you've still got from the show will drain from your body like blood from a severed carotid artery. You'll be asking yourself, Is this the same schlub who had me bent over and pounding my fists on my knees? It simply cannot be! But, sadly, it is. The difference between the comedian onstage and the comedian offstage can sometimes be a chasm of indefinable proportions. Remember in grade school when you found out how far apart the planets really were? That's how different a comedian is onstage and offstage, so the best thing to do is move quickly. Buy a CD, take a picture, shake a hand if you must, but whatever you do—don't linger. And never hug.

How to Properly Receive a Compliment if You Are a Working Comedian

When someone is giving you a compliment, the first thing you have to realize is that they think you are talented, even if you're not. They're probably drunk. Or maybe it's their first time at a live comedy show. Or they're Russian. It's possible they saw you on a night when the comedian on before you was just bad enough to raise the collective hopes of the audience for the next act (you) but not so bad they made the audience lose hope in comedy, and perhaps even in humanity altogether. An act that drains the room of hope in humanity is a tough act to follow.

Comedians often have an urge to tell the truth not because they're exceptionally moral humans, but because the truth is uncomfortable and people who are uncomfortable can sometimes break out in nervous laughter. A comedian counts any kind of laughter as proof positive that they are funny. Regular folks might differentiate the kind of laughs into intentional, unintentional, laughing with, and laughing at. Comedians, on the other hand, count them all as valid payment into the empty abyss of their damaged souls.

For whatever reason—probably a lack of childhood attention or that thing that happened to you on the subway when you were fifteen—getting compliments can put a comedian very ill at ease. To alleviate this feeling, a comedian will sometimes try to dismiss the compliment, argue with the admirer, or even try to publicly ridicule the fan by snatching his hat and throwing it above his head to a buddy at the other end of the bar while yelling, "Monkey in the middle!"

Resisting the urge to say, "The first show was much better. I forgot a tag on two of my jokes just now," may be the hardest thing you ever have to do as a comedian, but it is well worth the effort. Disciplining yourself to receive a compliment properly could garner you up to a half dozen new Twitter followers a year.

Here's how:

The key to properly receiving a compliment is to nod slightly to the left at a thirty-six-degree angle, and smile gently without showing any teeth. This serves two purposes: one, you don't look like a jackass grinning from ear to ear, and two, you probably have bad breath. Be honest, have you brushed your teeth since you got up at the crack of noon?

A genuine, closed-mouth smile that also looks a little fake is the look you're going for. This tells the fan that you are flattered enough to turn on the charm, but not so excited you might pee on their leg. You want to convey an expression that says, "Yes, this happens to me all the time, but I am also grateful for my admirers, and, as celebrities go, I'm one of the nice ones. So yes, I'll take time out from my heated discussion with the bartender about the WNBA players' monthly cycles so you can have your moment with me." After the picture is taken or the boob is signed, you can say, "Have a good night!" to let them know you're finished with their nonsense. You don't have to share that you're not really a celebrity and that, despite spending up to forty-five minutes a night in the middle of a spotlight, you actually live in a one-bedroom, five-story walk-up with seven other people. However, during your brief interaction, should the admirer happen to mention that they have an extra room in their brownstone that no one is using, by all means, drop the facade and beg them to let you follow them home.

Acknowledgments

There's no way I could've written this book without the help of my editors, Hilary Redmon and Emma Janaskie, who've probably already corrected seventeen grammatical errors in this sentence alone. Their expertise, patience, and senses of humor are truly admirable. I'd also like to thank my agent, Kim Witherspoon, who gently guided me through the process of writing proposals, closing book deals, and making deadlines without calling me an idiot. And since I value my marriage, I'd like to thank my husband, Rich Vos. He selflessly went golfing every day so that I might write my daily pages in peace. Thanks to my daughter, Rayna, who was extraordinarily interested in what I was endlessly tapping out on my keyboard and in when, exactly, I'd be finished. I'd like to thank my mom, who guided me with insight and clarity on my memories growing up and who provided her own fascinating stories of what happened before I'd come along. Also, many thanks to the rest of my family for allowing me to write so openly about their lives without their harboring any anger or resent toward me. (Fingers crossed!) I need to thank my friends Jacqueline Novak, Lynsi Hughes, and Lynn Shawcroft, who read early versions of my work and encouraged me to put the bottle down and continue writing. My thanks to Ecco

Books and HarperCollins for making my book a book. And last but not least, I need to thank Anthony Bourdain for thinking I could write a book and giving me the opportunity to do it. I am eternally grateful, although eternity doesn't quite seem long enough.

About the Author

Bonnie McFarlane is a comedian and writer who has appeared on *Last Comic Standing* and her own HBO *One Night Stand* comedy special, and cohosts the podcast *My Wife Hates Me* with her husband, comedian Rich Vos. She lives in New Jersey with her husband and daughter.